Use Your PC
to Build an Incredible
Home Theater System

BART FARKAS AND JEFF GOVIER

APress Media, LLC

Use Your PC to Build an Incredible Home Theater System
Copyright © 2003 by Bart Farkas and Jeff Govier
Originally published by Apress in 2003

ISBN 978-1-59059-057-7   ISBN 978-1-4302-5174-3 (eBook)
DOI 10.1007/978-1-4302-5174-3

Trademarked names may appear in this book. Rather than use a trademark symbol with every occurrence of a trademarked name, we use the names only in an editorial fashion and to the benefit of the trademark owner, with no intention of infringement of the trademark.

Technical Reviewer: Ron Tolton

Editorial Directors: Dan Appleman, Gary Cornell, Jason Gilmore,
  Simon Hayes, Karen Watterson, John Zukowski

Managing Editor: Grace Wong

Copy Editor: Nicole LeClerc

Production Manager: Kari Brooks

Compositor: Diana Van Winkle, Van Winkle Design Group

Illustrator: Tony Jonick

Indexer: James Minkin

Cover Designer: Kurt Krames

Manufacturing Manager: Tom Debolski

Marketing Manager: Stephanie Rodriguez

In the United States: phone 1-800-SPRINGER, email orders@springer-ny.com, or visit http://www.springer-ny.com. Outside the United States: fax +49 6221 345229, email orders@springer.de, or visit http://www.springer.de.

For information on translations, please contact Apress directly at 2560 Ninth Street, Suite 219, Berkeley, CA 94710. Phone 510-549-5930, fax 510-549-5939, email info@apress.com, or visit http://www.apress.com.

The information in this book is distributed on an "as is" basis, without warranty. Although every precaution has been taken in the preparation of this work, neither the author nor Apress shall have any liability to any person or entity with respect to any loss or damage caused or alleged to be caused directly or indirectly by the information contained in this work.

For Alison, Derek, and Adam

Contents at a Glance

Contents

Acknowledgments

WE'D LIKE TO thank everyone at Apress, including Grace Wong, Kari Brooks, Nicole LeClerc, and especially Dan Appleman and Gary Cornell—without their vision we wouldn't even be writing this! Thanks to Brent Sawatzky for his great ideas, Chris Brown for his audio engineering tips, and Ron Tolton for his help (we couldn't have done it without you, Ron!). We'd also like to thank Tom Genova, who offered his television expertise and runs the "Television History – The First 75 Years" Web site (http://www.tvhistory.tv). Finally, we'd like to thank the companies that lent us hardware to make this book the best it could be. These companies include ATI Technologies, Hauppauge, TheaterTek, and a host of others. Thanks to all who helped out!

Jeff

I'd like to thank my wife, Robin, and my daughter, Alison, for allowing me to work on this project. I'd also like to thank Bart for organizing many of the project details.

Bart

I'd like to thank my wife, Cori, and my two kids, Adam and Derek, for being supportive during the long process of producing a book like this. I'd also like to thank Jeff for working so very hard to ensure that this book is a valuable tool for the readers.

Introduction

HOME THEATER HAS become an increasingly popular entertainment venue for people all over the world. The last decade has seen giant leaps in the technologies available (and affordable) to the consumer at large. The recent DVD explosion has opened the public's eyes to the vast potential of very high-quality video and sound, and many people are jumping on this bandwagon.

As with all new technologies, components are expensive and consumers require a great deal of knowledge and research to make the proper choices. One area that is just now becoming a feasible option is that of using a computer to create a powerful, flexible, and cost-effective home theater system that is by its very nature adaptable to future technologies. The idea of using a home theater PC (HTPC) to manage an audiovisual entertainment system is not just a fringe idea for techno-geeks; there are genuine reasons for setting up a system like this in many homes.

What This Book Covers

In this book, we show how you can use a home computer to maximize the quality of video through processing incoming video signals (from DVD, broadcast television, HDTV, home video, satellite, and cable) and outputting them to your television at the highest quality the television can accept. Video, however, is only part of the experience, and using your computer's sound card (and/or sound system) gives you the best quality sound available for the money. We also discuss how to use your HTPC to play MP4 material and home video material such as home movies or slide shows in ultra-high resolution on a high-definition television (or any television). Finally, there has been a recent wave of interest in technologies such as TiVo, ReplayTV, and UltimateTV. We show you how to turn your HTPC into a homegrown, TiVo-like personal video recorder unit with unlimited expansion possibilities.

This book will show you how to select components and build an HTPC. We examine all of the various uses for an HTPC, including showing digital pictures on your television, improving your sound system, and using your HTPC as a jukebox for your MP3 collection. If you're interested in taking full advantage of your HTPC, we cover everything you need to know to get the ultimate home theater system up and running in your home with minimal fuss. Throughout the book, we use two HTPC examples (our own personal machines), HTPC 1 and HTPC 2, which we configure in different ways with different hardware and software. We use these two machines as our real-world examples as we explore various software and hardware options as they pertain to the their intended tasks (DVD playback, MP3 decoding, and so forth). The HTPC can take the home theater experience to the next level, and this book will help you take it there!

Who This Book Is For

This book is for those folks who are home theater enthusiasts and have some working knowledge of personal computers. This book will help these people create a new animal on the home theater landscape: the home theater PC (HTPC). You don't have to be an expert on hardware, and you certainly don't have to know how to program, but you *will* have to be able to spare a dozen evenings or so fiddling around with various software settings and such to get things running just the way you want.

The HTPC offers so very much in the way of improving the home theater experience that it's a viable option for anyone but the most technically challenged soul. If you like things to work 100 percent right out of the box with no fiddling, then an HTPC probably isn't for you (at least, not one you build yourself); however, if you like to tinker a little and spend a fair amount of time on your PC anyway, then you likely have what it takes to create your ultimate home theater system with the help of an HTPC.

Home Theater Basics

Part One

CHAPTER 1

Video

THIS CHAPTER CONTAINS basic background information about each of the key elements of a home theater. Without a doubt, you'll need to know where each technology originated from and how it has evolved to get the point where you can create a truly enjoyable home theater experience without having to re-mortgage your house to do it.

The genesis of home theater can be traced back not just to television and radio, but all the way back to the late nineteenth century when George Eastman introduced celluloid rolls of film for capturing moving images to create the first "movies." While we don't go all the way back to the earliest inklings of moving pictures and the inclusion of sound in movies, we give you a brief history of the key elements in any contemporary home theater system in this chapter. Here are the topics we cover:

- **Television:** What once was a novelty for the rich has become the staple information-delivery system for the industrialized world. We look at where television came from and how its origins have limited the quality of the images we see on it. We also look into the future to see what the next generation of television will be.

- **VHS and Betamax:** Since its victory over the commercial versions of Betamax format (Betamax is still widely used in pre- and post-production TV) in the mid-1980s, VHS has reigned supreme as the movie delivery and home taping system of choice for many years. With the advent and proliferation of DVD, however, the writing may be on the wall for this tried-and-true format.

- **DVD:** Starting as a collaborative effort between Sony and Philips as a way to get CD-quality digital information into a movie format, DVD has taken the world by storm and is well on its way to replacing videotape recorders such as VHS machines.

- **Laserdisc and Video CD:** Both of these formats have remained on the fringes, but it can be argued that Laserdisc is responsible for the success of DVD because it blazed the trail that showed a digital-quality movie medium could be successful.

- **Home video and video editing:** Home video recording is now over 20 years old, and all those tapes of children's first steps and family get-togethers in the heat of the summer are ready to be edited and turned into productions that can be enjoyed right at home in the new home theater PC (HTPC) home theater. The HTPC is just the tool to edit this material and turn it into a digital format where it can't degrade.

Television

The electronic television began as an experiment in 1908 by British inventor A. A. Campbell-Swinton. Eventually, the technology became the staple information delivery system for nearly the entire world. In fact, in North America there is nearly one television for every person, which translates into multiple televisions for every household. Television's capability to quickly dispense important information, from national crises to weather reports to financial information, has made it an indispensable tool that most societies around the world have embraced wholeheartedly. Not only would life without television of any kind cut off most people's main contact with the world outside of their communities, but it would also remove other key information-delivery systems, such as the television monitors in airports that tell you if your flight is on time.

A Little Television History

While the basic principles on which television would ultimately be created were discovered in the 1870s, the first practical uses of television didn't begin until the 1920s when a Scotsman by the name of John Logie Baird was able to give the first functional demonstration of electronic television where images were transmitted electronically onto a screen. Although these early demonstrations showed only crude, flickering images, this research was enough to inspire others to pick up the torch and work on improving on the concept.

By November 1936, the first public broadcasting of television programs began in London. These early broadcasts were sent out in two competing formats: the Baird system of 240 lines at 25 frames per second and the Marconi system of 405 lines at 25 frames per second. These early British broadcasts were of events such as the Wimbledon tennis championships and the marriage of King George IV. The crown for the first public broadcast, however, goes to the Germans, who put the 1936 Summer Olympic Games on the tube, complete with the tyrant Adolph Hitler standing on a podium giving a speech to open the proceedings.

In 1939, the European community adopted the broadcasting standard of 625 lines and 50 frames per second. Two years later, the United States set their standard at 525 lines and 60 frames per second, and thus the era of modern television was born. While there were no public broadcasts during World War II—indeed, there were only 400 television sets in the United States in 1941—the broadcasts resumed in 1946 and have been going strong ever since. To give you an idea of the explosion of television in the United States, by 1951 there were over 13 million television sets in operation.[1]

Also in 1951, the Peter Goldmark color system televisions were introduced, but these sets were not backward compatible with existing 525 line black-and-white broadcasts, and since very little content was being broadcast in color, this system was doomed to failure. The color/black-and-white conundrum was ironed out in 1953 when the United States and Canada adopted the National Television Systems Committee (NTSC) standard for both black-and-white and color broadcasts that is still enjoyed today. In other parts of the world, different systems were developed, specifically the phase alternation line (PAL) and système électronique couleur avec mémoire (SECAM) formats.

In 1954, all stations began broadcasting a portion of their content in color using the NTSC standard, but it took until 1965 for the National Broadcasting Company (NBC) to have their entire lineup broadcast in color (and even then there were a couple of exceptions). By 1974, over 95 percent of all households in the United States were equipped with television sets,[2] and as the cost of owning a television set has fallen, the number of Americans buying televisions has continued to rise through to the present day. In fact, by 1990 there nearly 1,500 stations were broadcasting television signals in the United States alone.[3]

---

1. This statistic comes from Tom Genova's Web site, "Television History – The First 75 Years" (http://www.tvhistory.tv).

2. This statistic comes from Tom Genova's Web site, "Television History – The First 75 Years" (http://www.tvhistory.tv).

3. This statistic comes from Tom Genova's Web site, "Television History – The First 75 Years" (http://www.tvhistory.tv).

The Evolution of the Television

As you can imagine, the television has evolved a great deal over the last 75 years or so. The evolution and development of televisions and their features could be a book unto itself, so we do not try to cover this fascinating topic. If you are interested in the history of the television, we suggest that you check out Tom Genova's Web site, "Television History – The First 75 Years" (http://www.tvhistory.tv). This Web site is an excellent resource and contains many pictures of antique television sets such as Tom's very own 1939 RCA TRK-12 (see Figure 1-1).

1939 General Electric HM-275

(c) TVhistory.TV Library

Figure 1-1. Tom Genova's Web site, "Television History – The First 75 Years," includes some great pictures of vintage televisions.

That said, we would like to mention a few key milestones in the development of the television. The following milestones are just too significant not to mention in the context of the history of television and its development:

- **Color television:** This advance changed television from something that approximated the way we see the world into something that looked like the way we actually see the world. To many of us, color is a very important aspect of what we see, and the addition of color to televisions took the medium to new heights.

- **The remote control:** The remote control is significant in that it changed the way television was watched forever. Instead of having to get up and change the channel manually, users could now simply press a button on a small device from wherever they were sitting to change the channel.

- **Transistor television:** Roughly around 1972, the traditional vacuum-tube circuitry of the television was replaced by the solid-state technology of the transistor. This enabled televisions to be smaller, lighter, and more reliable.

- **High-definition television:** The latest and greatest in television's evolution is the development of high-definition television (HDTV). HDTV increases the amount of information that can be displayed on the screen many times, thus creating a much sharper picture.

Of course, the milestones in the preceding list are only the major stepping-stones in the evolution of television. According to Tom Genova, "Along the way there have been *hundreds* of minor circuit design changes, improvements, and enhancements. These enhancements include brighter picture tubes, better signal control, easier computerized tuning, multilanguage capabilities, closed captioning, onscreen station identification, visual menus, timers, auto shut-off, built-in game modules, and even compatibility with computers, telephones, and the Internet."

Television Signal Delivery

For many years, the way in which consumers received the signal into their televisions was via television stations that broadcast signals from television towers that basically could deliver the "product" to any television set with an antenna within the line of sight of the station. In today's market, however, television users have a number of choices that enable them to tailor both what they watch and the quality of the signal they receive.

Radio Frequency Television Signal

Up until the advent of cable television delivery in the 1960s, most houses had what are called "rabbit ear" antennas on top of the television. These antennas could be adjusted to get the best picture possible for each channel; unfortunately, sometimes there would need to be adjustments made for *each* channel! Some enterprising folks got around this by having larger aerials on top of their houses to improve television reception, but these aerials didn't necessarily solve all of the problems associated with television reception. Surprisingly, this method of watching television is still used a great deal, especially in rural areas.

Cable

Eventually, there were enough problems with television signal reception that coaxial cable technology was developed to carry the television signals in a manner that wouldn't be affected by weather or physical obstructions. By the 1960s, local cable companies were supplying television signals to residents in urban areas where tall buildings were making reception degrade. This idea quickly caught on and by the mid-1970s there were many cable systems offering more channels than had previously been available to the average television user. Indeed, cable television is the de facto standard in North America and is used in more televisions than any other means of signal delivery.

In the last few years, a new kind of cable, *digital cable*, has crept into the marketplace and is becoming quite popular in some areas. Digital cable increases the number of possible channels that coaxial cable can carry, and in some areas of North America, as many as six channels are already being broadcast in HDTV all the time. This is currently greater than the number of HDTV channels available by digital satellite dish, so it will be interesting to see if digital cable surpasses digital satellite dish in the future.

NOTE *Although we discuss TiVo further in the "Direct Satellite" section, we'd like to state now that TiVo can be used with regular cable systems as well as satellite systems—it just doesn't integrate as smoothly. That said, services such as TiVo can be integrated very well with digital cable.*

Satellite

In 1965, the Early Bird satellite was launched to enable broadcasts of television signals between Europe and the United States. Older readers will remember that the Beatles sang "All You Need Is Love" on the program that commemorated the first transatlantic broadcast. With the proliferation of satellite signal delivery over the next few decades, some users began to set up their own (rather large) satellite dishes (see Figure 1-2) that could capture all of the signals coming off of any one television satellite and pipe them right into their home. This means of delivery has several drawbacks, including a very large dish, a high initial cost, and a complicated process for finding the programs you want to watch because there are now many satellites and the dish must be moved between satellites to receive all the stations available. Large-dish satellite systems are still available today, but they are less popular than the other satellite delivery system, direct satellite.

Figure 1-2. Analog satellite dishes are huge compared to the pizza-sized DBS dishes.

Direct Broadcast Satellite

The latest craze that has taken North America by storm is direct broadcast satellite (DBS). Launched in 1994, these small, pizza-sized dishes (see Figure 1-3) are able to receive over 200 channels of digitally compressed information that produces exceptional quality and convenience for users. Because DBS is computer based, it has a system of onscreen menus and provides newer technologies such as TiVo and ReplayTV that allow users to automatically (and easily) record whatever content they want from a selection of 200 channels. The upside to DBS systems is that they are relatively cheap, the dishes are small and unobtrusive compared to standard satellite systems, and the vast array of channels is organized neatly through the use of a computerized menu system. As of 2001, it was estimated that over 15 million homes in North America had DBS systems installed (according to *Encyclopedia Britannica*).

How Televisions Work

While our mandate is not to go into excessive detail about how the various electronic devices we discuss work, we feel that in the context of the home theater and the choices you as the consumer have, it is worthwhile to cover the basics of how the various kinds of televisions bring the picture to your eyes.

Figure 1-3. DBS (or DSS) services such as DIRECTV offer digital quality and a small, convenient dish, although in Northern Canada, larger DBS dishes are needed (18 inches or 21 inches) to get acceptable reception.

Picture Tube Televisions

Picture tube televisions make up the vast majority of televisions in use today. Today's picture tube televisions are descended from the original televisions that were used in the 1920s and 1930s. There are several reasons why this kind of television has remained popular:

- The prices of picture tube televisions have consistently fallen.

- The picture tube has a bright, clear image and can be watched from almost any angle without loss of brightness.

- The cost of tube-based televisions is significantly lower than projection, rear-projection, and flat-screen plasma televisions. That said, some rear-projection televisions are cheaper than high-end tube-based systems such as Sony's WEGA.

- With picture tubes, the color is more accurate than with flat panel televisions, and the convergence and geometry problems common to projection televisions are not an issue.

Picture tubes follow a basic design that hasn't changed a great deal in the last 50 years (since color television came online). The television consists of several key components: the power supply, the tuner, the picture tube, and the electron gun (which sits in the back of the picture tube). The tuner receives the video signals and sends them to the electron gun in the back of the television. Color televisions have three electron guns, one for each primary color (red, blue, and green). The images from the video signals are beamed (in an electron beam) onto the back of the picture tube, or in other words, the opposite side of the viewing surface of the television. The inside of the viewing surface of the television is coated with phosphorus, which glows when bombarded with electrons from the electron guns. In a standard NTSC television, the electron guns "paint" the image onto the phosphorus screen in 525 lines at a rate of 60 times a second. This constant painting of the video signal on the phosphorus screen creates the images that we recognize as television. Of course, this is a simplified explanation, but it shows the basic mechanics of how a picture tube television works.

 **NOTE** *In color televisions there is another component that enables the colors to be sorted out and displayed on the screen. This component is called a shadow mask. In short, the shadow mask is a nontransparent layer of material that has small holes in it. These holes are designed to ensure that electron beams of one color do not hit the phosphorus dots that are being hit with another color. Colors other than red, green, or blue (colors that are displayed from the electron guns) are created by having primary color dots displayed very close together. When this happens, your eyes and your brain combine the information to create other colors.*

Projection Televisions

Another method of video delivery is through projection. There are two types of *projection televisions:* front projection and rear projection (see Figure 1-4). The most common of these is by far the rear-projection television, which you can see at any audio/video store with large televisions on display. Projection televisions actually date back all the way to the mid-1940s (the RCA 8PCS41 projection television is a prime early example), but for practical purposes the first projection televisions arrived on the scene in the 1970s and allowed for much larger screens than the tried-and-true picture tube television sets.

Rear Projection

Generally speaking, conventional picture tube televisions do not exceed 36 inches diagonally (although Sony recently released a 40-inch diagonal tube-based television), so in order to get larger screens into a home theater, you must move to the realm of projection televisions. Rear-projection television screens get as large as 70 inches diagonally, which makes their size limits considerably greater than tube-based televisions. As a rule, rear-projection televisions are also somewhat cheaper than large tube-based televisions, especially when HDTV comes into play. With all these positive comments about rear-projection televisions, you may be asking yourself why everyone doesn't jump on the rear-projection bandwagon and do away with their tube-based televisions. The limitations of rear-projection television are as follows:

- There's a "sweet spot" on projection televisions where the screen looks fantastic, but if you're not sitting in the exact position to view the sweet spot, the quality and brightness of the image isn't as good.

- Viewing a rear-projection television from the side often means that it is difficult to properly see at least a portion of the screen.

- When a roomful of people is watching a rear-projection television, each person is seeing a different level of quality of image depending on where he or she is sitting or standing.

- Brightness suffers with rear-projection televisions, relegating them to darkened rooms where little natural light can enter.

Figure 1-4. This is a 50-inch rear-projection HDTV-ready set in action.

 **NOTE** *The new Digital Light Processing (DLP) projection systems in rear-projection and front-projection systems don't suffer from many of the effects described in the preceding list. Still, DLP systems are significantly more expensive right now, making them less likely to be an alternative for the average buyer.*

This is where people get divided into camps; some people absolutely love rear projection, and others can't stand it and prefer tube-based televisions. Your authors are also split on this point, with Jeff using a Toshiba 50-inch rear-projection HDTV television and Bart using a Sony WEGA 32-inch tube-based flat-screen HDTV television. In short, it's purely a matter of opinion as to which you will prefer, and we suggest going to your local electronics store to compare tube-based and rear-projection televisions to see which you like best.

Front Projection

The other type of projection television is one that requires an entire room to be effective—that is to say, the pieces are spread out across an entire room. Generally speaking, the projector is at one end of the room and the screen is at the other. The projection units can be on the floor in front of the screen, or high on a table in the back of the room, or even suspended from the roof at the back or middle of the home theater room. The advantage of *front-projection televisions* is that they produce a picture that's not unlike that of a real theater. The sweet spot issues that can plague rear-projection systems are almost nonexistent in front-projection systems, but these systems can be extremely expensive when compared to rear-projection or tube-based televisions. Still, the costs of front-projection systems are decreasing constantly, and if you're willing to buy a used unit, it's not inconceivable to purchase a complete system for about the same price as a new rear-projection television.

Flat Panel Televisions

The last decade has seen huge advances in technology in flat panel monitor technology. Initially used for laptop computer screens (see Figure 1-5), flat panel technology has made the leap into the realm of television, and with high-definition broadcasts just around the corner (and in existence in many areas already), these televisions are poised to become the standard by which all others are judged.

Figure 1-5. This 15-inch flat-screen computer monitor from Apple can also work as a high-resolution television.

Flat panel technology is basically a very advanced version of the liquid crystal display (LCD, the primary display in most digital watches). The advantages of flat panel television are both obvious and not-so-obvious:

- Flat panel televisions are very thin, and as a result they're much lighter than both projection and tube-based televisions.

- Color reproduction is more accurate in flat panel televisions, with whites looking whiter and so on.

- Flat panel televisions are physically more robust than their contemporaries. Not having electron guns and cumbersome projection systems means that they can take a bump or two without needing to be adjusted. They are also immune to damage from magnets, which is always a fear with tube-based televisions.

- Even huge flat panel televisions with 50-inch viewable areas can be hung on the wall, saving a great deal of space.

- Flat panel televisions use considerably less power than conventional televisions.

Of course, there are also some drawbacks to flat panel televisions:

- There can be dead zones that don't display the same as other areas on the panel.

- Dead pixels can occur. A *dead pixel* is a single pixel that has been turned to one color or is dead (black) and won't change. If this happens, the entire television set must be replaced, not an individual component. Most flat panel televisions have some dead pixels, but since the pixels are so small, they're usually unnoticeable.

The two competing flat panel television technologies are plasma and LCD. While an LCD television costs less than a plasma television, it can't produce a picture like a plasma television can. Some of the advantages of a plasma screen over an LCD television are a brighter picture, a wider viewing angle, better color purity, and a higher contrast ratio. Not surprisingly, plasma televisions are more expensive than LCD televisions (as a rule).

Not all is rosy, however, when you're looking to purchase flat panel televisions. While flat panel televisions are excellent performers and are light, crisp, and ready for HDTV, they're unbelievably expensive. At the time of this writing, a 50-inch flat panel television was easily over $10,000 (U.S.)—many times what a comparable projection or tube-based television would cost. That said, the future is definitely in flat panel technology, and it's only a matter of time before prices fall sufficiently to make them affordable to a wider market.

NTSC Broadcast Standard

The NTSC worked feverishly in the early 1950s to develop a broadcast standard that would enable both black-and-white and color transmissions to be viewable on one television. Up until the NTSC standard came into effect in 1953, there were other color standards (such as the Goldmark standard) that did not comply with the current black-and-white broadcast standards, meaning that the consumer had to literally have two televisions to watch both color and black-and-white programming. Of course, in 1953 only the very rich or the die-hard technology aficionados had more than one television set in their home, so the development of a standard was critical to the progression and growth of television in North America.

The NTSC standard involved breaking the black-and-white information and color information into two different signals. This method didn't degrade the black-and-white quality, but rather allowed both systems to work off of the same signal. The actual specifications of the NTSC standard call for 525 vertical lines of resolution (stacked on top of one another) displayed at 59.94 fields per second. A *field* is a set of either even or odd lines, so in this case it would be either 263 or 262 lines. These odd and even fields (basically half the lines on the screen) are displayed in a sequential manner, one after the other, thus painting alternate lines to create the full frame. One full frame, with both sets of lines painted, occurs roughly every 1/30 of a second, so even though every second line is being painted at 1/60 of a second, the entire amount of information streaming off the television screen is displayed only 1/30 of a second.

Amazingly, the NTSC standard has been the television standard in North America and Japan (and numerous other countries) for 50 years, and it hasn't changed at all. The only differences in the quality of television is in the sets that the signal is watched on, not the signal itself. That, however, is finally changing with the advent and integration of HDTV.

The Future of Television

There have been a few dramatic changes in television in the last 50 years, but most of those changes have involved the quality and features of the televisions themselves, not the way that the signal is delivered to the television or the quality of that signal. Of course, in recent years the acceptance of DVD and more recently the popularity of progressive scan DVD players (players that output the signal at maximum resolution) has made it possible for those with high-definition television sets (and even those without) to enjoy a much clearer picture than they've been otherwise used to. The real leap in television is scheduled to occur in North America by 2006. The Federal Communications Commission (FCC) has mandated 2006 as the year that all broadcasts must be in digital format, which in turn means that HDTV signals will be the norm rather than the exception.

High Definition Television

High-definition television (HDTV) is best described as digital television that provides a significantly clearer picture than the 525-line standard of North America or the 625-line standard of Europe. There are several reasons why it has taken nearly 50 years to finally get the ball rolling for a higher resolution television signal. First, there's such a huge installed base of analog televisions that the switch would be slow as consumers sluggishly adopted the new technology. The second reason is that it's very expensive for broadcasters to upgrade their equipment and broadcast equipment to capture images, process them, and then broadcast them in digital format. Nothing about the digital format is similar to the old analog system, and as a result the costs of switching over are significant. The last, and perhaps the most significant reason why we haven't seen a leap to HDTV sooner, is that digital picture images require a massive amount of information for every second they're on the screen. Until a compression algorithm came along that was able to reduce the bandwidth needed to produce HDTV, we weren't going to be watching anything different at all. Eventually, in 1993, the MPEG-2 standard solved the bandwidth issues associated with HDTV.

Because the FCC had some difficulty settling on a single HDTV standard, they decided on multiple formats that came from a "grand alliance" of companies, including AT&T, Zenith, Philips, Sarnoff, and Thomson. Ultimately, the FCC settled on a combination of formats including 1080i, 1080p, 960i, 720p, and 480p. The *i* means "interlaced," and the *p* stands for "progressive." *Interlaced* displays work on the same principle as old-fashioned television—that is to say that the screen is painted twice to get one full picture image, with odd or even lines being painted at any one time. *Progressive* scan technology paints the entire picture at once, thus eliminating any flicker there might be while creating superior picture quality.

Most high-definition televisions today come with the capability to handle all of these formats (1080i, 960i, 720p, and 480p), so you don't have to worry a great deal about whether or not your television can take advantage of high-definition broadcasts. Most older televisions (2002 and earlier) don't support all of these formats—most only manage 1080i and 480p (960i is 480p and 540p is basically 1080i), while others offer 540p and 1080i and then up convert 480p to 540p to support it. Many of the 2003 models support all of these modes, but you should inspect the fine print before you commit to buying one. At the time of this writing, two major networks are broadcasting their HDTV in 1080i, a third is broadcasting in 720p, and yet another network is broadcasting in a nonstandard 540p format. Still, this should not be a concern to consumers, because chances are that all HDTV and HDTV-ready televisions (see Figure 1-6) sold in North America will work with what's being broadcasted.

Figure 1-6. This Sony WEGA 32-inch HDTV television has a completely flat screen, is tube based and can handle all current North American HDTV standards.

MPEG-2

As mentioned in the previous section, it quickly became clear that if high-definition digital television was to be broadcast, the bandwidth issue would have to be addressed. In short, if there was no compression technology employed with HDTV broadcasts, the number of channels available would be very limited indeed. When you consider that one minute of 640×480 video in digital form takes up 1.8GB of memory, it isn't hard to see why some sort of compression is necessary to make digital television work.

In 1993, engineers from the 18 countries participating in developing the HDTV standard agreed on MPEG-2 compression technology as the standard for video compression for the HDTV format. MPEG-2 uses redundancies in the image to reduce the amount of bandwidth needed to display the image. In other words, MPEG-2 compressed signals only display what has *changed* on the screen, not what has remained the same. Therefore, if a scene in a movie takes place in front of an orange wall, the orange wall information is actually only received once, and it doesn't change until the area of the screen displaying the orange wall changes images. By only transmitting "new" information to the screen, a great deal of bandwidth is conserved. MPEG-2 is also compatible with AC-3 Dolby sound, and it contains enough bandwidth to include auxiliary information as well as voice-image syncing.

 **NOTE** *MPEG-2 is the same compression technology used for DVD technology, although the bit rate (the total amount of information flowing) is higher for DVD than it is for HDTV. MPEG-2 is the compression method for DSS service as well as DVDs. MPEG stands for Moving Pictures Experts Group, and there are several incarnations of MPEG compression, including the popular MPEG-3 (or MP3) compression used for audio files such as music available on Gnutella and other online forums.*

VHS and Betamax

Since the inception of television in the 1940s, the only way in which the average consumer could watch a show was to catch the programming as it was broadcast. That is to say, if a show was scheduled to broadcast at 5:00 P.M., you had to be in front of the television at 5:00 P.M. or you would miss part or all of the show. The ability to tape television shows was available by the late 1950s, but it wasn't until 1960 that Sony introduced a "compact" videotape recorder (VTR). These early video recorders were cumbersome because they could only record 1 hour at a time, and they employed a reel-to-reel methodology that meant users had to be able to thread the delicate tape through the machine in order to watch a show. The other drawback to these early machines was that only the very rich could afford the high-tech (at the time) equipment. As videotape technology became more sophisticated, the ante was upped and there were ever-smaller video recording devices on the market throughout the 1960s. It wasn't until 1975, however, that Sony introduced what could be considered the first successful home video recording system: the Betamax.

The Betamax quickly dominated the market (selling over 30,000 units in 1975) and was a success from the start. It owed its success largely to the fact that it was cassette based, but also because the units were relatively small and delivered a high-quality picture. The celebrations would have to be cut short, however, because the good old boys at JVC and Matshushita (Panasonic's parent company) had secretly been developing a new home video format, the Video Home System (VHS). While the quality of the VHS system was not as good as the Betamax, the VHS system could record *twice* as much information on one tape. The VHS 2-hour limit fit nicely with the standard 2-hour timeframe of most movies, whereas the Betamax limit of 1 hour meant that a movie was out of the question without a cartridge swap. While the term "Betamax" became synonymous with home video recording devices, by the early 1980s Sony's market share was a third of the market, while VHS continued to flourish both because of tape length and the much lower cost of the VHS recording units.

NOTE *Quality does not always win out over quantity. The Sony Betamax system was noticeably better than the VHS format when it came to picture quality, but the public did not care about this and they showed this by spending their money on VHS machines rather than Betamax machines.*

The war between the two formats continued for years until in 1988 the first Sony VHS machines went on sale in North America. By 1994 the Betamax format was actually still around, but it was relegated to an extremely small portion of the market and VHS (see Figure 1-7) had clearly won the battles and the war. With the dawn of DVD players and with home DVD recorders now starting to enter the market, the use of videotape is beginning to decline. As DVD recorders become cheaper, the advantages that DVD can offer will mean that DVD recorders will begin to supplant videocassette recorders (VCRs) in homes all over the world. Still, VHS tapes are a large part of many home movie collections, and the VCR continues to be the television recording machine of choice.

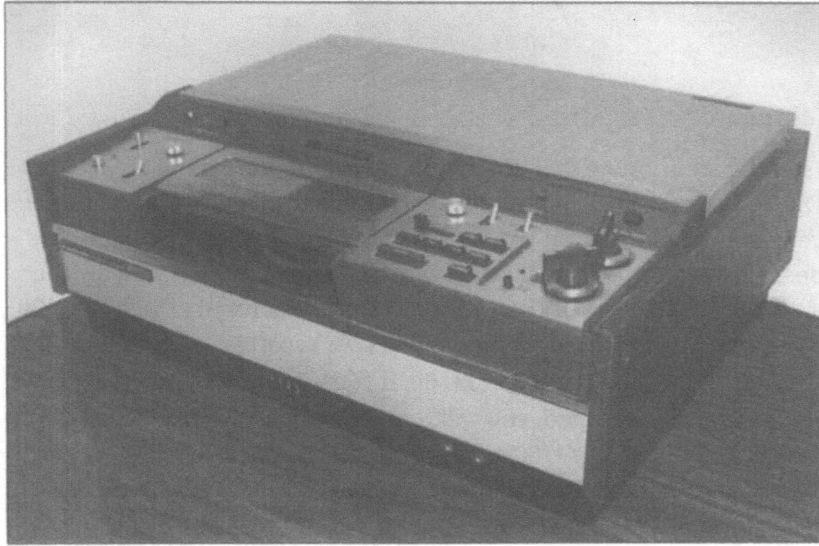

Figure 1-7. A VHS VCR circa 1985

How VCRs Work

VCRs have become so ubiquitous that most of us take their technology for granted. The development of videotape technology required many years and had numerous seemingly insurmountable obstacles in its path over the years. Still, it made it to the point where you can buy yourself a VCR for $50 *new!* There are two main parts of the VCR that we discuss in this section: the tape (and tape cassette) and the mechanism that reads the tape (including the VCR head[s]).

The Tape

Although VHS tapes vary in length and quality, the basic VHS tape is a magnetic oxide-coated piece of plastic that's about 800 feet long and 1/2 inch wide. To give you an idea of how long 800 feet is, it's nearly the length of three football fields, and that's a lot of tape in one small cassette! This tape is wound up on two spindles much like a cassette tape that's used for audio purposes, but the video cassette also contains a door that keeps the very fragile and thin videotape from being damaged by the environment.

The Heads

We need to start by mentioning that VCRs in North America are designed to work with the NTSC television standard; that said, we can continue the explanation. If you have ever glanced inside a VCR you may have noticed that there is a circular device inside. This device is a circular drum with at least two heads on it, one on each side of the drum 180 degrees apart. This circular drum rotates once every 30 seconds so that each head meets the tape 30 times per second—the total number of times the heads hit the tape per second is 60. If you remember back to when we were discussing the NTSC standard, you will remember that the interlaced screen is drawn one-half at a time every 1/60 of a second, making for one complete picture every 1/30 of a second. The two heads in a VCR are literally writing the information to the tape in the same way that information would be displayed onscreen if it were receiving an NTSC broadcast signal. The audio portion of the content is recorded on a narrow portion on the outer aspect of the tape. This information includes such details as what speed the information was recorded at and the sound for the video content.

NOTE *When you adjust the* tracking *on a VCR, you are using a content strip to line up the tape for proper playback. Tracking adjustment is sometimes necessary because the tape can degrade, stretch, or even shrink a small amount.*

NOTE *We now see the limitation of VHS tape, specifically, that it is tied to the NTSC standard, which uses a 525-line interlaced format. This relatively low-resolution image cannot compete with DVD and the HDTV technology that is to come.*

DVD

DVD stands for *digital video disc* or *digital versatile disc,* depending on whom you talk to, but for our purposes we'll just refer to it as DVD. DVD is fast becoming the standard for videophiles everywhere. Capable of storing over 4 hours of information on one side of the disc, the DVD (see Figure 1-8) can offer up superb picture quality, digital sound, and a plethora of extra features such as alternate sound tracks, a director's commentary, multiple viewing angles, and even deleted scenes and outtakes. The other huge advantage of DVD technology is that the user can hop from one scene to another almost instantaneously. With VHS tapes, the user must fast forward or rewind the tape to get to specific areas, and this can take minutes.

Figure 1-8. A DVD looks much like a compact disc (CD), but it can hold nearly 70 times more information.

NOTE *Most modern DVD players can serve a variety of functions now; they are able to play video CDs, audio CDs, DVDs, and even PC-formatted CD-Rs with MP3 audio files on them. Because of its power and versatility, the DVD player has become the focus of the home theater/stereo in just a few short years.*

DVDs also offers a permanency that videotape cannot; videotapes begin to degrade from the time they are recorded, and of course close proximity to a magnet will damage them significantly and irrevocably. In short, DVD is a far superior medium for viewing video of any kind. With the recent arrivals of DVD recordable and rewritable (DVD-R/RW) VCR-like machines, DVD is poised to supplant videotape forever.

DVD History

Although videotape and VCRs have dominated the scene for many years, the limitations of video have started to rear their ugly heads. For example, we have a store-bought copy of a popular movie from the early 1990s on VHS. In the decade since we purchased that movie, the quality of the picture has degraded markedly to the point where it is not enjoyable to watch anymore. This and the 2-hour limit for high-quality video (among other factors) precipitated the need for a video format that could be purely digital and be distributed on a disc the same size as a standard audio CD.

NOTE *It can also be argued that DVD exists in large part because of Moore's Law. Moore's Law states that the power of a computer processor doubles every 18 months, and it has been this huge explosion in the power of computer processors that has precipitated the development of DVD technology. Certainly, the vast amount of information that must be moved and uncompressed requires powerful processors, and without these DVD would be only a theory instead of reality.*

In 1994, Sony and Philips working together came up with the specs for a digital disc that was one sided and dual layered and could hold many hours of video. There were other formats proposed, including a super-density disk (SD), but ultimately there was an agreement reached in 1995 that allowed for DVD to move forward. The fact that an agreement was reached was perhaps in part because of lessons learned over the protracted VHS/Betamax battle in the 1970s and 1980s. By 1997, the first DVD players hit the shelves in North America, and they sold better than anyone could have expected. Perhaps helped in part by the adoption of DVD/CD-ROM drives in computers, DVD players became the fastest-adopted new technology in history, and DVD technology is poised to push VHS right out the door in the next 5 years.

How DVD Works

DVDs are actually closely related to CDs in size, appearance, and basic concept. The main exception for the *standard* DVD versus the CD is the amount of information that a DVD is capable of holding. A standard DVD can hold over 130 minutes of MPEG-2 video, plus up to eight audio tracks, the menu systems, and text screens. A standard single-layer DVD can hold 4.7GB of data, a double-layer single-sided DVD can hold 8.5GB, and finally a double-sided double-layer DVD can hold a whopping 17GB. The way data is stored on DVD is almost exactly the same as it is in the CD format—that is to say that the data is represented on the disc by a series of pits and bumps that are run out in a long, contiguous layer. This layer is so long that a single-sided DVD's data track, if laid out in a straight line, would be nearly 7.5 miles long.

The way this information is read is by laser. A DVD player has a laser that can focus on the pits and bumps and read them as they zip by (DVDs spin inside a DVD player). The size of these pits and bumps is so small that it's difficult to impress just how tiny they are. When you consider that a DVD is capable of holding nearly 70 times more data than a standard CD, the tiny size of these pits and bumps becomes apparent. Earlier we mentioned *dual-layer* discs. These DVDs have two layers of information, both on one side of the disc. On a single-layer DVD, there is a reflective coating on the top portion of the disc that reflects the laser back and allows the data to be read. Dual-layer DVDs have this same layer, but there is also an in-between layer that is semireflective. This semireflective layer can be penetrated by altering the focus of the DVD player's laser, thus allowing for twice as much information to be stored on one side of a DVD.

MPEG-2 and DVD

Even though DVDs can hold a massive amount of information, when you consider that 1 minute of 640×480 color video takes up 1.8GB of space, you can see that uncompressed, even a double-layer DVD could only hold about 4 minutes and 40 seconds of video. How do they get 4 hours of high-quality video and sound on one side of a DVD? The answer is MPEG-2 compression, which we discussed earlier in this chapter.

When a DVD is compressed, it is not simply compressed at a particular rate; rather, each frame is compressed one at a time to maximize the compression without compromising quality. There appears to be an art to compression of video, because some DVDs are simply not encoded as well and the quality is noticeably lower than others. Not to worry, however, because most DVDs on the market are well encoded and won't disappoint. Some DVDs are thoroughly optimized and are sold at a premium, such as the Superbit collection that is currently available for true aficionados.

Laserdisc

Back before there was DVD, there *was* a video medium that had excellent quality and came on a laser-read disc. The Laserdisc was never a huge success, but video aficionados adopted this format and lovingly kept it alive. Many of the features now available on DVD, such as alternate soundtracks and director's commentaries, were pioneered on Laserdisc long before they became a reality on DVD. Laserdisc was invented back in the 1960s and patented by David P. Gregg in 1961. Back then he thought of it as a "videodisk," but the basic principles of this technology are clearly the genesis of all subsequent disk designs (CD, DVD, and so forth). While Mr. Gregg's original idea was an analog product, the same basic principles were ultimately used in the creation of the CD and also the DVD.

The RCA Videodisk

Back in the early 1980s, RCA came out with a videodisk technology that used an analog disk that was read by a stylus much like a record player uses. Like the Laserdisc, this disk had to be flipped halfway through a movie, but that was the least of its problems. The area at the end of the disk (near the inside of the disk) had a tendency to wear out faster than the rest of the disk, causing video breakup sometimes after only a few uses. The result was a fuzzy picture right before the movie reached the point where the disk had to be flipped. Needless to say, this technology, which was introduced to compete with the VHS and Betamax, quickly failed.

The Laserdisc technology that was sold by Pioneer (and is still available today in a limited way) involved a reader, and large Laserdiscs that were the size of old-fashioned audio records. The biggest drawback to Laserdisc is that the discs themselves only hold 1 hour of video per side, which requires the user to flip the disc halfway through a movie. The availability of movies for this format has also been an issue, and today Laserdisc movies are limited mostly to specialty stores if they are sold at all.

Video CD

Video CDs are basically a product that was created when computers met the CD-R format. The Video CD uses the same technology and basic data reading/writing that CDs use, making them easy to create on today's home PCs. In the late 1980s, a few Video CDs were actually released, but they were limited by the CD's size constraints and could only hold about 20 minutes of video. Video CDs today use MPEG-1 compression to give about 1 hour of video per CD. This is mostly used for putting home video on a permanent format, but unfortunately some less scrupulous people use this technology to put copyrighted movies on Video CDs. The quality of these CDs, however, is certainly lacking and can't compete with DVD or Laserdisc.

 **TIP** *If you're interested in finding one of these old Video CDs, you can try to find David Bowie's Sound + Vision four-CD set that included a Video CD of his "Ashes to Ashes" music video.*

For now, Video CDs are bridging the gap for people who have home video that they would like to have available on a convenient CD rather than on digital video-tape. Most contemporary DVD players can play Video CDs, making them a viable option if you need to archive some midrange-quality video.

There is also Super Video CD (SVCD). This format is similar to Video CD and is capable of holding 30–60 minutes of very good quality, full-motion video as well as two stereo soundtracks on a 74-minute CD-R.

Table 1-1 provides a comparison of the resolutions and bit rates for Video CD, Super Video CD, and DVD formats.

Table 1-1. Resolutions and Bit Rates for Video CD, Super Video CD, and DVD

ENCODING	FORMAT	RESOLUTION	BIT RATE
MPEG-1	VCD	352×TMS240 (typical)	1.5 mbit
MPEG-2	SVCD	480×TMS480 (NTSC)	2.6 mbit (typical)
MPEG-2	DVD	720×TMS480 (typical)	2–8 mbit (typical)

Home Video and Video Editing

Home video has been around in one form or another for many years. Heck, Bart's grandfather used 16mm film back in the 1920s to record life in rural Saskatchewan! More recently, 16mm color film was used, and by the mid-1980s the videotape camcorder had become ubiquitous with families and tourists alike, and people were recording millions of hours of footage every year. It is hard to imagine how we have come from the giant videotape recording units of the 1950s to the tiny handheld digital camcorders of today, but the technological advancements have marched on, and now many camcorders are actually called *palmcorders* because they are so very small. With the recent flood of digital camcorders that have found their way into the average home, using the PC as a video editing tool has become increasingly popular, and with the HTPC the newly edited home videos can be streamed right off the HTPC's hard drive and onto a high-definition television screen.

Analog/Digital Cameras

Up until 1998, the standard cameras were not digital, they were analog, and as a rule they used 8mm (also called Hi-8) tape to record. Since 1998, however, more and more of the cameras sold are digital cameras. These cameras often use the same tapes, but they record the information digitally rather than in an analog fashion. Why is this good? Digital information is more permanent than analog, because error correction algorithms can account for any degradation in the quality of the digital information on the magnetic tape. With an analog tape, that degradation is seen right on the screen. Digital video is also very handy if you have a computer that can edit and manage digital video. Computers with this capability can create professional-looking movies with multiple soundtracks and digital effects, and then output them to Video CD, VHS, or even burn them onto record-able DVDs (DVD-Rs).

 **NOTE** *While digital camera connectivity and digital video editing technology is just emerging on the mainstream PC, the Apple Macintosh line of computers has been doing it for years now. If you're interested in making incredibly professional-looking movies easily and then burning them onto your own DVD, think about picking up one of the new iMacs or a Mac with a Superdrive DVD player in it. These drives can burn DVD-R media so that you can make your own home movie DVDs easily. These Macs also come with iDVD and iMovie, two pieces of software that turn the chore of video editing into a treat. Lastly, all Macs come with IEEE 1394 Firewire ports for easy connection to digital cameras. Very few PCs have this built in. Unfortunately, we don't feel that the Mac is a viable computer for creating a kick-ass HTPC, so we don't cover it in this book, but if video editing is your main passion, the Mac is worth looking at.*

While importing movies onto an HTPC with a digital camera is a breeze, it's not impossible or even difficult to get yourself an adaptor that will allow you to stream your analog video source (even from a VCR) into your computer and turn it into digital footage. The quality won't be as good, but at least your precious home movies will be moving into the permanent realm of digital rather than degrading on analog tape. There are many devices and video cards, such as the ATI Radeon 7500, that are capable of importing video sources, but we won't go into detail about that now—you can read about that in Chapter 6.

Summary

While a background in the history of television, DVD, and audio/visual technology isn't absolutely necessary for creating a home theater PC (HTPC), the history of these technologies *is* interesting and can provide a frame of reference for the novice, especially when terms such as "NTSC" and "high definition" are being bandied about. Figure 1-9 shows a timeline of important developments in television, video, DVD, and so forth from 1900 to 2002.

The following chapters examine what an HTPC is and explore the ins and outs of the components that go into making one. The next chapter covers HTPC uses.

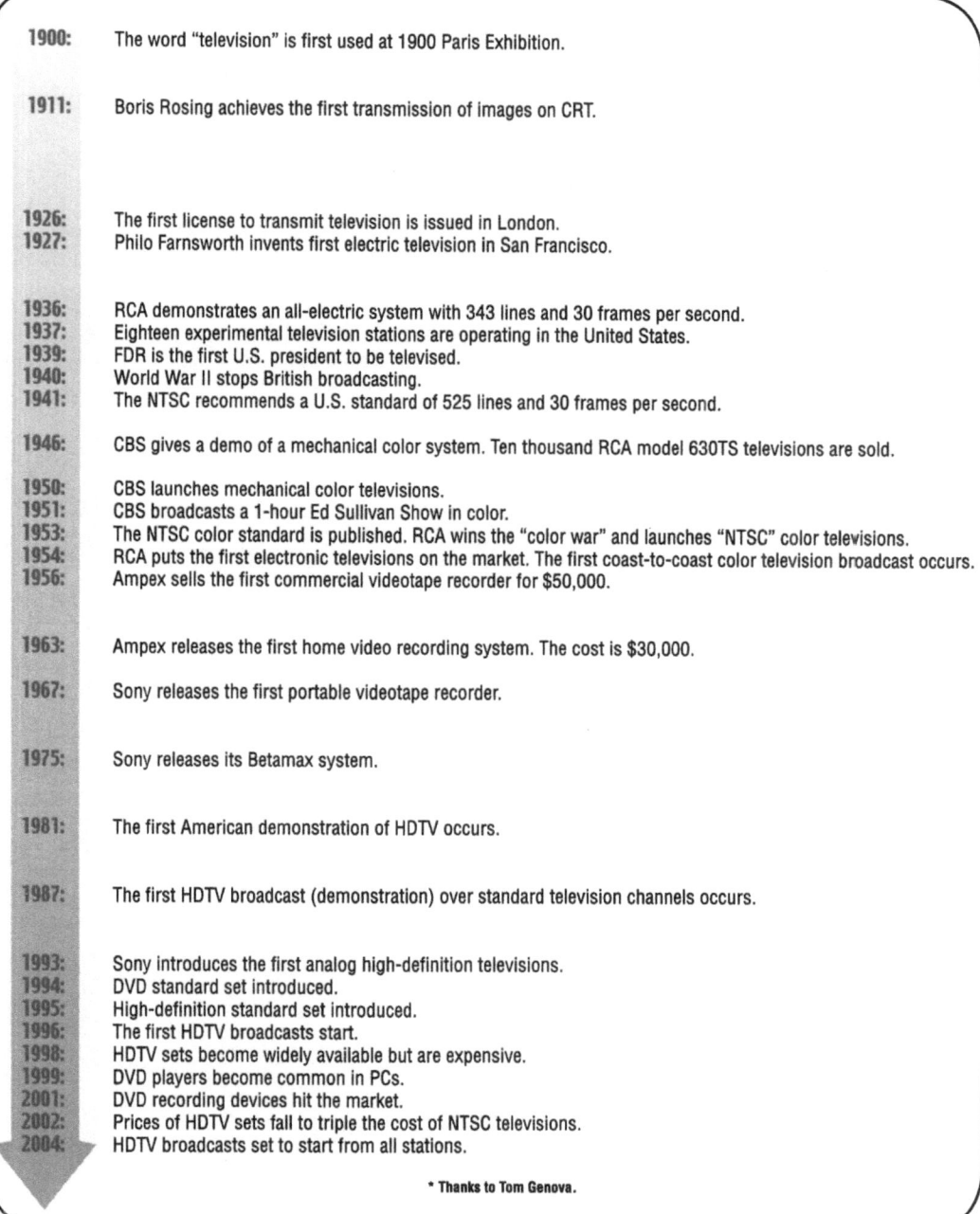

1900:	The word "television" is first used at 1900 Paris Exhibition.
1911:	Boris Rosing achieves the first transmission of images on CRT.
1926:	The first license to transmit television is issued in London.
1927:	Philo Farnsworth invents first electric television in San Francisco.
1936:	RCA demonstrates an all-electric system with 343 lines and 30 frames per second.
1937:	Eighteen experimental television stations are operating in the United States.
1939:	FDR is the first U.S. president to be televised.
1940:	World War II stops British broadcasting.
1941:	The NTSC recommends a U.S. standard of 525 lines and 30 frames per second.
1946:	CBS gives a demo of a mechanical color system. Ten thousand RCA model 630TS televisions are sold.
1950:	CBS launches mechanical color televisions.
1951:	CBS broadcasts a 1-hour Ed Sullivan Show in color.
1953:	The NTSC color standard is published. RCA wins the "color war" and launches "NTSC" color televisions.
1954:	RCA puts the first electronic televisions on the market. The first coast-to-coast color television broadcast occurs.
1956:	Ampex sells the first commercial videotape recorder for $50,000.
1963:	Ampex releases the first home video recording system. The cost is $30,000.
1967:	Sony releases the first portable videotape recorder.
1975:	Sony releases its Betamax system.
1981:	The first American demonstration of HDTV occurs.
1987:	The first HDTV broadcast (demonstration) over standard television channels occurs.
1993:	Sony introduces the first analog high-definition televisions.
1994:	DVD standard set introduced.
1995:	High-definition standard set introduced.
1996:	The first HDTV broadcasts start.
1998:	HDTV sets become widely available but are expensive.
1999:	DVD players become common in PCs.
2001:	DVD recording devices hit the market.
2002:	Prices of HDTV sets fall to triple the cost of NTSC televisions.
2004:	HDTV broadcasts set to start from all stations.

* Thanks to Tom Genova.

Figure 1-9. A timeline of television/video/DVD development from 1900 to 2002

CHAPTER 2

Home Theater PC Uses

THIS CHAPTER WILL answer the question, "Why should my DVD player be an HTPC?" To the computer hobbyist, this question needs no answer: Building a machine to play movies is much more fun than just purchasing one. For the rest of us, however, this question needs to be answered to provide some justification for investing time and money to create a machine that on the surface looks like it could easily be replaced by a low-cost DVD player. Of course, there is a lot more to an HTPC than just playing DVD movies, but since DVD technology represents the state-of-the-art for home theater, it is an ideal topic for comparing an HTPC to the alternatives and showing how the HTPC has many advantages over conventional DVD players.

Under the best conditions, an HTPC can provide better picture and sound than an off-the-shelf consumer DVD player. With the imminent arrival of high-definition television (HDTV), many people are already considering (or have made) the purchase of a new, larger television that is capable of displaying HDTV formats. In order to get the best possible high-resolution picture quality on an HDTV, many home theater enthusiasts use a *line-doubler* to increase resolution. These devices are available in a range of quality and prices, but an HTPC can output a comparable or better quality video picture for less money.

The output from an HTPC is much more adjustable than that from a dedicated DVD player, and in addition to precise adjustments to color levels and saturation, the HTPC allows for a variety of ways to convert the 24 frames per second (fps) of film to the 30 fps of television and to scale up the image for high-quality monitors. On a small display, this conversion is hardly noticeable, but on larger displays it becomes a much-discussed and debated issue. Even those home theater systems that include only a standard NTSC-capable television can benefit from the picture quality fine-tuning that can be accomplished with an HTPC (see Figure 2-1).

Figure 2-1. The HTPC looks like any other PC, but when configured properly it can make all the difference.

Improving Picture Quality

Standard television picture quality is quite poor compared to the newest movie and digital television formats. The NTSC television format specifies 525 lines of resolution at 60 fields per second, which is composed of 30 interlaced frames per second. On a standard direct-view television tube, this looks acceptable, but when the picture is bigger, the interlaced scan lines are visible. The NTSC television format was never meant for the large screen displays that are becoming popular today—after all, the NTSC standard was developed in 1953!

NOTE Progressive scan *means that all the lines on the monitor are being painted at the same time. This is different from* interlaced *pictures, where the scan lines are painted every second row.*

On a 36-inch or larger display, you can see the scan lines plainly from even an average 6-foot viewing distance. To counter this problem, newer television formats either increase the resolution or up-convert it to a progressively scanned picture. High-definition digital television uses progressive scan for all resolutions below 960 lines. Computer monitors can switch between interlaced and progressive modes, but consumer television sets do not switch. It is very easy to tell the difference between an interlaced picture and a progressive scan picture when comparing large television sets side by side in a store, and most people who can afford to do so prefer to buy the progressive scan set.

Converting Interlaced Video to Progressive Scan

Converting the NTSC interlaced picture to a progressive scan picture is not simple, and this is why the HTPC is a great tool for this problem. Remember that an interlaced picture shows half the picture lines each time it draws the screen. Even though the next set of lines follows right away, moving objects on the screen will not be in exactly the same spot as they were when the previous set of lines was displayed. The two sets of lines that make up the interlaced picture are not simply two halves of the same frame; they are each half of a separate frame (though NTSC is still referred to as 30 fps). Converting interlaced television pictures to progressive scan pictures cannot be done properly by simply drawing both sets of lines at the same time. The edges of moving objects look distorted by "stair steps," and fine detail will appear to flicker and vibrate.

A better method of converting interlaced to progressive scan is to double each interlaced line. This creates a full resolution picture for every field by repeating each line in the field, which means that the field becomes a full frame of information. The new frame does not have as much information as the combined interlaced frame, since it is made from half the lines of the full interlaced frame, but it has no motion-induced distortion. Thus, the resulting video signal has lower resolution and a higher frame rate.

These two methods of converting interlaced video to progressive scan video are called *line doubling*. A high-quality line-doubler also does some extra processing to eliminate motion distortion or increase resolution, depending on which method is used to convert the video signal. Though the resulting video quality is better than the original interlaced video, it is never as good as a native progressive scan signal. Though most high-quality progressive-scan televisions up-convert interlaced video to progressive scan, an HTPC can perform this function with more options to fine-tune and configure the video quality.

Image Scaling

Converting the resolution of a standard NTSC video signal to a high-resolution display device is almost as complicated as the interlaced to progressive scan conversion. Some display projectors require an up-conversion, though this is not usually needed, since almost all HDTV-ready televisions sold today will display NTSC just fine. However, many digital projectors and LCD or plasma displays have a *native resolution*. This is the resolution that the set was manufactured to display, and all other resolutions are either converted or not displayed at all. Therefore, in some cases it is desirable to convert the resolution, and doing so requires complicated digital processing.

NOTE *Although the NTSC video standard is 525 lines, only about 480 of those lines are visible to the viewer. The rest are used to synchronize the display to the signal and carry the closed captioning information.*

If the picture resolution is not converted to a simple multiple of the native format (i.e., 480 lines converted to 960 lines), then some lines are converted unevenly to the new resolution. Converting 480 lines to 540 lines means that every eighth line is repeated. This would make the resulting image look pretty odd, so instead of just doubling some interval of lines, a good converter will average the information on each line and use that information to draw the new lines. Such a video converter is called an *image scaler* and is quite costly. Low-quality scalers start above $700.00, and prices go up to $20,000.00 for high-quality units.

The HTPC Advantage

The HTPC will do the interlaced-to-progressive-scan conversion and video scaling at a high quality for considerably less cost than an external scaler. Using an HTPC to output to a high-definition display device is a great solution to the prohibitive costs of an image scaler. The HTPC can be set to the best image resolution that the display can handle—such as 720p or 1080i for an HDTV—and it will convert everything else up to that quality. Even DVD movies, which are encoded at 480p, can be displayed at HDTV resolution.

TIP *Scaling an NTSC (480i) or DVD (480p) video image to 1080i does not make it as good as a native 1080i video image. The original video signal does not gain extra information—the extra lines in the high-definition image are just filled in with detail from the original lines. The only advantage to scaling an image up is to keep the display at its native resolution. It may also be convenient to leave the television set at one display resolution setting and use the HTPC to switch between video sources with different resolutions.*

Many DVD movies are presented with an *anamorphic picture*. This means that the picture is not the same shape as a standard television screen, which has a ratio of width to height of 4:3. An anamorphic picture is usually wider than a standard television, and these wide-screen movies are meant for wide-screen televisions. When an anamorphic movie is shown on a 4:3 television, black space is visible above and below the picture. Some viewers find this distracting, and even an HTPC cannot do much to alleviate it. However, the anamorphic movie shown on a 4:3 television has another problem, and most home theater enthusiasts consider it a much bigger problem than the black bars: resolution loss. Since the movie picture is squeezed down to fit into the display area, it loses resolution. To put it another way, those black bars above and below the picture are using up lines of resolution that the picture in the middle of the screen should use. The effects of this are subtle, but disturbing to those who are fussy about picture quality.

The simple solution is to use a wide-screen television to watch anamorphic DVD movies. Since the television is the same shape as the movie picture, the picture fills the whole screen and is shown at maximum resolution. The problem now is that watching a standard television broadcast suffers from having blank areas on each side of the picture, since it was intended for a 4:3 television and is too narrow for the wide-screen set. Another solution is to buy a 4:3 television set that can squeeze the scan lines into the visible picture area when displaying 16:9 video. This feature is called *vertical compression* or *anamorphic squeeze,* and it is becoming a more common, though expensive, option on new 4:3 HDTV sets.

The HTPC can provide a solution for those with a 4:3 high-definition television. By up-converting DVD movies to 720p or 1080i, anamorphic video pictures will be displayed at maximum resolution. The black bars are still present at the top and bottom of the screen, but there is enough resolution left in the picture area to show the movie without distortion. No off-the-shelf consumer DVD player can do that!

 **NOTE** *Some high-definition televisions, such as Sony's tube-based HDTVs, have a built-in feature that ensures that the black bars on the top and the bottom of the picture are not painted at all and that resolution is maximized. Unfortunately, televisions like this are few and far between, thus bringing the HTPC to the forefront to solve the problem.*

Improving Audio Quality

Traditionally, computer audio has been poor, more often the subject of ridicule and jokes than the standard benchmark of quality. Some bright spots in the history of computer audio exist, however, such as the sound capabilities of the Commodore Amiga or the futuristic tones of digital keyboard synthesizers, but in the past, most home computers had sound that was poor, bad, or nonexistent.

Digital Sound

In the later 1990s, computer processors became fast enough to handle digital sound (and indeed, even digital video). This led to a revolution in computer sound hardware. By the late 1990s, most avid computer users were disconnecting their PCs from the small, cheap speakers that came with the system and were instead connecting to high-quality sound systems and even their home stereo. Many people began to use the CD-ROM drive in their computer to play audio CDs, and then to decode and play back digitally compressed audio such as MP3 and WMA files. With the increase in hard disk capacity over the years, it is possible to store many hundreds of hours of compressed audio in a home computer.

When CD digital audio was introduced in the mid-1980s, it set a new standard of quality for sound and storage media. It was not until the early 1990s, when many new PCs were sold with CD-ROM drives, that computer buyers started to ask for sound capabilities in their new systems that could match the quality of sound stored on a CD.

Sound quality was important to computer game players, too. It is a little-acknowledged fact that the amazing innovation in computer games during the 1990s sold a lot of computer hardware and increased demand for graphics and sound capabilities. Each new generation of computer games needed faster computer processors, more memory, faster video hardware, and higher quality sound. These great advancements in video and audio capabilities pay off in a big way for home theater enthusiasts who want to build an HTPC because the home computer is now powerful enough to create a high-quality theater experience—and it can still play all those fantastic games!

CD Audio

The quality of CD audio has recently been surpassed. Chapter 3 explains how higher bit rates, increased sampling frequencies, and denser storage media have all led to new digital audio formats that store and re-create music at a higher quality than CDs. Newer sound hardware also supports digital inputs and outputs, so that recording and playing back high-quality soundtracks is possible. For the HTPC hobbyist, this means that upgrading to a new sound card capable of supporting 24-bit/96 KHz digital sound is more appealing, since it can now take advantage of more than just DVD movies.

A huge benefit that arises from using a PC to reproduce music is that when a new digital format is released, the computer can be upgraded or adapted to support it. With a large market of computer users who want premium-quality sound reproduction for computer games, home theater, presentations, and professional audio editing, it is a safe bet that the HTPC will remain at the leading edge of audio technology for years to come.

Networking the HTPC

Since the HTPC is still a PC at heart, it is perfectly suitable to networking with other computers. It is becoming common to find homes with more than one PC and to find high-speed Internet access available in many large cities. Adding computer networking capabilities to the HTPC (see Figure 2-2) is a great idea for many reasons.

Figure 2-2. A network can add functionality to your HTPC, such as allowing it to bring audio files over from another PC.

A Media Player

First, the HTPC is essentially a media player, and it can benefit from the extra storage capacity that a computer network allows. In these days of digital convergence, when many media formats are digital, the computer can record, store, and play back these digital media. From CD audio music or digitized LP records to home movies or downloaded digital video clips, the media files use up a lot of space on a hard disk. The HTPC is a great machine to use as a media server in the home, where every computer connected to the same network can play the audio and video files stored on the HTPC.

The HTPC can also be used as just a player, with another computer on the network serving out files. By reducing the number of hard disk drives in the HTPC, the heat is reduced, and therefore the number and speed of fans needed to cool the system is reduced. This makes for a much quieter HTPC, which is a major consideration for most home theater rooms. It also allows for better performance for the HTPC, since it is dedicated to home theater tasks, instead of also serving files out to other computers on the network.

Internet Access

Second, the HTPC can benefit from networking where broadband access to the Internet is available. An HTPC with an Internet connection can be used for convenient access to e-mailing and Web browsing, and streaming media formats for Internet radio or video clips.

Even broadband Internet access cannot provide the minimum video quality that most people would find acceptable, though for some functions many are willing to make a sacrifice. The great thing about having the HTPC connected to the Internet is not to stream video, however, but to download it to the hard disk before playing it back. Many feature films and television shows provide preview video clips and movie trailers, which are of high enough quality to benefit from playback in the home theater. Watching a trailer on a conventional PC with a small screen and poor sound system is no match for the HTPC connected to a big television and digital home theater audio receiver.

Communication

The third major reason for networking an HTPC is for online chatting or videoconferencing. It is far more comfortable to gather people around the television in a home theater room for a videoconferencing session with distant relatives than to crowd around a small PC monitor stuck in the corner of a spare bedroom or office. It is also more convenient to participate in Internet chats or instant messaging on a large display, where you can resize video from broadcast television to a smaller area of the screen while the chat takes place.

Gaming

The final reason for networking an HTPC may apply only to a portion of those who are interested in building and operating such a system. Computer games have become widely popular since the availability of multiplayer sessions on the Internet. Most games released these days allow a small number of players to connect to each other over the Internet and play a round or two. It is an experience unlike anything a player could find in a single-player game. Also, several massive multiplayer games are available on the Internet now. These games do not start and end when a few friends decide to have a session—they continue 24 hours a day as people come and go from the game server. The HTPC is quite capable of the performance needed to play most modern multiplayer computer games.

 **NOTE** *The HTPC is a great system for game playing. Most gamers desire a video card that is optimized for speedy 3D graphics, and these features also give the card excellent MPEG-2 and DVD playback capabilities. No single video card is able to claim the best features and performance for games and video playback, so the HTPC must compromise on one or the other. However, the HTPC is still capable of playing modern computer games, and having the games presented on a big-screen display with ground-shaking audio can go a long way toward making up for the marginal loss of cutting-edge graphics performance.*

Using an HTPC

The HTPC is more than just a glorified DVD movie and CD audio player. It is a computer that specializes in high-quality audio and video, but it is also a computer that can perform all the functions of any other PC. Since this PC is located in the home theater, it often becomes the most convenient computer to use. In this section, we make some suggestions for uses of an HTPC and the hardware and software required for these functions. The functions intended for the HTPC will determine the size and shape of the system case, the location of the system, and the attachment of external peripherals. Intended functions will also affect the software that needs to be loaded and configured. The HTPC is very adaptable, but as with all computer systems, planning ahead can save effort and frustration later on.

Putting the excellent audio and video capabilities of the system to good use requires some knowledge and time on the part of the HTPC hobbyist. Unlike off-the-shelf consumer equipment, an HTPC does not simply plug into the wall, connect to the television, and start playing movies. The system must be put together—sometimes right from scratch (this is the way most hardcore hobbyists prefer it!)—and then configured. Often this configuration needs several tweaks in order to find the optimal settings. An HTPC can be set up to behave like any other home theater component—point the remote and click a button—but achieving this level of simplicity takes a great understanding of the complexity inherent in the system.

TIP *Actually, the HTPC can be a "plug-and-play" device now. Several manufacturers have introduced HTPC products to the retail market. Though these machines never have the same balance of cost and perform-ance that each individual prefers, they are just as configurable and upgradeable as custom-built systems. For those with limited technical skill, or little interest in assembling their own machine, the retail HTPC is a great solution.*

Each function of the HTPC requires hardware and software to support it. Many functions use the same hardware, such as the video card and sound card. Some functions require specialized hardware, such as a computer game that may require a joystick or game pad. Later chapters of this book explain precisely how to configure major components such as the video card and sound card. This section serves as an overview of what's available to you and what you should consider when planning an HTPC system.

Playing DVD Movies

This functionality is perhaps the most popular use for the HTPC. It is also a great measurement by which to assess the capability to perform other functions. A system that can play back DVD movies with optimal video and sound will also be able to perform most other home theater tasks with excellence.

We discussed the advantages of using an HTPC to play movies earlier in this chapter. With the low cost of DVD-ROM drives today, almost all PCs shipped to consumers include them. This does not guarantee that the system is suitable for

DVD movie playback in a home theater, however, and it may not mean that the system can play DVD movies at all.

Required Hardware

In addition to a DVD-ROM drive, the HTPC requires a sound card. Sound hardware is usually added to a computer system by including an add-in component called an *expansion card,* or more specifically, a *sound card.* Sometimes the sound hardware is added to the main system board, also called the *motherboard,* instead of adding it separately. This saves some cost and makes the system cheaper, but it is notoriously difficult to upgrade systems that have sound hardware on the motherboard. Instead of simply swapping one sound card for another, the system must be configured to switch off the built-in sound hardware before a new sound card is added. Switching off such built-in sound hardware may require a jumper to be moved or a system BIOS setting to be altered, and unfortunately there is no standard regarding this procedure. The good news is that some motherboards are available with very high-quality sound hardware built in, including digital audio output and surround-sound analog connections for full surround sound speaker sets.

Sound

The digital surround soundtrack from a DVD movie can be read by the DVD drive and sent to the sound card, and then sent directly to an external digital decoder such as a digital receiver that supports the Dolby Digital 5.1 and DTS 5.1 formats. This is usually the preferred way to configure the home theater, since the digital receiver/decoder has more power to drive the speakers than the PC. For such a setup, the sound card needs to have a digital output. This may be either a coaxial S/PDIF connector or an optical Toslink connector. Be aware that some sound cards with the S/PDIF connector use a nonstandard voltage to send digital information because they are meant to be used only with the manufacturer's external hardware. Some Creative Labs sound cards are like this. Also, most computer sound hardware with a digital audio output uses a mono DIN output connector, which requires a converter to connect a standard RCA-type digital audio cable.

Some sound cards do not preserve the quality of the digital audio from the DVD. They down-sample the 24-bit/96 KHz sound to a lower rate supported internally by the sound processor, and then up-convert it again when it is output through the digital output port. This causes some degradation in the final sound quality. A lot of cheaper sound cards, such as the low-cost cards from Creative Labs and C-Media, will do this.

Video Output

Most computers are not capable of sending video output to a television, since a standard television requires an analog video signal that is very different from the normal Video Graphics Array (VGA)–type signal that is sent to a computer monitor. For an HTPC that will be used to display on a standard NTSC television, a video card that has an NTSC output port is required. This is not an uncommon feature for computer video cards, and it adds only a small extra cost to the hardware, but many systems do not include such features.

For the serious home theater enthusiast, the HTPC must be able to output video compatible with the high-definition television standards that have recently been introduced. Computer users familiar with the display settings of their computer will notice that the PC has the capability to output a great variety of resolutions and refresh frequencies, many of which are even higher quality than the highest HDTV standard. For those HDTV sets with a VGA input, connecting the HTPC is only a matter of plugging in the video cable and setting a compatible display resolution and refresh rate. For the vast majority of HDTV sets without a VGA connector, another piece of hardware is required.

The device that converts the VGA output of a computer to the component inputs used by an HDTV set is called a *transcoder*. It is also known as a *converter*, a *component adapter*, or a *break-out box*. It is a little box with a VGA input and a component output, and inside it converts the VGA signal to the Y-Pb-Pr signal of the three-line component output. It is an external device that sits behind the HTPC. Transcoders are not widely available or easily found at local electronics retailers. The normal method for acquiring one is to order it from an Internet merchant. Though inconvenient to procure, the transcoder is one of the most critical components of the HTPC system.

ATI has recently begun to offer a special transcoder for their Radeon 8500 and 9700 series of video cards. This transcoder is much less expensive than other converters, though it only works with the ATI hardware and it has some output limitations. Overall, it seems to be well received and offers a very high-quality video picture.

Many front projection televisions and some rear projection televisions do not require a transcoder; they require an RGBHV cable connected directly from the HTPC to the projector or television. The RGBHV cable is a cable that converts the VGA-type connector on the back of the PC to the red-green-blue connectors on the display. This cable is also expensive and relatively difficult to find, but it is cheaper than a transcoder since it does nothing more than reroute the wires from the VGA connector to fit into the inputs on the television set.

Required Software

With all of the required hardware installed, the HTPC still cannot play DVD movies without software. The HTPC needs a DVD movie player application to read the movie information from the DVD player, decode it, and display it on the screen and output the sound to the sound card. Software players are not commonly included with computer operating systems, so you must purchase the application. Since not all software DVD players are created equally, it is helpful to know the features of the available applications and which ones are considered best. Chapter 9 of this book includes information about popular DVD movie players.

NOTE *The reason that DVD movie-playing software is only available for purchase is that DVD movies are encrypted on the disc, and only licensed manufacturers have the keys to decrypt the movies. Each brand of consumer DVD player has a unique key that can play an encrypted DVD movie, which the manufacturer has to pay licensing fees to use. Publishers of software DVD players must also pay to license a decryption key, so not many of them are keen to give their products away. Even video card manufacturers that provide DVD playing software for their hardware are careful to ensure that the player is either not easily accessible to noncustomers or does not work on other types of video hardware.*

You need to install and configure all of the hardware and software needed to play DVD movies. We provide complete details about installing hardware and the software drivers that support the hardware and installing software applications in later chapters in this book.

Using the HTPC As an Audio Jukebox

The convenience of converging audio formats into an HTPC is unmatched by any other device currently available. Even a massive 200- or 300-disc CD audio carousel cannot store as much music as the hard drive of an HTPC (see Figure 2-3). Plus, when it comes time to find a desired audio piece among such a massive collection, only the HTPC has the versatility of indexing and instant play that a computer can offer.

Figure 2-3. Portable MP3 jukeboxes, such as the Creative Labs Nomad Jukebox shown here, can't touch the functionality and storage space of an HTPC.

The key to storing large amounts of music and other audio in a computer is digital compression. The benefits and drawbacks of using psycho-acoustic sound compression, such as the MP3 or WMA format, are discussed in Chapter 3. Some audiophiles find the concept of digital compression unacceptable—for those not willing to digitally compress music, the storage capacity of the HTPC is markedly reduced. Whatever the format, however, the limits of storage are only set by the capacity of hard disk drives installed in the computer.

Required Hardware

The HTPC will have a sound card—without one it would be little more than a video player. This may suit some special purposes such as business presentations or slide shows, but the machine of interest to this book is for a home theater, and so the need for a sound card is unquestionable. However, the performance and specifications of the sound card may be questioned.

An HTPC that is meant primarily for playing music may not require anything more than an average sound card. Because CD audio quality is measured at 16-bit/ 44 KHz, and sound cards sold today (and indeed for many years now) are all compatible with this standard, most audio playback will not benefit from more expensive sound hardware. The only requirement is to select a good quality unit that is compatible with the operating system with which it is intended for use and that has the appropriate connectors to support the desired function of the sound system.

CAUTION *Some sound cards have compatibility problems when they are used with certain motherboards in combination with certain operating systems. See Chapter 5 for specific details about problems that we encountered when researching this book.*

Sound Card Connections

The connectors on the sound card will determine what uses the HTPC has for audio jukebox functions (see Figure 2-4). The sound card will have, at the least, a speaker output to connect the system to external speakers. This is not usually the desirable way to configure an HTPC in the home theater, however. The sound card should therefore have a *line-out* connector to send audio to an external receiver/amplifier, which has more power to drive larger speakers. This line-out connector is almost always a ministereo jack (1/8 inch), and it is easy to confuse the speaker jack with the line-out jack, so you should take care to note that the sound card includes a line-out connection. The line-out is an analog port that sends audio at an appropriate level for the external receiver/amplifier. Although you can use the speaker output if there is no line-out, a proper line-out connector is preferable.

Figure 2-4. The sound card will determine how the HTPC performs with jukebox functions.

Digitizing Audio Sources

To use the HTPC to digitize other audio sources such as an LP record or an audio-cassette, the sound card should have a *line-in* connection. This is similar to the line-out port in that they both handle analog audio at the same voltage level, but the line-in allows the sound hardware to receive sound connected from an external receiver/amplifier. Without a line-in connection, there will be no way to convert analog sound sources to digital format for playback on the HTPC.

Most sound cards include a microphone jack. Not all HTPC hobbyists will need one, but there are a few uses for the microphone jack that we discuss later in this chapter. An important point to remember is that the microphone jack is not the same thing as a line-in jack—they operate at different voltage levels, and confusing the two can cause damage to the sound hardware in a computer.

CAUTION *Never plug a line-level input meant for the line-in port into a microphone input connector. The microphone connector uses a very low voltage, and sending the higher line-level voltage into it can cause damage to the audio circuitry and will cause painfully loud distortion to be heard. The microphone jack and the line-in jack are the same size, and they are often not well labeled, so you must take special care when connecting line-level inputs.*

Connecting Speakers

Some sound cards feature an extra set of speaker outputs for use with extra speakers. The surround sound formats for computer games are not all compatible with home theater surround sound, and these extra speaker outputs are generally not useful for an HTPC. Some sound cards are capable of outputting standard 5.1 surround sound to speakers connected directly to the system, so in that case the extra speaker connectors may be desirable if the HTPC is not intended for use with an external digital audio receiver/amplifier.

More expensive sound cards also feature extra line-in connectors (see Figure 2-5). These allow the HTPC to be used to mix audio sources in real time, which is the common method of producing professional video and audio segments. These extra connectors are not necessary for the home user wishing to mix audio, since there are other methods of doing so, but for those hobbyists who need to combine audio from multiple sources simultaneously, a sound card that features multiple line-in connectors is worth the extra cost.

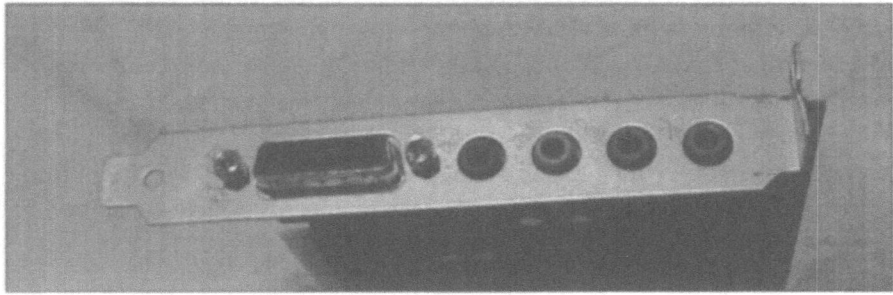

Figure 2-5. Modern sound cards have an entire row of connections.

The final type of connector to consider is the *digital input and output port.* Chapter 3 has more information about the development of the S/PDIF and Toslink digital connectors. These are becoming more common on sound cards, though digital input connectors are still quite rare. Even cheap sound hardware can be used to reproduce high-quality digital sound since the sound card does very little processing of the digital audio stream, except to pass it through the output port to the external receiver. A digital input port requires more processing to accept an audio stream from an external source, so this audio hardware remains relatively expensive.

For the Future

If you're going to use the HTPC for newer digital audio formats, such as DVD-Audio or Super Audio CD (SACD), it is worth investing in a higher-quality sound card. Where CD audio specifies a quality of 16-bit/44 KHz stereo, newer formats reach up to 24-bit/96 KHz with 5.1 channel sound, and beyond. Playing such formats through a standard 16-bit/44 KHz sound card will cause the high-quality digital sound to be down-sampled before it is output by the sound card, thus losing all the benefit of the higher-quality format. For such uses, you should use a 24-bit/96 KHz sound card. Since DVD movies feature audio that can reach up to the 24-bit/96 KHz measurement, the investment in such a sound card is not purely for audio formats, though such high-quality bit rates are extremely rare on DVD movies.

The high-quality 24-bit/96 KHz sound cards all feature digital output ports, which are the preferred way to send digital audio to an external digital receiver/ amplifier. The line-out port on a sound card sends the analog sound that has already been decoded to the receiver. This analog sound is susceptible to interference and degradation as it travels through the cable between the HTPC and the receiver, and other electrical fields from other home theater components may affect what finally reaches the speakers. A digital signal is not affected as badly, since the bits are correctly decoded in the external receiver/amplifier as long as they arrive with enough coherence to be read as bits. Since the HTPC can output all audio through the digital connection, the best quality of sound is preserved for all formats.

Required Software

You have several choices of software applications that play various types of audio on the PC. Some of them can only play back one file and must be requeued for each successive piece, and some of them can play file after file, continuously, repeating a track or the entire program infinitely. Some audio players can only play CD audio, while some can play CD audio and compressed audio files, and yet others can play all those types plus video and streaming media from the Internet. An application that can play back various media types, file formats, and audio sources is called a *software jukebox*.

The jukebox you choose to play back audio files depends on what features you prefer and what cost is acceptable to you. Several of the jukeboxes are free but require registration and potentially undermine privacy. Some of them can automatically convert a CD audio disc to a digitally compressed audio file, and some require extra steps to do so. To see some example jukebox applications and get more details about them, see Chapter 9. Whatever your preference, the HTPC will need some kind of software jukebox to organize, record, store, and play back audio files.

A growing trend for digital audio enthusiasts is to convert all media formats to compressed audio files on the PC. To compress a digital audio file recorded from an analog source or CD audio disc, the jukebox application requires special software called a codec. Some codecs are included with jukebox applications, and some can be added separately from the Internet or from other applications. The HTPC will likely acquire a long list of them through its lifetime.

There are various digital compression methods available to the HTPC, each one with its own codec. Some of the more common ones are MPEG-1 layer 3 (MP3), Windows Media Audio (WMA), and RealAudio (RA). With good jukebox software, the HTPC can record and play each format easily. With an Internet connection, the jukebox application can even look up the album title and song names of CDs that are being converted to compressed audio files, saving you the time and effort of typing the information into the HTPC manually.

The greatest advantage of using the HTPC to play audio is its capability to store, organize, and access a massive collection of music. It does not require a specialized, expensive sound card to start a system capable of CD audio quality playback. Yet you can configure the HTPC with the highest quality audio hardware available to reproduce new digital audio formats without losing a single nuance. Though the HTPC may be considered primarily a DVD movie player, it is also an unmatched audio player.

Using the HTPC As a Television Tuner and HDTV Tuner

As mentioned earlier in this chapter, the HTPC can scale up any video source to match the highest quality available from the display device. This makes the HTPC a good way to receive standard television broadcasts and scale them up to a high-quality television or projector. If the display device is a standard NTSC-compatible television, then the HTPC is still a convenient device to use as a television tuner, if only to avoid switching between different input settings on the television.

Most HDTV sets sold do not have an HDTV tuner built in. This is partly because of the extra cost (HDTV sets are already much more expensive than standard televisions) and partly because the broadcast standards were not agreed upon until quite recently, as we noted in Chapter 1. Instead of purchasing an external HDTV tuner for high-definition-capable sets, you can add this functionality to an HTPC for a lower cost and with more configuration options.

Required Hardware

Television tuner cards for PCs are becoming quite inexpensive. Most of them not only provide a tuner for cable or over-the-air broadcasts, but they also have video inputs to accept video from VCRs or camcorders. The quality of a computer television tuner card is usually quite good (easily comparable to a good television set or VCR), and they are capable of tuning the more than 100 channels used in some markets today.

Television tuners for computers are available in two physical varieties: internal expansion cards and external devices. The external television tuner usually plugs into the computer via the USB bus, which causes some problems. The USB 1.0 bus specification allows for a maximum data transfer rate of 12 megabits per second, which is not enough to send the full 525 lines of NTSC television to the computer, so the video is scaled down to reduce the amount of digital data that needs to move across the bus. The newer USB 2.0 specification allows for a much higher data rate (480 megabits per second), which will make newer USB television tuners better.

Internal Tuners

Internal television tuners look like other computer adapter cards, and they usually use the faster PCI bus inside the system. These tuner cards are able to send the full 525 lines of resolution to the PC, so they provide better picture quality. It is preferable to use an internal television tuner card for HTPC purposes, since the quality of video is a prime concern for the HTPC hobbyist. Some video cards have television tuners built in, which also provides optimum television quality.

HDTV Tuners

Tuning HDTV is a more complicated subject. Tuner cards for HDTV are just like internal television tuner cards for standard NTSC broadcasts, but the HDTV signal reaches the home in only a few restricted ways. Over-the-air broadcasts of HDTV are available in a few markets, and only a few channels are currently being broadcast even in the largest markets. The HDTV tuner card can only tune these over-the-air broadcasts. The HDTV channels on digital cable boxes and digital satellite services are not accessible to the HDTV tuner card. Though this may seem to make an HDTV tuner card a rather useless accessory, it is for this very reason that the HTPC is a good place for receiver HDTV: Why pay a lot of money for an external HDTV receiver of limited use, when HDTV tuner cards for the PC are much less expensive?

NOTE *It is hardly worth putting an HDTV tuner card into an HTPC that is not connected to a high-definition television: The high-resolution video will be down-converted to standard NTSC-quality video, which is available from a cheaper NTSC television tuner card.*

It seems that all HDTV tuner cards also tune standard NTSC broadcasts, not only from over-the-air antennas, but also from the coaxial cable television service in most homes. For those interested in experiencing HDTV in the home theater, an HDTV tuner card for the HTPC is a great way to do so economically.

NOTE *Television tuner cards cannot replace digital cable boxes or digital satellite receivers. The security features of these components do not allow PC component manufacturers to make adapter cards for them. Though some are available from foreign distributors, they cannot be legitimately activated for domestic systems. The best solution is to get a television tuner card with a video input so that the output from these external decoders can be routed through the HTPC.*

Required Software

All television tuner hardware comes with the software necessary to watch television on the computer. Also, there are some third-party software applications available that you can use with many different brands and models of television tuner cards. This third-party software is usually pretty good because it includes extra features and configurations that give you more control over picture quality or other card features. For this reason, when you select a television tuner card, you should evaluate the software that works with the card.

Using the HTPC As a Digital Video Recorder

In the late 1990s an alternative to the VCR was introduced to the consumer market. The *digital video recorder* (DVR) is also known as a *personal video recorder* and by the brand names TiVo, ReplayTV, and UltimateTV. The DVR is a video recorder that digitizes the audio and video signal from a television and stores it on hard disk drives inside the unit.

The DVR is much more versatile than the VCR. Not only can the DVR play back the video that it has recorded, but it can also play it back *while* it is recording. This means that the viewer can pause the playback while the DVR continues recording the live broadcast, and then continue the playback while the unit is recording. This allows for some other neat functions, such as the ability to skip commercials by tuning into a show 10 minutes after it starts and the ability to jump ahead when the commercials are played, eventually catching up to the live broadcast just as it ends.

The DVR is finally becoming very popular, and adding this capability to an HTPC is an attractive option because the system already has most of the hardware necessary. It is largely a matter of selecting the best software to use for personal video recording.

Required Hardware

There are a few points to note about hardware that an HTPC should have to function as a DVR. The capability to output video to a television or high-definition television has already been discussed, and as a core component of the HTPC it is necessarily included so that the DVR has a way to output video to the home theater.

To get video into the DVR the HTPC may include either a television tuner card (or HDTV tuner card) or simply a video input. This choice affects the way the HTPC can be used as a DVR to record television or other video programs. With a television tuner card, the HTPC can be used to tune channels for recording, allowing for convenience when setting up a recording schedule or when channel surfing. In contrast, a simple video input also allows the DVR to record video, but it cannot select what channel is being recorded; it can only record what is being fed into it. The external video source may be configured to switch channels and programs automatically, but the DVR can only be set to record at scheduled times.

For those interested in using the DVR like a conventional VCR (i.e., setting a recording schedule for later viewing), a television tuner card is more appropriate. If the primary purpose of the DVR is to pause live programs or replay segments of a live program, then a television tuner card is not necessary, since the HTPC can be connected to whatever video source is being watched.

Hard Drive Requirements for the DVR

Hard disk drive performance has a large bearing on the quality and performance of the DVR. A standard NTSC video is usually rendered on the computer at a resolution of 640×480 pixels (remember that the 525 lines specified by the NTSC standard are not all visible—only about 480 horizontal lines are actually used for the image) and at a color depth of 24 bits, which is required for true color representation. This means that the video stream will be digitized to 27,648,000 bytes per second! Most hard disks will have trouble keeping up with this data rate.

There are some ways to improve the hard disk performance. One way is to digitally compress the video before it is written to the hard disk. This helps because less information is written, so the disk performance is not as taxed. Compressing video takes a very fast PC, though, so unless the HTPC features a top-of-the-line CPU, it will not be able to compress the data fast enough to capture it at good quality.

 **TIP** *Since HDTV has a much higher resolution than NTSC television, recording it to a hard disk must be almost impossible, right? Actually, recording HDTV data to a hard disk is easier than recording standard NTSC video. The HDTV broadcast is already compressed to MPEG-2, and the compressed data stream can be recorded before it is decompressed for display. An HDTV broadcast at 1080i quality actually uses less bandwidth than a standard television channel.*

Another way to improve performance is to scale down the picture size. Instead of capturing 640×480 video, the DVR can reduce each dimension by half and capture 320×240 video. This has the effect of reducing the data rate to one quarter of the full size rate. Unfortunately, this affects the quality of the video being captured. For some purposes it may not matter, but there may be some programs for which preserving maximum quality is essential.

The most effective way to improve disk performance is to build a disk array called a *striped volume* or *RAID 0*. A RAID is a *redundant array of inexpensive disks*, and RAID 0 is the technical term for using two or more disk drives as one logical drive. The computer data is striped evenly between the disks, and since the computer can read and write to each drive at nearly its full performance, the performance of the logical volume is essentially doubled compared to using one hard disk drive.

To build an HTPC with the ultimate performance, you should consider a disk array. Even a two-disk striped volume is fast enough to capture full-quality NTSC video without losing any data. Adding another disk drive to the HTPC does have some consequences, including higher costs and a louder system, but it cannot be matched for disk performance. Chapter 8 provides more details about this method of improving disk performance.

Required Software

The field of DVR software is a very new topic, but there are already some great choices available. Some DVR applications even allow you to record HDTV broadcasts, which is otherwise impossible—there are no consumer devices available on the market to record HDTV. For more information about DVR applications, see Chapter 9 of this book.

 **NOTE** *The consumer electronics industry is struggling with HDTV recording. It is a difficult issue because it would allow consumers to make perfect digital copies of high-quality television shows and movies in their home. Broadcasters are reluctant to allow this, and they are putting pressure on manufacturers to find ways to protect digital content from unauthorized recording and distribution, which is causing the release of recording products to the marketplace to be delayed.*

Editing Video

As we mentioned in Chapter 1, the HTPC is an excellent tool for importing analog (and thereby converting it to digital) and digital video. Once in the HTPC, you can edit the video using a number of software packages. The resulting edited video can look remarkably professional and you can even burn it onto DVD or Video CD to keep it forever. Several devices on the market allow you to import analog video at a low cost, and of course digital video cameras come complete with an IEEE 1394 port (a FireWire port) that allows the camcorder to be connected directly to the PC (see Figure 2-6). FireWire is an extremely efficient communication channel, and it can handle the huge amount of information that must flow between the camcorder and the HTPC.

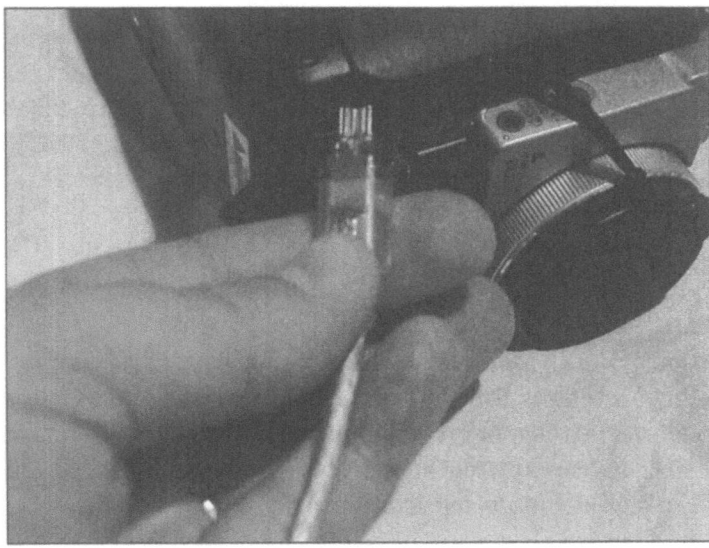

Figure 2-6. Digital camcorders are a breeze to connect to a properly configured HTPC.

After you've placed the video on the hard drive of your HTPC, you can edit the resulting files into large or small clips and put them in any order you desire. You can add in multiple audio tracks, music, and even special digital effects such as ghosting and sepia tone. If you have a large enough hard drive on the HTPC, you can have these movies sit there and play them right off of the HTPC onto your home theater screen (whatever it may be) whenever you need a little nostalgia. See Chapter 11 for details on how to use your HTPC as a home movie (or business presentation) workshop.

Viewing Slide Shows

Storing a huge collection of images digitally on an HTPC makes a lot of sense. Digital images do not fade or lose color over the years, and gathering friends and family in the home theater room to view images on a large screen television can be more fun and intimate than passing around a photo album or a stack of prints. Just like with a music collection, digital pictures can be indexed and accessed very quickly on the HTPC, and the whole picture experience can be enhanced with background music. It is also easy to switch from home movies to pictures and back again, providing a rich multimedia display to document camping trips, graduations, and other life events—even just really good parties!

Required Hardware

Using an HTPC to show digital pictures on a television is pretty trivial if the HTPC is already connected to a display device. It is important to realize that still pictures, more than video, benefit from higher resolution displays. Connecting the HTPC to a high-definition television makes quite a difference in quality compared to a standard television.

There are two main ways to get pictures into the HTPC: you can scan them from film prints by a picture scanner or you can take them with a digital camera and download them into the PC. A scanner is often the least expensive way to digitize an existing collection of prints. Many people have photo albums and family pictures that go back for generations. Even low-cost flatbed color scanners are capable of digitizing pictures at a very high resolution and color quality. In fact, most consumer scanners can scan a picture at many times the resolution that can be reproduced even on a high-definition television.

Digital Cameras

Digital cameras (see Figure 2-7) are more expensive than scanners, but they are becoming comparable in price to film cameras. Shooting pictures with a digital camera is very convenient and cheap—you don't have to wait until the pictures are developed to see how they turned out, and you don't have to pay for developing the pictures, either. Most people find that shooting with a digital camera motivates them to take many more pictures than they would with film, where each picture costs a little bit to develop. However, unless digital pictures are taken with a fairly high-resolution camera (which means a fairy expensive camera), they won't have as high a resolution as scanned film prints. This may not be a problem if you plan to only show the images in the home theater, but it is a problem if you want to make prints from the digital images.

Figure 2-7. Digital cameras are fast becoming the default method to get pictures into digital format.

Required Software

Several image viewing applications are available that can display digital images at full screen size, scaling small images up and large images down to fit the display. Good viewing software also allows you to jump from one picture to the next easily and without distraction. In this manner, you can show all the images in a collection in sequence without having to find each file in turn. You can configure automated slide shows to flip to the next picture at a specified interval, which makes a nice display while listening to music on the HTPC.

For capturing and processing images, an image tool that allows rotation is essential. Images from a digital camera that are shot in *portrait orientation*—that is, the camera is rotated 90 degrees to make the image taller than it is wide—must be rotated after they are captured in the computer so that they display the right way up. Some image editing tools also provide neat picture filters that make the image look black-and-white, drawn with crayon, etched in metal, or painted with watercolor paint. With digital images, you can also add captions and speech bubbles to snapshots of friends and family.

Videoconferencing

The average quality of video streamed over the Internet is relatively poor when compared to the quality of standard television, but the entertainment value is arguably much higher. Even those fortunate enough to have access to broadband Internet connections still suffer low video resolutions, poor sound quality, and annoying glitches and delays. Putting this experience into a home theater seems pointless, but you must not underestimate the fun to be had with friends, kids, grandparents, and pets all trying to see each other in the home theater room!

The home theater really is a great environment for videoconferencing with groups of people, since there is generally more room to sit and be comfortable than when the videoconference is done in a spare room, office, or basement with everyone crowded around the computer monitor. And if broadband Internet access is not available in your area, you can still use the equipment to record messages and short videos to e-mail to your friends and family.

Required Hardware

In addition to the usual HTPC requirements of displaying on a television or large display device, videoconferencing requires a video camera of some sort. Generally, when people think of videoconferencing, they think of *Webcams*, small cameras that connect directly to a computer. These are suitable for videoconferencing on the Internet, since they usually support only the low resolutions that can be streamed back and forth. They are also small enough to be placed on top of the television, which is the ideal place from which to capture video, since everyone will be looking at the television.

Camcorders and other analog consumer video cameras are also suitable for videoconferencing, but because they cannot connect directly to the HTPC, they must be connected to a video input port or video capture device attached to the system. Though the video quality may be too high to stream efficiently across the Internet, the HTPC can down-sample it to a more suitable data rate. The nice thing about using a camcorder is that you can use it for more than just videoconferencing.

TIP *Using a camcorder as a video camera for videoconferencing may be inconvenient if the camera has a default time-out to shut itself off. Unless it is recording, a video camera may stop capturing video after a few minutes to save battery power. In this case, you may have to keep a "scratch" tape handy to record your sessions to keep the camera turned on.*

Unless the camera has a microphone built in, you will need to provide audio for the videoconference. This microphone may be connected to the microphone jack on the sound card. You should place the microphone away from speakers in the home theater room to prevent audio feedback. Also, many cheap microphones are only meant to be used at a close range—within a few feet—and are too weak to pick up sound from across a room. The specifications on the microphone's packaging should indicate its effective range.

Required Software

Videoconferencing software is not difficult to find or expensive to acquire; it is mostly free, in fact. Don't expect to get high-quality video streaming across the Internet, though, no matter what the cost. The limiting factor is the speed at which the HTPC can send and receive information on the Internet. A video image at 320×240 pixels is quite good, even for broadband Internet subscribers. The video-conferencing software should optionally scale the video up to the size of the screen, though the result may be very blocky or blurry. A better suggestion is to use one half of the screen for the received video and the other half to watch the video that is being sent.

Instead of sending video and audio, some software allows people to connect with each other with only audio. Using the Internet to make phone calls, and especially to make long-distance phone calls, has become popular as Internet connection charges have dropped. It is cheaper to talk for hours on the Internet with someone in a different city than to make a long-distance phone call, and a broadband Internet connection is not even necessary.

E-mailing and Web Browsing

Using the HTPC for e-mail is very simple. It requires no special hardware or software that would not normally be found on a conventional PC. The only advantage to using the HTPC for checking e-mail is the convenience of having it on a PC that is always nearby and usually turned on. Since there is not likely to be much privacy for reading or composing messages, it is a good idea to use the HTPC for a general e-mail account shared by members of the household. It is also a good idea to turn off any audible message warnings so that new e-mail doesn't play a loud ping or a "You have new mail!" greeting during a movie or television show.

E-mail

Many e-mail programs are integrated with scheduling and calendar software, which is another convenience that the HTPC can bring to the home theater. Having a daily schedule in the home theater room where it is conveniently accessible is a great help, and having critical reminders and notes pop up on the screen can save embarrassment and problems for even the most absentminded.

Web Browsers

Web browsing on the HTPC is a great function for sharing Web site information with others in the room. The display is usually conveniently visible to other people in the home theater, and those people do not have to look over someone else's shoulder to see what it is that the person is trying to show them. Many Web sites feature entertaining animations and movies, which are also conveniently displayed with the HTPC.

Using the HTPC for e-mail and Web browsing makes having a high-definition display very appealing. Standard televisions do not have enough resolution and cannot show enough detail to make reading text on the screen comfortable or easy. While image detail may be blurred without much notice, the display of large amounts of text demands a high-resolution television.

Remote Controls

In Chapter 7 of this book we discuss various remote controls for the HTPC and wireless keyboard and mouse features (see Figure 2-8). Generally, most features of the HTPC only require simple commands, such as play, stop, change volume, next picture, previous picture, next audio track, and so forth, which can be mapped to a button on a remote control unit. If the HTPC is to be used for e-mail and Web browsing, a wireless keyboard and mouse are essential for comfortable use of the system. It would be time-consuming and tedious to try to write an e-mail message with a simple remote control. Being constrained by a keyboard and mouse cord to within a few feet of the HTPC may not be convenient, either, if the HTPC is located right beside the large screen display.

Figure 2-8. A wireless keyboard can make for the ultimate remote control.

Playing Computer Games

Most computer game enthusiasts are excited by the idea of playing their favorite titles on a big-screen HDTV, and the HTPC can make that idea a reality. Any genre of computer game can be played on a high-definition television via the HTPC, but the most visually impressive games are the ones that use 3D graphics to create rich virtual environments. These can include sports games, first-person shooters, auto-racing games, and even 3D adventure games. All these types of games benefit from the larger display and more powerful sound available in the home theater.

Required Hardware

Computer games that use 3D graphics depend largely on video cards that enhance and accelerate such graphics. The development of 3D computer games has driven the graphics card industry forward relentlessly, and indeed many gamers are serious enough about it to pay $500.00 or more for a top-performing video card.

As we discuss in Chapter 4, not all video cards are equally suitable for use in an HTPC. A PC that will be outputting video to a high-definition television must have a video card that can be set to custom resolutions and refresh rates, and most 3D video cards that are optimized for games concentrate on the standard PC display sizes. They also tend to favor high refresh rates, as this is desirable for computer monitors, but not for a high-definition television. The HTPC must sacrifice either game performance or video output performance, and most hobbyists prefer to sacrifice games in favor of DVD movies.

High-performance 3D graphics cards also generate a lot of heat, which must be dissipated with fans inside the computer case. Fans make noise, and noise is undesirable for an HTPC, especially one that sits in a quiet home theater room.

That is not to say that the HTPC is unusable for 3D video games, however. There are several good HTPC video cards that have acceptable 3D performance. Many computer game players will find the HTPC to be a great machine for computer games. Only the most hardcore 3D graphics fanatics will be unhappy with the trade-off of graphics quality for screen size.

For the past few years, computer games have featured 3D sound to go along with the 3D graphics, but the sound standards are not all compatible with home theater 5.1 surround sound. To hear the surround sound effects from a computer game that uses a noncompatible 3D sound process, the computer must have a sound card that supports the game's sound and speakers connected to the sound card. Unless such a sound card also supports the Dolby Digital 5.1 or DTS 5.1 surround sound audio from a DVD movie, it is unsuitable for use in an HTPC. Thus, some players may lose some of the gaming experience when playing on an HTPC.

As with e-mailing and Web browsing, a wireless keyboard and mouse are a great convenience when playing computer games on the HTPC. A wireless joystick is a nice game controller to have for flying games and flight simulators in the home theater. If a wireless keyboard and mouse are not available, the HTPC could be located closer to the seating positions in the room, or extensions for the connecting cables could be used.

Required Software

Playing computer games on an HTPC requires little extra software. Many computer games are published for the Windows family of operating systems. Such games generally require the DirectX software included with the operating system or available as a free upgrade for Windows. Games that use surround sound formats also need the software for the sound card installed to activate this feature. Instead of trying to accommodate a noncompatible surround sound format in a home theater, a game can be played in stereo sound, which diminishes the game's realism but accommodates its use with the existing sound system.

Summary

This chapter outlined several uses for an HTPC in a home theater. Its capability to play DVD movies at a quality matching the best high-definition television makes the HTPC a great investment. Even when it's connected to a standard television, the HTPC can provide advantages that surpass the capabilities of a conventional DVD player. Personal video recording and audio jukebox functions are a wonderful convenience of the modern home theater, and combining them into one versatile unit makes sense. This is especially true when the ability to upgrade hardware and software is considered. The HTPC need never become antiquated or obsolete; as consumer electronics makers innovate new "must-have" digital technologies, you can integrate them into the HTPC with relative ease. Because the HTPC is a fully functional computer, you can also use it for any task a computer is capable of, including word processing, video editing, and even chatting online. It is, in effect, the ideal home theater device.

The next chapter covers audio specifications in the HTPC.

CHAPTER 3

Audio Specifications

SOUND REPRODUCTION IS not normally the first thing most people consider when planning a home theater. What impresses most people about seeing a movie in a modern theater is the size and quality of the image. Few think about any other element of their experience, even if they notice the deep thumping of the low-range sound effects or the shrill piercing of a terrified scream. Yet, without the soundtrack of a modern movie, the experience is much less involving. Movie makers spend a great deal of time and effort to make the soundtrack of a motion picture a high-quality, realistic reproduction of the sounds meant to accompany the picture. In order to achieve the ultimate home theater experience, this high-quality soundtrack must be treated as a vital component of the home theater system.

Sound reproduction is a complex topic. The audio formats for movies have changed and improved over the years, so the home theater enthusiast must understand the newest technologies and strive to stay current. Most home theaters are used for more than just watching movies, so audio formats for music and television also have a bearing on the configuration of the system. Additionally, the use of a home theater PC (HTPC) allows for the integration of even more audio sources such as CDs, a telephone, video conferencing, an intercom, and everything else that you can imagine.

Fortunately, the HTPC is a great way to converge different audio formats. From the newest DVD audio formats to your collection of vinyl LPs, the HTPC can record, store, and play back almost anything. The greatest thing about it is that the only limit to the size of the collection is the available hard disk space.

Audio Terms and Techniques

The most basic measure of a soundtrack is how many channels it has. Each channel is a separate audio signal. Early movies with audio (the first "talkies") had only a single channel of sound, which is referred to as *mono* sound. Eventually, multichannel soundtracks were added to movies to make the audience feel more involved with the movie by giving the events on the screen a location in the sound field. For example, if you are watching a movie scene with mono sound and a car approaches from offscreen, you cannot tell from which direction it is approaching.

If the movie scene has a multichannel soundtrack, you can tell if the car is approaching from the left, from the right, or even from behind you. Multichannel sound allows the cinema to create a sound field and immerses the audience more deeply into the action of the film.

Though multichannel soundtracks with four sound channels have been common in movie theaters since the 1960s, most home theaters in the 1980s only had two-channel sound, which is referred to as *stereo* sound. This is because until recently, most music and television audio had, at most, stereo sound. Since the late 1980s, the number of channels has increased, mainly because consumer equipment capable of playing back multichannel soundtracks has improved and has become more affordable.

The Digital Era

The most important development in audio formats in the past 30 years is the switch to digital storage. Digital information can be converted to sound (and video) at a very high quality, and digital storage has become the standard for all recent and emerging consumer media such as CDs, DVDs, and computer media such as diskettes, hard drives, and CD-ROMs.

Before digital storage, sound information was stored as an analog waveform on the media. Briefly, all sound is composed of vibration, which is transmitted by pressure waves through the air. A microphone has a diaphragm, usually a cone of paper or other light material that vibrates with the air movements and converts the vibration to an electrical signal. This signal is then recorded onto the storage media. To play back the sound, the process is reversed and a larger diaphragm (a *speaker*) is used to push more air around and make the sound louder.

Digital storage adds a step to the analog process. After the sound is converted to an electrical signal, it is measured, and the measurements are stored on the media. The measuring process is called *sampling* and it is usually performed by a dedicated computer chip. In order to measure the analog signal, the chip has to be told how to sample it. There are two important measurements that affect the quality of the signal stored digitally: the sampling rate and the sampling resolution. The *sampling rate* determines how many times per second the measurement will be taken, and the *sampling resolution* states how finely the analog wave will be measured. The numbers that represent the values of each measurement are stored as *bits* (binary digits), 1s and 0s, which, depending on the physical media, may be represented by positive and negative magnetic fields, or by pits and bumps on an optical disc.

 **NOTE** *It is an oversimplification to state that bits are represented by pits and smooth sections on the compact disc media. Actually, each data bit is represented by several pits and* lands, *the name for a bumpy section. Further, it isn't the presence of a pit or land that represents a bit, but rather the transition from pit to land (or absence of that transition) that the laser detects as a bit. The bits on the surface of the disc are combined to make a data bit.*

Obviously, the higher the rate and resolution, the better the sound quality you can expect. Unfortunately, higher rates and resolutions also mean more digital information needs to be stored. In order to reproduce that analog wave perfectly, the digital sampling rate and resolution would have to be infinite, and there's no way to store that much information. Fortunately, sound engineers and human perception researchers have determined that most people cannot perceive the difference between sound sampled at an infinite rate and resolution, and sound sampled at merely a high rate and resolution. Though this topic continues to be controversial for experts in the digital audio industry, most home theater enthusiasts are satisfied with the current state-of-the-art in digital audio. (Though it should be noted that every time a newer, higher-quality format arrives, the former state-of-the-art suddenly seems inadequate!)

Why Is Digital Storage Better Than Analog?

First, the reproduction does not degrade as the media gets worn or ages. In the case of optical digital storage, such as a CD, the media itself is almost immune to the effects of aging, but even digital audiotape (DAT) allows for reliable, high-quality playback. On magnetic media such as computer hard drives or audiotapes, the strength of the magnetic fields that store the information on the surface of the media deteriorates over time. If the media is exposed to a strong electro-magnetic field, the information is degraded further, and it can even be completely erased. If the signal stored on the media is analog, it will sound only as good as the strength of the remaining magnetic fields. With a digital signal, it doesn't matter how strong the magnetic fields are—if the media reader can tell what the bits are, it can reproduce the digital signal. Thus, an analog tape with 80 percent of its magnetic strength remaining will sound 80 percent as good as the day it was made, but a digital tape will sound exactly as good. Table 3-1 lists various media types and their life expectancies.

Table 3-1. Storage Media Life Expectancy

MEDIA TYPE	LIFE EXPECTANCY IN YEARS*
Magnetic tape (audio and video)	10–20
Digital magnetic tape	30
CD recordable (CD-R)	70–200
CD (commercially produced)	100–200

* Information about life expectancy is difficult to find, and it's often vague or conflicting. Some CD-R manufacturers claim upward of 200 years of shelf life under ideal conditions, but who's going to own a CD player in the year 2203?

NOTE *A CD-R can degrade within a few years if it is labeled with an ink pen or a felt-tip pen. The ink in many permanent pens eventually leaks through the CD-R and will fill many of the pits and lands, rendering it useless. Using a proper CD label can prevent this early degradation.*

Another advantage of digital storage is that most media contain the digital signal plus some error-correction information. Even if a part of the media is destroyed, the original signal can be reconstructed. This is highly effective in counteracting the effects of scratches on CDs, though obviously it cannot re-create an entire soundtrack if half of the media is missing.

Let's do some math: The format of an audio compact disc (CD) is defined by the *Red Book,* a specification for audio discs released by Sony and Philips in 1980. This specification defined digital audio sampled at 16-bit resolution and 44.1 KHz frequency (44,100 samples per second). This means that each second of audio on a CD uses $16 \times 44,100 = 705,600$ bits per second per channel. It is conventional to discuss storage capacity in terms of bytes, which are equal to 8 bits, so 705,600 bits per second divided by 8 is 88,200 bytes per second. Remember that a CD holds two audio tracks, the left and right stereo channels, so double the bytes per second to 176,400. The original Red Book specification allowed for 78 minutes per disc, which is 4,680 seconds (see Table 3-2). Thus, the data stored on an audio CD is $176,400 \times 4680 = 825,552,000$ bytes. This number is only an illustration of the capacity of an audio CD, however, as there are extra bits for error correction and tracking.

 **NOTE** *Computer data on a data CD is not encoded in the same way as data is on an audio CD, so the capacities are not directly comparable. Since a data CD needs to store all the computer data very reliably, there is more error-correction information in each block.*

Table 3-2. Information About the Capacity of a Compact Disc

CD AUDIO FORMAT	CAPACITY
16-bit resolution × 44.1 KHz sample rate	705,600 bits per second
705,600 bits per second	88,200 bytes per second
88,200 bytes per second × two stereo tracks	176,400 bytes per second
78 minutes per CD	4,680 seconds
4,680 seconds × 176,400 bytes per second	825,552,000 bytes
825,552,000 bytes/1,024 bytes per KB/1,024KB per MB	~787.3MB

Digital storage has one aspect that some people consider an advantage and others consider a major problem. When you copy an analog signal, you always lose some quality because the reproduction is never as good as the original performance. Each generation is successively worse than the preceding generation (a "copy of a copy of a copy" is not as good as a "copy of a copy"). Digital information, however, may be copied without any loss of quality for any number of successive generations.

If you are in the business of making and selling digital recordings, this is obviously not welcome news. Uncontrolled copying and distribution of audio recordings on the Internet have prompted publishers to find ways to protect audio CDs from such copying. Various copy-protection schemes have been implemented on various types of digital media, with mixed success. Sometimes the copy protection affects the performance of the media, so publishers must tread a fine line between protecting their content from copying and allowing consumers to enjoy it.

Digital Compression

A neat thing about digital signals is that they may be compressed to fit more information into the storage space. In the digital world, there are two main types of compression: lossless and lossy. These terms mean pretty much what you might guess. *Lossless* compression reduces the size of the stored digital signal without losing any of the information. *Lossy* compression eliminates redundant and unnoticeable data to save space. For digital audio information, lossless compression doesn't help much, so digital audio engineers have concentrated on lossy compression techniques. Audio compression was researched and developed in the mid-to-late 1980s at the Fraunhofer Institut in Germany, but it only became popular with consumers in the mid-1990s when personal computers became powerful enough to decode highly compressed audio signals.

Lossy audio compression depends on a *psycho-acoustic model*, which is a set of guidelines that tells engineers which sounds are not noticeable in a soundtrack. For example, if two sounds with nearly the same pitch occur simultaneously, or even almost simultaneously, then the softer sound can be eliminated without most people noticing. Audio compression is sort of like haggis: You feel better about it if you don't know what's in it!

Though the actual compression process is very complicated, and different technologies with varying degrees of complexity and efficiency yield differing degrees of compression, most people cannot tell the difference between uncompressed digital audio and audio that has been skillfully compressed. Technology has continued to progress, and the best coders today achieve the same sound quality that previously required double or quadruple the amount. This is what makes it possible to economically deliver 5.1 sound over satellite and cable television systems, for example.

An appreciation of these audio terms is helpful when you consider how to build a modern home theater and when you look back at how modern home theater audio technology has evolved in only a few short decades.

A History of Home Theater Audio

It may be argued that "home theater" has existed since the first days of motion pictures, as the wealthy only required a film projector in their house to have a home theater. Not many people could afford the cost or space for such equipment, however. For our purposes, "home theater" means recreating the theater experience at home with equipment that is so affordable that the majority of people can do it. Thus, home theater really began when home videotape recording units hit the consumer market at a price the average person could afford.

From a confusing medley of early VCRs emerged the dominant videotape format: VHS. Though some of the major competitors to VHS actually had a higher quality of picture and sound, VHS exploited the balance of quality, cost, and marketing that appeals to the masses. Not everyone was happy about VHS's compromises (even to this day!), but there is no question that by the late 1980s VHS was the dominant home entertainment video format based on market share.

Early VCRs could only record and play back a single, mono audio soundtrack. Stereo VCRs were introduced in the late 1970s, but they were not attractively priced until the mid-1980s, about the same time as stereo television broadcasts began. The quality of stereo sound on a VHS VCR tape is exactly comparable to stereo FM radio. Connecting a stereo sound VCR to your home audio system made a lot of sense, and for the first time people began to get enthusiastic about home theater.

We must make special mention of one of VHS's competing formats: Laserdisc. Though it carried an analog picture, Laserdisc did have the capability of carrying digital sound, and even the analog sound on a Laserdisc was better than VHS. As a physical medium, a Laserdisc is large (12 inches wide) and doesn't hold much capacity (a 2-hour movie could barely fit onto a double-sided disc), but since it is an optical disc format, it does not degrade with time or use. Though DVD has now made the Laserdisc obsolete, many people feel that the "serious" home theater of the 1980s was not complete without a Laserdisc player.

Laserdisc and VHS battled for consumers' loyalty into the mid-1990s, but in 1997 a new digital video disc format was introduced with picture and sound that clobbered everything that existed in the home theater. Originally named digital video disc, but later changed to digital versatile disc, DVD has a higher quality picture than VHS or Laserdisc, and it has the same high-quality digital audio capability as Laserdisc has had since 1995.

Surround Sound

By 1987, VHS players were available with the capability to play back a four-channel Dolby® Surround encoded soundtrack via its two-channel audio format. This was the first access most people had to a true movie theater experience in their home. Dolby Surround was originally available in VCRs in 1982, but with the introduction of Dolby Surround Pro Logic®, a home theater could have as many audio channels as most movie theaters. To hear the Dolby Surround Pro Logic soundtrack on a VHS movie, the VCR must be connected to an external decoder, such as a Dolby Surround audio receiver, which became popular and affordable in the 1990s.

Dolby, Pro Logic, and the double-D symbol are registered trademarks of Dolby Laboratories.

Figure 3-1 shows the Dolby Surround trademark, which denotes Dolby Surround encoding in an audio track.

Figure 3-1. Dolby Laboratories' trademark denoting Dolby Surround encoding in an audio track

The four channels of sound were arranged to allow for the most realistic spatial effects in a motion picture. The traditional left and right channels provided great stereo sound for music accompanying the action, a center channel placed the sound of dialogue near the video screen where the people were speaking, and a single rear channel (usually connected to two rear speakers) filled in the room with offscreen sound effects, echoes, and reverberations.

How Important Is Surround Sound?

Two speakers seems to be the optimal number for reproducing sound meant to be heard by a listener with two ears. Some sound experts contend that only two speakers are needed to re-create a complete sound field for audio recordings and for motion pictures. Why spend so much effort and expense to build an HTPC capable of outputting more sound channels than that?

A human listener can perceive the direction from which sound arrives using many clues, noticeable and unnoticeable. The most important is by detecting the volume level and delay between hearing in the left and right ears. A sound wave from the right side will travel directly into the right ear, but only indirectly into the left ear, and so it is slightly softer in the left ear than in the right. The sound wave also arrives in the left ear slightly later. Though this delay is barely a few microseconds long, it is enough to determine whether a noise came from the left or right—sounds that come directly from the left or right are the easiest to locate.

This detection can even reveal if a sound is located to the front or back of the listener. Locating a sound to the front or back is more difficult, though. The ear is shaped to capture sound in front more clearly than in back, so only subtle auditory clues about the clarity and sharpness of the sound can reveal its location ahead or behind. Similarly, noise above or below is slightly differentiated as it is blocked by the body and external parts of the ear, though most people find it very difficult to locate a sound coming from above or below them. Still, with only two ears, most people can tell from which direction sound is coming. If the soundtrack from two speakers could re-create these audible location clues, it seems that the optimum surround sound arrangement would require only two speakers.

The ability to detect sound coming from any direction is greatly affected by the environment into which the sound exits, and since enclosed rooms are about the worst place for distorting sound, extra speakers are needed to ensure proper perception of the sound field. Sound is reflected by flat objects such as walls, floors, and ceilings, which are usually the main structural features of a movie theater or a home theater. Reflected sound is perceived as a softer echo that reaches the listener within milliseconds of the primary sound, obscuring the auditory clues that indicate its location. A room full of reflected sound is a confusing environment in which to listen to an audio track, since the clues about sound location are washed out in the cacophony. To understand this concept, just think about what it sounds like to sing in the shower, where hard tile floors and walls reflect noise so much that a voice seems to be amplified and filled in from all directions.

Many movie theaters use fabric on the walls to dampen sound reflection, which helps to trap and disperse the echoes. Even with proper sound treatment, however, it is hopelessly difficult to eliminate all destructive sound reflection in a large movie theater or a small home theater. By adding extra speakers placed around the audience, the sound engineer hopes to overcome the remaining subtle reflected sounds with those from a stronger primary source. The audience still perceives the movie soundtrack with two ears, but the location clues in the soundtrack are controlled more precisely by using the surround speakers.

Note that Dolby Surround Pro Logic is an analog format, decoded from the analog audio signal on the videotape. Though it was a huge step forward at the time, it did have some severe limits—for example, the inability to keep sounds from "leaking" across the channels. Since the rear channel was a single audio track played through two speakers, it could not do much to position sounds to the left or right behind the listener. For some home theater enthusiasts, the worst thing about Dolby Surround Pro Logic was the quality limits of the source content itself, often marked by annoying hissing and lack of dynamic range of the analog audio signal; the loudest and softest sounds were not separated enough, and if you turned it up to make it louder, you heard the hissing. Digital audio from Laserdisc set a remarkably high standard that even VHS hi-fi could only approximate.

Surround Sound Becomes Digital

In 1992, Dolby Laboratories introduced a new purely digital sound format to movie theaters, Dolby AC-3, which has since been renamed Dolby Digital 5.1. This new format had five discrete digital channels: left, right, center, left surround, and right surround, as shown in Figure 3-2. It also had a special sixth channel for low frequency effects (LFE). Since the LFE channel was only used for low-pitch sounds, it needed much less information, so it was referred to as the ".1" channel. The first movie in theaters to use the Dolby Digital 5.1 soundtrack was *Batman Returns.*

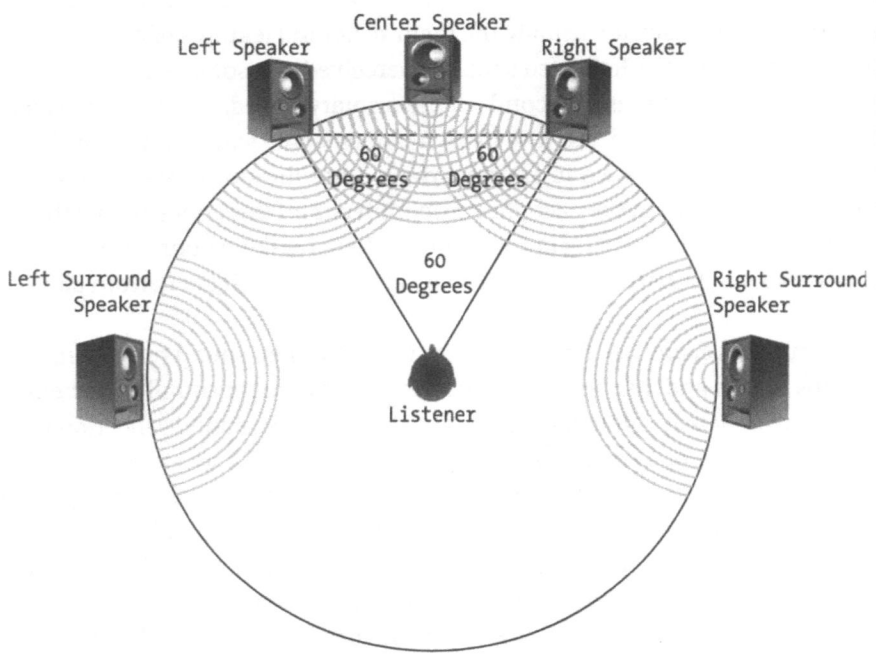

Figure 3-2. The optimal location for speakers in a five-speaker surround sound environment. Each speaker is the same distance from the listener, and the left and right stereo speakers form an equilateral triangle with the listener.

Dolby Digital 5.1

The great thing about a digital surround sound format is that there is no sound leakage across audio channels. The analog surround formats always have some of the sound meant for one speaker coming through in the others. Discrete digital channels are not susceptible to this problem, however, as the digital decoder can send the correct information to the correct audio channel flawlessly.

By 1995, Dolby Digital 5.1 was available to the home theater enthusiast on new Laserdisc players. The Laserdisc format would have a short reign of glory, however, as DVD soon eclipsed Laserdisc in quality when it was introduced to the consumer market in 1997. Figure 3-3 shows the trademark denoting Dolby Digital sound encoding.

Figure 3-3. Dolby Laboratories' trademark denoting Dolby Digital sound encoding

At first no one knew how well DVD would be accepted by the home user. Though DVD could match or beat Laserdisc in every audio specification, it was a new and unknown format with high player costs and little variety from which to choose. One aspect of the DVD that helped it to gain favor was that the discs are the same size as CDs—12 centimeters, or just under 5 inches—and this small size made them ideal for home computers and especially notebook computers. The convenience of having a high-quality movie player in a laptop appealed to many early adopters of the technology and helped propel it into the mainstream. It is ironic that this popular way of enjoying DVD movies doesn't even allow the viewer to experience the full digital surround sound, since most computers have only two (usually poor quality) speakers. But if you have headphones, Dolby has new technology, aptly called Dolby Headphone, which allows you to simulate the 5.1 experience with just headphones. This is available in most PC DVD players.

Digital Theater Systems

While DTS was around before DVD hit the marketplace, it probably was not as well known in the home until it showed up on home DVDs. Digital Theater Systems (DTS) still uses lossy compression, but with less compression, so at a much higher bit rate. Whereas Dolby Digital compresses all the sound channels down to 384 Kbps or 448 Kbps, DTS only compresses down to 882 Kbps for movie theaters (using a different technology altogether) and 1,509 Kbps or more commonly 754 Kbps for DVDs.

NOTE *In order to fit the audio information onto a DVD loaded with extra scenes, multiple audio tracks, and other features, the quality and bit rate of the surround-sound audio track is sometimes reduced. For this reason, many movie purists prefer special DVD movie releases that remove the extras in favor of a high bit rate for the audio and video information stream. It turns out, however, that even lower bit rate sound tracks can be excellent, and the quality varies so much from disk to disk that no generalities can be stated accurately.*

NOTE *CD audio is a digital audio format with 16-bit resolution and sampled at 44.1 KHz, as specified by the Red Book standard. The Dolby Digital audio track from a DVD movie is sampled at 48 KHz for slightly better quality. While all DVDs that include DTS support 48 KHz playback, DTS can support up to 24-bit resolution at 96 KHz sampling rate.*

The DTS surround-sound format uses a higher bit rate, but it also uses a different model to compress sound. Those home theater enthusiasts with sensitive ears swear that the DTS-encoded movies sound clearer and more natural than Dolby Digital soundtracks, but many others are hard-pressed to tell the difference. It appears that a well-encoded Dolby Digital audio track is just as good as a DTS track for most listeners. Figure 3-4 shows the trademark denoting a DTS-encoded soundtrack.

Figure 3-4. The DTS trademark indicating a DTS-encoded soundtrack

To some it appears that a well-encoded Dolby Digital audio track is just as good as a DTS track, but we feel subjectively that DTS has a slight edge. DTS movies are not as common as Dolby Digital movies, for various reasons, the primary one being that DTS is optional in the DVD format, whereas Dolby Digital is mandatory. Some DVD movies have both the Dolby Digital and DTS soundtracks on one disc, and some come in two different versions. To date, no movie has been released on DVD without a version with a Dolby Digital soundtrack. Still, if you have an amplifier that can decode DTS, and many can, it is worth keeping an eye out for DTS encoded DVDs.

NOTE *The Dolby Digital and DTS trademarks on a DVD movie only indicate the digital sound encoding process. They do not promise that the soundtrack has full multichannel surround sound. Digital encoding can be applied to a mono audio track or a stereo track.*

The newest development in the surround sound industry is the addition of yet another sound channel. As mentioned previously, the term "5.1 surround" applies to both Dolby Digital and DTS and means there are five main channels and one low-frequency effects channel. These soundtracks are often played back on a 5.1 speaker system, but the signal feeding the subwoofer is not just the LFE channel, but optionally also the bass from the five main channels that is too deep for the satellite main speakers to reproduce properly. Bass management in the decoder takes care of all this. The five main speakers are arranged with one speaker in the center front, two speakers for left- and right-front stereo, and two surround speakers for left and right surround sounds. The surround speakers are supposed to be located beside and slightly behind the listening audience to provide ambience and sound effects. Both Dolby Laboratories and DTS have added a rear surround channel for sound effects placed behind the audience. Though the rear surround channel is a mono audio track, it may optionally be reproduced by two speakers: a right- and left-rear speaker.

The Dolby rear surround channel has been added on top of the existing Dolby Digital 5.1 specification by the use of matrix encoding. This means that a Dolby Digital 5.1 sound processor can properly decode and play a Dolby Digital EX soundtrack, though the rear surround channel will be heard equally from both surround speakers, a very similar experience to that of other 5.1 soundtracks. To hear the full Dolby Digital EX spatial effect, a new digital receiver capable of decoding it must be used with the extra back speakers.

DTS has also created a sixth audio channel by deriving it from the left and right surround channels. The consumer name for this audio format is DTS-ES Matrix, where the term "matrix" is used to denote that the extra rear surround channel is made up from a matrix of the sounds in the left and right surround channels. However, DTS also has a "6.1" format with a digital rear channel, called DTS-ES Discrete 6.1. Proper playback for either of these new DTS formats also requires a new digital audio decoder.

It is easy to see that consumer home theater audio follows what is happening in professional movie theaters. As more audio channels are added in theaters, new audio formats such as Extended Surround are introduced by manufacturers of audio receivers to appeal to those home theater enthusiasts who want to be on the cutting edge. These new formats are all based on digital encoding and are compatible with previous digital formats, so a good digital audio receiver is an important addition to any serious home theater. Thanks to the adoption of digital audio technologies, home theater enthusiasts can have real theater-quality sound, and the technology now seems to be available very soon after it hits the professional theaters. In order to re-create the optimal cinema experience, then, the HTPC should be capable of handling the digital audio data from DVD.

Pure Audio

The soundtrack from a movie isn't the only audio that the HTPC may be used for, and indeed for some people, it isn't even the most important use. The convergence of media onto the personal computer has been heralded for years, and now the results of convergence are yielding great advantages to those who choose to use a PC as an entertainment system.

Since the PC is fundamentally a digital device, it is able to read, store, and play back almost every popular digital audio format. Audio CD is the most popular format for music (and other audio performances) today, but before CDs there were a variety of analog formats. Whereas the home computer is useless for playing vinyl LP records or audiocassettes, the HTPC can convert these old formats to digital information and bring the benefits of digital storage to a history of analog media.

Predigital

For those hi-fi enthusiasts who swear that vinyl LPs sound better than modern digital CDs, converting an LP to a digital format would seem to be heresy. But for those listeners with stacks of wax that have been collecting dust for the past few decades, such a conversion is a great way to get more life out of an unused record collection. The HTPC can record the audio from an LP record to a digital file, which can be saved in the HTPC or recorded onto a CD-R for playback in an audio CD player. Although the resulting sound will be only as good as the quality left on the LP record, it will never pick up any additional scratches, pops, or hissing, and it will not deteriorate with use.

The sounds on an LP record can vary in pitch from about 7 Hz up to 25 KHz, though sounds in the higher frequencies are muted intentionally to keep the record player's stylus from jumping out of the record groove. For comparison, the Red Book CD audio standard specifies that audio CDs sample sounds at 44 KHz, so it appears at first that CD audio has a much better high-frequency response than an LP. However, with digital audio, the sample rate should be twice the audio frequency in order to accurately reproduce it, so the effective range of pitch for a CD only goes up to about 22 KHz. Thus, vinyl LPs can actually reproduce a higher pitch than a CD. The advantage for CD audio is that it has full dynamic range and frequency response up to its frequency limit. The high-pitch sounds on a vinyl LP are "rolled off," or muted, so most LP records will not lose any quality when digitally sampled and stored at CD audio quality. Audiocassettes have a smaller range of pitch than LPs, and they drop off at high frequencies too, so converting these to a digital audio format using CD quality specifications is also quite effective. Table 3-3 lists the frequency ranges for common audio formats.

Table 3-3. Frequency Ranges for Common Audio Formats

FORMAT	LOWEST	HIGHEST	ROLL-OFF
FM radio	20–50 Hz	15 KHz	Not significant
Audiocassette	30 Hz	13–20 KHz	Above 10 KHz*
LP record	5–20 Hz	25 KHz	Above 12 KHz
CD digital audio	20 Hz	20.5 KHz	none

*The quality of the magnetic tape determines the frequency response.

NOTE *The upper range of hearing for most people is about 20 KHz. Frequencies above this are inaudible, so no matter how well an LP or CD audio system can reproduce them, they are lost to the listener.*

The HTPC can do more than just convert LPs and cassettes—it can convert almost any audio source to digital audio. No matter what the source—reel-to-reel tapes, 78 rpm records, radio broadcasts, or even the audio portion of videotapes and video broadcasts—it can all be digitized. Though the Red Book audio CD specification specifies a bit rate and sample resolution that allows these digitized recordings to be put on an audio CD (the HTPC with a CD burner can create an audio CD from recordable media), the HTPC can digitize sound at lower or higher bit rates and resolutions if the source is lower or higher quality.

TIP *Most computers have a sound card inside that allows sound to be input and output. The sound card determines the maximum quality of digital sound that can be recorded and played back. As we discuss later, most common sound cards support the CD audio quality of 16-bit/44 KHz, but sound cards that support higher bit rates and resolutions are available. Recording at better-than-CD quality requires a better-than-average sound card in the HTPC.*

Once you've converted these analog formats to digital computer files, you can store them on your computer's hard disk drive, archive them to CD-R or tape backup, or convert them to audio CD.

Digital Convergence

In the discussion earlier in this chapter about digital storage, we looked at CD audio and the Red Book specification. Almost every computer with the capability to play sounds is able to play at least CD-quality sound. Even the least expensive computer sound card supports at least 16-bit/44.1 KHz sound, and it has been almost a decade since less-capable sound cards were sold. Still, it is important to point out that the HTPC should include sound hardware capable at least of this standard.

The playback capabilities of the HTPC are at least equal to a good CD audio player, but many people find that they listen to music played from CDs less and less. This is due to the convenience of storing digital audio files directly on the hard drive of a computer instead of leaving them on a CD. Instead of hunting through a rack of CDs or digging through stacks of CDs in a drawer to find the music you want to listen to, you can play CD audio tracks directly from directories on your PC. This is even more convenient when you want to hear tracks from several different CDs during one session. Even a CD disc carousel cannot switch between tracks on different discs as quickly and easily as an HTPC with all the music stored on its hard drive.

The convenience of using an HTPC for playing music depends greatly on the new digital compression techniques that have been developed in the past decade. It has become very popular to compress audio files using the lossy compression specified by the MPEG-1 layer 3 protocol. This protocol is commonly known as MP3 compression, and it is similar to the compression described previously for DVD audio. Most listeners do not notice any sound degradation in MP3 compressed audio, and since this compression can reduce the space needed to store the audio to less than 10 percent of the original space, it is a great way to store vast amounts of audio.

For audio tracks that have been digitized from analog sources, MP3 compression is a good way to store the audio. Instead of lowering the sample rate or resolution, the audio can be sampled at the highest quality then compressed to fit into less space. For a given amount of space, MP3 compression of high-quality sound will yield better quality than lowering the sample rate.

MP3 is not the only lossy audio compression method available for digital audio. Competing formats such as WMA, OGG, and RMA all use the same basic idea of psycho-acoustic modeling to remove unneeded information without degrading the sound. The implementation of each method on a PC is known as a *codec*, a combination of the words "code" and "decode." Thus, to use computer files that store audio tracks compressed with the MP3 method of compression, the computer must have the MP3 codec installed. Likewise for those other formats. Later chapters cover these codecs in greater detail, but we must note that compressing and decompressing an audio track takes a lot of computer power, so the HTPC must be built around a modern computer, and the faster, the better.

TIP *It takes a lot more computer power to compress audio (and video) than to decompress it. An HTPC that will be used to record and compress a lot of audio data will be much more efficient and enjoyable if it is the fastest affordable computer available.*

New Audio Formats

The future of digital audio is in dispute; its existence is guaranteed by its merits, but its format is uncertain. There is little doubt that the now-antiquated audio CD can be improved, and consumers are becoming more knowledgeable about digital audio and the limits of CDs. However, there are at least two competing formats fighting to provide the next generation of optical disc digital sound. We describe these formats in the sections that follow.

Super Audio Compact Disc

Super Audio CD (SACD) is based on the physical DVD optical disc format, which allows much more information to be stored on a disc than is allowed on a CD, since the pits can be smaller and closer together and the tracks are closer together. The SACD specification, called the *Scarlet Book*, allows for frequencies up to 100 KHz to be accurately reproduced in each audio channel and can support two stereo channels or up to five surround channels and a low-frequency effects channel (5.1 surround sound, in other words). The SACD does not state the number of bits per sample, but it does specify a total sample rate of 2.822 MHz.

The SACD disc can be manufactured with two layers, the DVD layer and a conventional CD layer, so that older CD audio players can still play the CD layer. Only new SACD players would be able to read and reproduce the higher-quality SACD soundtracks.

DVD-Audio

DVD-Audio is based on both the physical DVD optical disc format and the DVD video format. This new specification allows for two audio channels (stereo sound) at 24-bit resolution and up to 192 KHz sample rate, or 5.1 channel (surround sound) at 24-bit resolution and up to 96 KHz sample rate. Obviously, this sound quality is much higher than CD audio.

NOTE *The two new digital audio formats, SACD and DVD-Audio, do not use the same method of sampling sound to convert it to digital information. DVD-Audio uses the traditional method that CD audio uses called* pulse code modulation *(PCM), whereas SACD uses* direct stream digital *(DSD) encoding. The SACD specification seems better technically, but both formats are expected to produce about the same quality of sound. Needless to say, they are not compatible.*

DVD-Audio allows for images, lyrics, and other text notes to be stored on the disc, while SACD does not. Presumably, the players for these new discs will allow the listener to access this information while enjoying the performance. Both new formats are also heavily copy-protected.

Although the new formats are incompatible, the players are compatible with existing CD audio media. Also, they both strive to exploit the surround sound speakers and audio channels that home theater enthusiasts are using for movie soundtracks. This makes setting up a theater at home more appealing since it can have multiple uses. This also makes having an HTPC at the heart of your media center more appealing as the ultimate convergence of all digital media.

It is worth mentioning that virtually all DVD-Audio discs include compatible material, usually the entire album, in 5.1 Dolby Digital, so that they can be played on any existing DVD video system. So it is possible to build a library of DVD-Audio discs, enjoying superb surround sound, and then step up to a DVD-Audio player in future to extract even more features and higher sound quality from the same discs. SACD allows the option to include a Red Book CD layer, making the discs compatible with regular CD players, but not many discs do this so far.

The HTPC Sound System

Few home theater or audio experts think that their newest CD player, DVD player, digital receiver, or video recorder will be the last one they'll ever need to buy. The consumer electronics industry couldn't last long if it didn't constantly innovate new technologies to sell to enthusiasts hungry for the latest and greatest equipment. Deciding to be a home theater lover is deciding to constantly spend money, it seems. This sobering realization discourages current enthusiasts and keeps many out of the hobby altogether.

The HTPC is a great way to mitigate the high cost of constantly upgrading home theater equipment. When a new sound format appears, it is often accommodated simply by adding new software to the system, and at most by upgrading one or two components, instead of replacing the entire HTPC. For example, buying a DVD video player for a home theater costs more than buying a DVD-ROM drive for a PC, because the player needs to include a case, power supply, video decoder chipsets, and other subsystems that a DVD-ROM drive doesn't include. By letting the HTPC handle the housing, power, and decoding, the DVD-ROM drive is a much simpler (and less expensive) device. When new DVD drive technology is available, only this drive needs to be replaced.

The HTPC is ready for the future, but since the specifications for future technologies are obviously unavailable, let's look at what high-quality sound systems should be included in today's system. The most basic thing to know is that sound in a PC is usually handled by a component called a *sound card*. In some computers, the microchips and sound processors are not located on a separate card; rather, they are part of the main board (motherboard). Either way is fine, as long as the sound components meet the quality desired.

Meeting Specifications

Since the DVD-Audio specification states that the highest quality sound will have 24-bit resolution at 192 KHz, the ideal sound card for an HTPC will be able to reproduce sound at this quality. This is an unusually high specification—it is more common to find high-end sound cards that support 24-bit resolution at 96 KHz sample rate. As discussed earlier in this chapter, this is the highest quality for DVD video and the quality specified for 5.1 channel DVD-Audio.

An acceptable alternative to the finest quality sound card when cost is a limiting factor is to build an HTPC to the CD audio specification. This means a sound card capable of processing 16-bit resolution at 44 KHz sample rate. Using such a sound card will cause the HTPC to down-sample the audio when outputting the digital surround soundtrack from a DVD movie. For sound cards without a digital audio port, the digital surround sound will be completely inaccessible, though the analog Dolby Pro Logic surround sound audio will still be available. This sound card will also play CD audio at its full quality, but newer digital audio formats will either be down-sampled or not played at all.

TIP *Most DVD movies that have a digital 5.1 soundtrack also have a stereo soundtrack. Software to play DVD movies on an HTPC will also convert the digital 5.1 soundtrack to an analog stereo track with Dolby Surround sound encoding. Either way, it is still possible to hear the sound-track for a DVD movie without a digital sound decoder or a sound card capable of passing the digital soundtrack to an external decoder.*

Using an External Digital Decoder

The way an HTPC is connected to the rest of the home theater system can determine the quality of the sound it reproduces. For the highest quality DVD audio—the digital surround soundtrack—the audio information is read from the disc and sent to an external digital receiver, where it is decoded and sent to the appropriate speaker. The HTPC handles the process by reading the DVD in its DVD-ROM (or DVD-RAM) drive. The software that plays DVD movies separates the digital audio information and outputs it through a digital interface to the external decoder.

S/PDIF Digital Audio Connector

One type of digital interface is a Sony and Philips Digital Interconnect Format (S/PDIF) port, which is usually found on the sound card. This is a pretty straight-forward connection—a coaxial cable connects from the digital output (the S/PDIF port) on the computer to the digital input on the digital receiver. However, not all S/PDIF ports are created equally! Some sound cards actually down-sample the digital signal to process it internally at a lower rate and then up-sample it to output it through the digital connection. Further, some sound cards with S/PDIF ports use a proprietary voltage level, so they are not even compatible with standard external decoders. You should be aware of the internal processing of the sound card you choose for your system. We discuss some popular brands and models in Chapter 5.

Toslink Optical Digital Audio Connector

Another digital interface that sends sound information to an external decoder is the digital optical port, known as the *Toslink port*. This is basically the same as the S/PDIF port, but instead of sending voltages through a metal wire, it sends information as pulses of light through a fiber-optic cable. This may be confusing for some who are new to the digital audio hobby—this *optical* link is sending *audio* information.

TIP *The S/PDIF port and the Toslink port send exactly the same digital information to the sound decoder. There is no difference in quality, because it is the same digital signal that is processed by the decoder. The only advantage to using an optical cable is that it is immune to the effects of electrical interference and cross-talk. If the S/PDIF cable is properly shielded, the resulting sound quality should be completely indistinguishable from an optical audio link.*

Some sound cards can decode digital surround soundtracks and send the audio channels to speakers connected directly to the HTPC. In this case, an external digital receiver/decoder is not needed. Since a new decoder is not necessary when a new sound format is available, it does save money and adds some convenience. However, most home theater enthusiasts prefer to use an external digital decoder because it includes an amplifier and can drive speakers with more power and volume than a sound card with powered speakers.

Analog Connections for "Digital Sound Ready" Receivers

Some early surround sound audio receivers had an input for each of the five surround sound channels. The receivers were marketed as "Digital Ready" or "Surround Sound Ready." Many early DVD players could decode the digital audio track and output each channel through an analog connection to the compatible audio receiver. This saved the cost of having to buy an audio receiver with a digital sound decoder, though the DVD player needed one, so the cost was not always less. One advantage of these "Digital Ready" receivers is that they are great for use with any new type of audio source that outputs analog sound information, such as MiniDisc players or the new DVD-Audio formats.

Creating an HTPC for High-Quality Sound

The quality of the sound produced by the HTPC depends on the quality of the sound card and the correct configuration of hardware and software in the system. This chapter has explained some concepts that are important to achieving high-quality sound reproduction. Hopefully it is clear that the HTPC is capable of creating the highest quality sound for movie soundtracks and other audio sources. By including an HTPC in the home theater, the enthusiast does not have to acquire separate components dedicated to the various audio forms.

An HTPC can also do more than just play the soundtrack from audio and video sources—it can record, store, and play back sound from a variety of analog and digital media. With enough disk space, the HTPC can be the home jukebox that aggregates the entire collection of LP records, audiocassettes, audio CDs, and other formats into a conveniently accessible location. Advances in the past decade for digital sampling and digital compression techniques make it possible to fit more sound into an HTPC than anyone could have imagined before the digital revolution.

An HTPC has the potential to reproduce sound at the highest standards possible for the home theater enthusiast, or at any level deemed an appropriate balance between cost and quality. Where cost is a factor, the sound card in an HTPC can be economized until money (or motivation) is available. The great thing about this is that upgrading the sound quality does not require replacing the whole system, just the sound card. No off-the-shelf consumer component can do that!

Perhaps the most impressive use for the HTPC is still its uncompromising video and audio playback quality for DVD movies in the home theater. Though many people consider the visual part of the movie experience most impressive, the audio capabilities of the HTPC help to create the magical movie experience desired in the home theater.

Summary

This chapter explained how the HTPC can be used very effectively to reproduce the highest quality sound using the latest and greatest technology and standards. In the next chapter, we discuss the realm of video cards. This area is absolutely critical to many aspects of the HTPC (for obvious reasons), so it's important that you make the right decisions around which video card to employ in your HTPC.

Hardware Components

Part Two

CHAPTER 4

Home Theater
PC Video Cards

THIS CHAPTER DISCUSSES the subject of video cards in the HTPC. Specifically, we discuss how video cards affect the quality of the viewing experience, what to look for in a card, and the primary features that are available in contemporary video cards. We'll look at the best card for your needs, be they gaming related, for video editing, or just for enjoying DVDs through your HTPC.

There are two main ways to connect an HTPC to a display device, the choice of which has a major bearing on which video card is best suited for the system. In turn, the manner in which the HTPC is connected to the display device is largely dependent on the display device itself. Since the display is potentially the most expensive part of the home theater, it is best to start assembling the HTPC after the display device has been acquired, or at least decided upon.

The Video Connection

The first way to connect the HTPC to a home theater display is through a standard S-video or composite video cable. This is suitable for virtually all television sets and most front projection display systems. Most televisions manufactured in the past several years have a composite video input, and those sets of sufficient size and quality for home theater use usually have at least one S-video input. These are the same inputs used for connecting VCRs, camcorders, DVD players, or any other typical video source.

NOTE *Many modern televisions have four, five, or even six video inputs, giving the user the ultimate in flexibility. As an example, Sony's XBR WEGA 32-inch HDTV television has seven inputs: two component, two coaxial, and three composite.*

Composite

In order to use the composite or S-video connection, the HTPC must have a video card with an S-video or composite video output connector. Typically, PC video cards do not have such outputs, so finding a suitable video card can be challenging. Often the selection of appropriate video hardware is limited, and finding one card that meets all of the desired requirements of performance, memory, and software may be impossible. Fortunately, with the rise of digital media convergence has come a great range of video cards with stunning performance and the necessary video output connector.

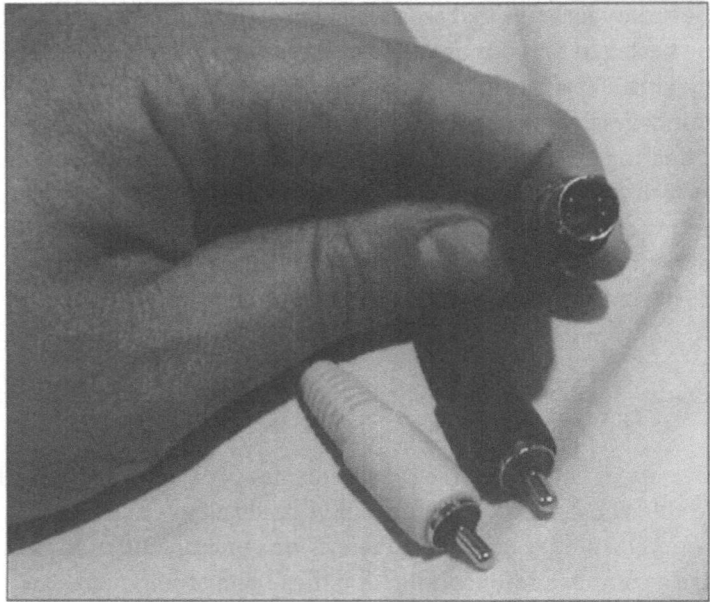

Figure 4-1. These are examples of composite RCA jacks and S-video cables.

Connecting the HTPC to a television with an S-video or composite connector limits the quality of the video image to the NTSC standard, since these connections were developed to work with regular television displays. There is a difference in quality between S-video and composite connections, however. The video signal is composed of brightness and color information. The composite connector sends video information to the set through one wire. The display device must separate the two signals before it can display a picture. The S-video connection sends the two signals separately on two wires, so the television does not have to process the video signal as much, and the result is a better picture with truer color and sharpness than the composite signal. If the home theater display can accept an S-video signal, it is preferable to select a video card that can output S-video instead of composite video.

Component

The second way to connect the HTPC to a home theater display is through component video cables. This method is suited to high-definition television displays, since the component cables can carry the HDTV video signal required for the high quality and resolution of HDTV displays. A component video cable is three separate cables with RCA-type jacks at each end, and though almost any cables with such jacks can carry component video information, most home theater enthusiasts prefer to use cables with a heavy gauge and shielding to protect against signal degradation. It is important to note that the component video signal is not digital—it suffers the same susceptibility to interference as S-video or composite video. In fact, given that the component cables carry much more information in high-definition modes than the NTSC formats, they are even more susceptible to electromagnetic interference.

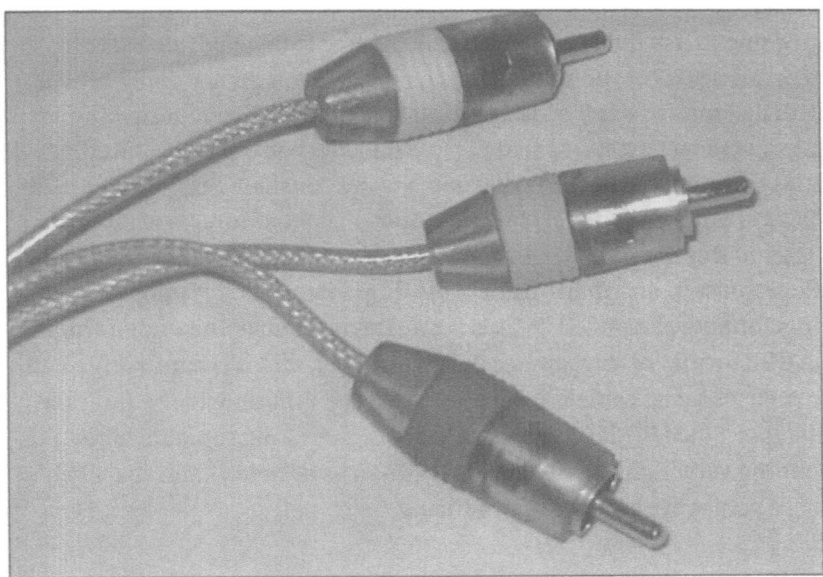

Figure 4-2. These jacks are examples of component cables.

All high-definition display devices have component inputs for use with high-definition video sources, but very few PC video cards have component outputs. However, the VGA connector sends a signal that can be converted for use with the component video cables needed for high-definition television display. To convert from VGA to component requires a transcoder, which some call a break-out box or simply a VGA-to-component converter. These small devices have a VGA input on one side and a component output on the other. The video signal is passed through the transcoder to the HDTV without any internal processing, so the PC controls the resolution and refresh rate of the video displayed on the HDTV. It is important to note that HDTV displays can only accept a few different resolutions and refresh rates, so setting up the HTPC to output through a transcoder is not an easy task. (At least, not an easy task without this guidebook!)

TIP *Many people are surprised to learn that the VGA connection between the PC and monitor sends an analog—not a digital—video signal. This is the key reason why a transcoder can convert the VGA signal to a component video signal without a lot of expensive processors or electronics. Though transcoders are notoriously expensive, this is because of the relatively low demand for them, not their complexity.*

If you are going to use the HTPC in a home theater with a high-definition display that can accept a component video signal, then you do not really need a video card with a composite or S-video output. Some video card manufacturers are starting to offer video hardware that can output component video, but there are some issues with these new cards that you should consider before you decide how the HTPC will output to the display. The topic of video output is explored in more detail later in this chapter.

Some television sets, and many front projection systems, have another type of video connector known as RGBHV. This is an analog video connection format similar to the RGB format of a computer VGA connector, and it is compatible with VGA output when a special cable is used to convert the VGA plug to the multiple coaxial connectors. Since RGBHV sends the video signal along separate wires, it is capable of sending very high-quality video—as good as or better than the video that component cables are capable of producing.

Video Card Features

After you've determined the method of connecting the video signal from the HTPC to the display, you have other video card features to consider. Home computer hobbyists generally regard the performance of a video card as the most critical issue, and the HTPC enthusiast should also consider this factor. Almost every video card made in the past few years is fast enough to play back DVD movies, but if you're going to use the HTPC for playing computer games, then good DVD playback may not be sufficient justification to choose a particular card. A few premium, full-featured video cards can capture video from analog or digital inputs and tune television channels from cable sources. The video hardware in an HTPC is one of the most critical subsystems, so careful selection is an important step.

Hardware Video Assistance

In the early days of DVD movies on a computer, the system processor and video card were barely fast enough to decode the MPEG-2 video stream from the DVD disc and display it on the computer monitor. To make DVD movies smoother and enable full-screen playback, extra hardware was dedicated to decoding and displaying the video. This extra hardware was usually a separate computer adapter card, but in some cases it was an add-on or daughterboard for the video card.

Modern PCs are capable of decoding the MPEG-2 video stream and displaying the video full-screen without a hardware decoder, but most decent video cards still have some hardware features to assist in DVD playback. These features are no longer added on with a daughterboard but are instead included right in the video card processor itself. Features such as deinterlacing, motion compensation, and filtering all improve the picture quality of DVD video without adding an extra load on the system processor. Some premium video cards such as the NVIDIA GeForce4 MX have an MPEG-2 decoder built into the video hardware so that the system CPU is relieved of much of the work involved in showing DVD video.

Gaming

The most visually stunning computer games on the market today require a video card with excellent 3D rendering capability. The virtual worlds into which the player is drawn are realistic, detailed, and smoothly animated environments that look more and more like real life with each new generation of games. The relationship between PC game software and video hardware is intimate and dynamic— new features are introduced by hardware vendors that are almost immediately exploited by the game makers, so it is difficult (and expensive!) to stay on the cutting edge of video hardware. The best 3D video card on the market last year is only a midrange performer this year, so the HTPC hobbyist who hopes to play "Medal of Honor" or "Doom III" on the big screen in the home theater must find a video card with the features and performance to match those games.

There are, of course, countless PC games that will look great and perform splendidly on any average video card currently available, so the HTPC without a top-notch 3D video card is not wholly useless for gaming. Many gamers enjoy older 3D games, strategic titles, or even just playing solitaire. Those hobbyists with kids to please should keep in mind that most children's games do not require expensive systems, and the entertainment value is increased when the kids get to play on a big-screen display.

The definitive advantage to using an HTPC as a gaming machine is that no other hardware can output the high picture quality of an HTPC connected to a high-definition display device. Since the HTPC can display a picture at resolutions up to 1080i (or whatever limit the television can handle), it can take full advantage of the quality of the home theater system to improve the gaming experience. Even if you do not intend to play PC games on your HTPC, you may feel tempted just to see how it feels to score a goal, win a race, or shoot an alien in a darkened room with a big-screen display and full surround sound pulling you into the experience.

Capturing Video

A video card that has an input for capturing video from analog sources is a very convenient way to digitize old home movies from VHS, a Hi-8 camcorder, or any other analog source into your HTPC for editing and storage. There are a few video cards available that can accept an analog video input in the form of either a composite video signal or an S-video signal. Though the current trend in camcorders is digital, many people have older analog recordings in formats that are incompatible with digital camcorders. An analog video input adds versatility to the HTPC system.

The video input feature of a video card is not a critical feature for most hobbyists. Considering that most HTPC computers will include a television tuner, an analog video input on the video card may be redundant. Since the television tuner card will almost certainly have a composite and an S-video input (in addition to the coaxial cable inputs), having a video card that can accept analog video is not worth considering for most HTPCs. However, if a television tuner is not part of the plan for the HTPC system, the video input feature on the video card may be a worthwhile addition.

Digital video is usually sent to a PC through a digital input known as an IEEE 1394 port (see Figure 4-3). The IEEE is the *Institute of Electrical and Electronics Engineers,* an organization that creates standards for many different electronic components and devices. IEEE 1394 is called FireWire by Apple Computer and i.LINK by Sony. Some video cards feature an IEEE 1394 port, as do some sound cards, and increasingly more and more motherboards. For this reason, it is not usually necessary to get a video card with such a digital input, unless it is to be used in an HTPC that has no other IEEE 1394 port.

Figure 4-3. Digital camcorder with an IEEE 1394 cable ready to plug into an HTPC

 **NOTE** *The FireWire connection to a digital video camera carries both audio and video information, which makes it a very convenient way to import high-quality digital information from a camcorder.*

Tuning Television

Many hobbyists considering an HTPC will want to include the ability to tune television stations from analog cable or over-the-air sources. This chapter includes a detailed examination of the available hardware later on, but we should mention one category of television tuner during this examination of video cards. There is a popular line of video cards from ATI called "All-In-Wonder" that feature a tuner built into the card. This combination video card and television tuner has some interesting benefits and drawbacks worth discussing.

Combining the video card and tuner into one card can save space in a cramped HTPC case. Most enthusiasts will want to find an inconspicuous PC case for their HTPC, so size and interior room can be a big issue. Further, this combination can potentially save some cost since a separate television tuner is not needed. Perhaps the best advantage is the fact that there will be no compatibility issues between the video card and television tuner, since they are a single unit from one manufacturer.

Broadcast television is about to undergo a huge transformation in the coming years as digital channels start to multiply, and this leads to a major drawback to using a combination video card and television tuner: To change the tuner, the video card must also be changed. An HTPC is a great machine because it is versatile and upgradeable, so it is a weighty decision to combine two features inside the system when one of those features is likely to be swapped out during the lifetime of the machine.

Fan Noise

Some PC hobbyists that are new to the HTPC topic may be surprised to learn that one of the most important issues for an HTPC system is the noise it makes. A PC sitting in an office or den may seem quiet when you are surfing the Web or playing "Dungeon Siege," but put that PC into a home theater room during the quiet suspense of a horror movie or the soft atmosphere of a love story and the fan noise will drive you mad. We discuss this topic in more depth in Chapter 8, but it is worth addressing during this discussion of video cards.

Most of the new high-performance 3D graphics processors run very fast and generate a lot of heat. Almost all video cards with competent 3D performance have a heat-sink fan attached to the processor, and this fan can be quite large in some cases. Generally, the faster the graphics processor, the better the video performance, but the bigger and louder the fan required to dissipate all the heat generated. Most HTPC enthusiasts forego cutting-edge 3D processor performance in favor of a video card with good DVD playback capabilities and medium-to-low heat generation. Some people even prefer older versions of video cards from previous years when heat-sink fans were not necessary.

If the noise of a small fan spinning inside the case of the HTPC doesn't seem unduly distracting, consider the fact that most cooling fans have a lifespan of only a few years. Anyone who has listened to a dying fan for a while can testify about the annoying sound it makes as it slows down, speeds up, and grinds out its bearings. Also, an HTPC that is set up to record programs, report alarms, or play reminders is necessarily turned on most of the time. Even when no video image is displayed, the video card cooling fan will still be spinning its life away. A video card that does not require a cooling fan could save a lot of aggravation and maintenance.

There are some novel and extreme ways to cool an HTPC without increasing fan noise that might be worth considering for home theater rooms that must be as quiet as possible. Water cooling kits are available to cool the CPU, video card, and hard drives inside a computer case. These kits include heat sinks for the major heat-generating components, tubing to circulate the water or other coolant, and a nearly silent pump. Kits that include a refrigeration system are also available, but if the refrigeration compressor motor is not located in a separate room, it will make more noise than a fan. Some special cases with extra ventilation and some special modifications to standard cases are also available.

Drivers

You can save quite a bit of frustration if you research the quality of drivers and support for the video card before you make a final selection. Each video hardware manufacturer provides the software that makes the video card work with an operating system, and every video hardware manufacturer has its strengths and weaknesses in supporting these drivers. Experienced PC hobbyists often have favorite manufacturers or brands, but using a video card in an HTPC adds some points to consider that don't apply to conventional PCs. We detail these extra considerations in the sections that follow.

Resolution

Most video card drivers allow the user to select a display resolution. The *resolution* is the measure of the number of pixels horizontally and vertically on the display screen. The display screen always stays the same size, but the size of the pixels changes.

 **NOTE** *Actually, you can configure some LCD displays so that when you change the resolution, the size of the display area shrinks. The resulting image appears as a smaller window inside the display, around which the screen is blank. The reason for this is that the pixels in an LCD display do not scale well because of the very sharp screen resolution. This is the same reason that all LCD displays have a native resolution at which the picture looks best.*

Common resolutions for computer displays are as follows:

- 640 pixels wide by 480 pixels tall

- 800 pixels wide by 600 pixels tall

- 1024 pixels wide by 768 pixels tall

- 1280 pixels wide by 1024 pixels tall

- 1600 pixels wide by 1200 pixels tall

This list does not include all of the possible resolutions for display on a computer screen, but it does illustrate some limitations that have an important bearing on an HTPC. The resolutions are all fixed at an aspect ratio of 4:3—that is, they are all multiples of 4 units wide by 3 units tall. This is the aspect ratio of standard television sets (NTSC or PAL), but high-definition sets allow a 16:9 aspect ratio, and many DVDs are even wider. Some computer monitors support 16:9 resolutions, such as the new Apple PowerBook and the new Apple Cinema HD Display, but the majority of personal computers are used with 4:3 displays, and the video software reflects it.

The other limitation shown in the preceding list is that there is no matching resolution for all of the digital high-definition television standards. Remember that HDTV can support 480p, 540p, 720p, and 1080i. These numbers would correspond to the number of pixels measured vertically up and down the display. The only match is at 640 × 480. This resolution is no higher than any off-the-shelf DVD player, so limiting the HTPC to this display measurement negates much of its display advantages.

Since the video card drivers do not support desirable aspect ratios and resolutions, the HTPC requires additional software to run the video card at the correct resolution for a high-definition display. The most popular utility for doing this is called PowerStrip, and Chapter 10 provides more detailed information about using it, but it is important to note at this point that PowerStrip is compatible with a finite list of video cards. Fortunately, must popular cards are supported, but it is wise to check the list before you select a card for an HTPC that will be used to drive a high-definition display. The PowerStrip software comes with documentation that lists all supported video cards and chipsets.

NOTE *The ATI Radeon 8500 has HDTV resolutions built into the system when you purchase the add-on dongle (DVI-to-component connector) so you do not have to use Powerstrip.*

Video Card Quirks

Researching information about video cards is essential to avoid problems when configuring the HTPC system. Some video cards have annoying quirks and bugs that aren't readily apparent from the manufacturer's literature. It is helpful to consult other sources of information (such as this book!) to find out all the dirty secrets of video hardware. For some suggestions about where to start looking, there is a list of (mostly online) information sources in the Appendix.

One quirk that we've found occurs with the drivers for ATI Radeon video cards. The HDTV resolution of 1080i is an interlaced video mode, but the ATI drivers do not allow an interlaced mode above 640 × 480. This isn't surprising, since few manufacturers do, and it's not a problem thanks to PowerStrip, which can set an interlaced mode of 1920 × 1080. Unfortunately, when you play video at this resolution, the picture is stretched to double the height of the display area so that only the top half of the video is visible.

There is no remedy for this situation except to drop the display settings to 1920 × 540 and set the refresh frequency to 60 Hz progressive. As we discuss in Chapter 10, this mode is equivalent to the 1080i mode and should work for most HDTV displays.

Another example of a video card quirk occurs in the NVIDIA line of video hardware based on the GeForce graphics processor. Although the GeForce is widely regarded as a premier gaming video card, it does not perform as well as the ATI Radeon line of video cards with regard to video quality from DVD movies. The Radeon video cards are (in our opinion) smoother and have better color than the GeForce-based video cards. This illustrates an important consideration when assembling an HTPC: Should it be optimized for gaming or for DVD playback? There is no right answer except to follow your own preference.

Video Output

Since outputting images to the display device is one of the most crucial tasks for the HTPC, a review of the major issues to consider for each method is important. As mentioned earlier, the home theater is often built around the display—a front projection system, a rear projection television, a large-screen direct-view television, or whatever display device is appropriate or cost-effective—so the method of connecting the HTPC to the display will depend on the features of the display. Fortunately, since the HTPC is such an adaptable machine, it is not difficult to build it to suit a number of different output methods.

Component Video

The recent introduction of large-screen televisions and high-definition televisions brought with it a new way to connect video sources to these advanced quality displays. Composite and S-video cables are engineered to carry the video signal for conventional NTSC- or PAL-quality sources, but they are not suitable for anything better (and, some argue, they are not even suitable for the best quality NTSC or PAL). A new connection was introduced to carry the higher quality images. The standard is published by the Consumer Electronics Association (CEA) and is known as EIA/CEA-770, though it is commonly referred to as component video.

The component video standard is actually a three-part specification: The first part, EIA/CEA-770.1, is for normal NTSC broadcast television and compatible video sources. The second part, EIA/CEA-770.2, is for standard-definition video sources that can output a 480i or 480p video. The third part, EIA/CEA-770.3, is for high-definition video at 720p or 1080i resolution. It is important to note that this component video standard is for analog video. Even though the standard-definition and high-definition video is digitally stored and transmitted, it is sent to the display device as an analog signal through the component video cables.

Component video separates the video signal into three lines. The first is the brightness information, called *luminance,* that essentially carries a black-and-white version of the video. The other two lines carry color information, or *chrominance,* in different color ranges; one is for yellow-red, and the other is for yellow-blue. All three lines are required to re-create the full-color video from the source.

TIP *Although the component video connection is defined as an industry standard, it is anything but that. The output line levels and the input levels vary from manufacturer to manufacturer so that each display device or output source must be tuned and calibrated to reproduce the video picture as close to the original quality as possible. This is one of the reasons why the HTPC is so versatile—no other device allows as much control over the output levels of color and contrast.*

The display device with component video inputs must sense the video format being input, since component cables can carry everything from standard NTSC video of about 480i up to the best HDTV resolution of 1080i, and anything in between. In most cases, a video display device will support a few modes in the HDTV specification. Commonly, 480i, 480p, 540p, and 1080i are compatible with any high-definition television, and 720p and the derived 1440i modes are less frequently supported. Since the HTPC configured with the PowerStrip software allows for extreme fine-tuning in a huge range of resolutions and frequencies, at least one compatible high-resolution mode can be found. Determining the correct settings for the video card to output a compatible video signal for the display device is one of the key challenges of configuring the HTPC.

Transcoders

To connect the HTPC to the component inputs of an HDTV-compatible display device, the computer VGA output must be converted to the three-line component input. The VGA signal is an analog video signal composed of luminance, chrominance, and timing signals that can be converted to component output through the use of a transcoder. The transcoder passes the video signal through without modifying the resolution or frequency, so the HTPC video card must be configured to output the proper resolution and refresh rate for the high-definition television.

Due to the specialized purpose of VGA-to-component transcoders, they are relatively rare and expensive. The only ones we could find were from Key Digital Systems (see Figure 4-4), Audio Authority, and RCA. They all have the same basic size and configuration: a small external device with a VGA input on one side, a three-line component output on another side, and a power socket for the power cord. Some models (the Key Digital Systems ones, for example) have a small knob for centering the picture, but this adds little value as the picture size, shape, and position can all be adjusted in the PowerStrip software. They also are all the same basic price, which may be regarded as expensive for a relatively simple device, though not astronomically so.

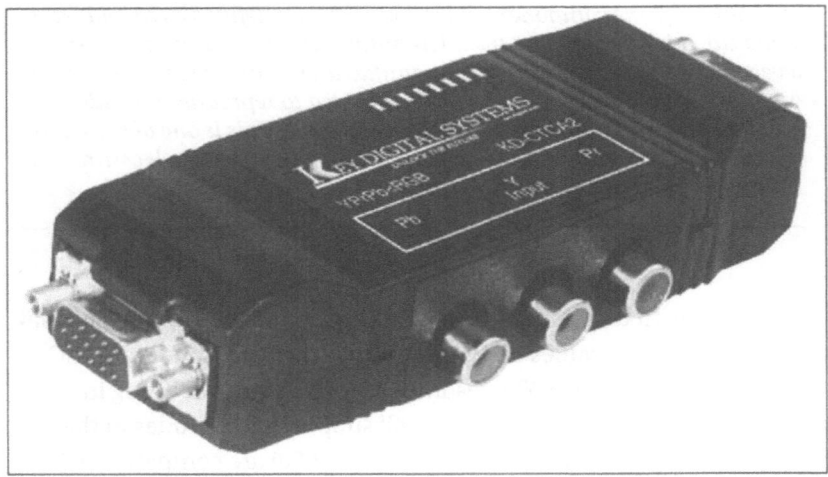

Figure 4-4. The Key Digital Systems VGA-to-component adaptor

A transcoder is essentially an adapter that gives your television a VGA port, but some televisions have a VGA port built right in. You should take care when considering a display device with a VGA-type connector. Unless the television or projector is made to work as a computer display device, it may support only one VGA mode: 640 × 480 interlaced. Though convenient, it pretty much negates any picture quality advantage of higher resolution modes.

TIP *A VGA connector is more correctly referred to as a* DB-15 RGB connector. *The term "VGA" is only relevant in the context of computer displays. Such a connector on a television or home theater projector will likely not be labeled VGA.*

The need for a transcoder makes the HTPC system a little more complex. Without it, the system is limited to outputting video at standard NTSC quality. Those HTPC hobbyists fortunate enough to have a high-definition device will probably find the advantages of using the transcoder outweigh the disadvantages of its cost and configuration challenges. The one great advantage to using the transcoder is that you can use any video card that outputs via a VGA connector.

 **CAUTION** *There are many products available that convert common PC display resolutions for use on any television. These devices actually down-convert all screen resolutions to the NTSC standard 480i in order to work on a television. This is* not *what a VGA-to-component transcoder does! The transcoder passes the video resolution and timing signal straight through to the display. The HTPC hobbyist should be aware that the device needed for use with an HDTV-compatible display is a transcoder and not a converter.*

Pure Digital Video Is Scarce

A few high-definition television sets and display devices have digital video inputs in the form of an IEEE 1394 digital connector. CEA published the specification EIA/CEA-775 for sending video signals over the IEEE 1394 digital wire. For televisions equipped with the proper IEEE 1394 connector, pure digital video can be sent to the display with absolutely no analog conversion until the last step when the picture is drawn on the screen.

Unfortunately, the industry does not seem to be picking up this "standard" very quickly. Though IEEE 1394 is fast enough for NTSC and other lower-res digital formats, it is not quite able to support the full quality of high-definition television, so already newer formats have been introduced to compete with this format. Very few display devices are available that accept a digital IEEE 1394 connection. Although it is a popular format for transferring digital audio and video from camcorders to computers, it is not widely adopted for televisions. There are a few other digital formats that allow a connection from a video source to a display device—DVI and LVDS, for example. These formats are also not widely available on display devices large enough for use in a home theater environment. The best solution for high-definition video from an HTPC is to use the analog format of component video, or for compatible front projection systems, an RGBHV converter cable.

Component Video Output from the Video Card

The need for a transcoder to use an HTPC with an HDTV has led some manufacturers to consider adding component outputs to their VGA cards. ATI announced an upgrade for their All-In-Wonder Radeon 8500 and 9700 that will allow the output of digital television formats of 480i, 480p, 540p, 720p, 1080i, and 1440i. It is supposed to be ready by the end of 2002. NVIDIA have also announced component outputs as part of their Video Performance Engine (VPE) feature for the GeForce4.

Unfortunately, because of pressure from the media-publishing industry, the ATI video card will not play DVD or other copy-protected material at a resolution above 480p. The NVIDIA GeForce4 MX will also respect the 480p limit for DVD playback. For those HTPC hobbyists with high-definition displays, this handicaps the capability of the HTPC to scale up a video to make use of the full resolution of the display. Many hobbyists in the HTPC community have voiced their frustration to the DVD publishers and to hardware manufacturers, but vendors can hardly be blamed for adhering to the contractual restrictions of the DVD consortium. In order to obey the requirements for Macrovision protection encoded into DVD video media, DVD playback is limited to 480p, and this restriction limits the value of any video card with component video outputs.

S-Video

For display devices that lack component video inputs, the S-video connection is the best choice for connecting the HTPC. Most large displays manufactured in the last decade or so have at least one S-video input, so it is widely compatible with television sets, rear projection televisions, and projection displays. S-video is therefore also popular on many video sources such as VCRs, DVD players, and camcorders.

S-video is used only for standard NTSC- or PAL-format video; it does not support any high-definition modes or even any progressive video modes. It is a little like component video because the luminance and chrominance signals are transmitted over separate lines, but there are only two wires instead of three, and they are wrapped into one cable. The difference in picture quality between component video and S-video is barely noticeable at the NTSC standard of 480i— it takes a very sensitive and well-trained viewer to notice any difference at all.

The HTPC that outputs S-video must have the appropriate connector on the video card in order to connect to the display device. This means that your choice of video cards for the HTPC is limited when your system must output to an S-video–capable display. There are external converters available that convert the VGA output of any video card to a standard NTSC signal via an S-video connector, but the cost of S-video–capable video cards is so low that such an external device is almost never worth the money.

It is worth mentioning that S-video has one or two advantages over the quality of component video. The software drivers that make the S-video output work with the HTPC often allow the system to be configured to use the VGA output at the same time as the S-video output. This allows you to connect a computer monitor in addition to the home theater display. You can use the monitor to set up the system and to select functionality while video images are sent to the main display.

The monitor is also easier to read than the relatively blurry television screen, so it makes using the HTPC a little easier.

The other advantage of building an HTPC with an S-video output is that you can use it on almost any display, anywhere. Many hobbyists use their HTPC systems for presentations, as portable gaming systems, or occasionally at a friend's house. For those who will be using their system in multiple locations, adding an S-video output makes the HTPC almost infinitely compatible.

Composite Video

S-video and component video are actually both types of "component" video—they carry a video signal separated into multiple components that must be recombined by the display device. *Composite video* is named as such because it carries a composite of the luminance and chrominance signals along one wire. The display device must actually separate these two signals (they are transmitted along the wire at different frequencies) before recombining them to form the picture.

This means that some picture quality is always lost using composite video because the parts of the video signal interfere with each other slightly and can never be perfectly separated. A video picture coming from a source connected via composite video looks less well focused (less sharp) and has color that lacks the saturation and purity of an S-video or component video signal. Although it is difficult to see the difference between S-video and component video signals, comparing either to composite video reveals noticeable degradation.

Composite video is, however, easily the most popular format for connecting video sources to display devices. Composite video comes in the form of a single cable with standard RCA-type connectors that are usually colored yellow to indicate that they are for video or from a coaxial cable used to transmit all of the channels from most cable television providers in North American cities.

Composite video output is included with virtually every video card that outputs S-video. Many video cards with the capability to output an NTSC video signal have only an S-video connector but come with an adapter to convert the S-video to composite.

 **NOTE** *The S-video to composite video adapter that comes with many S-video–capable video cards does not work with just any S-video source; it only works with computer video cards. The computer must be configured to output a composite video signal so that luminance and chrominance are sent at different frequencies.*

There are a number of great video cards with S-video and composite output connectors that are also perfectly suitable for use with a VGA-to-component transcoder. It is not necessary to sacrifice any DVD playback performance or gaming features in order to get a video card with an S-video connector. Even if you do not anticipate using your HTPC by connecting to an S-video display, you should consider finding such a video card in order to get the flexibility and compatibility such a connection offers. Many of the cutting-edge, full-featured multimedia video cards have composite and S-video connections even though they are primarily selected by HTPC enthusiasts for use in high-definition television display home theater systems.

Television Tuners

In the past, watching television on a PC has mostly been a novelty, but with the growing popularity of the HTPC, adding television to a computer seems like a natural step. Television tuner cards are a great way to add television channels to the PC desktop, but since the cost of an actual television is relatively low, it hasn't always made sense. Even a small television sitting beside a computer is more practical than a tiny window on the screen that's continuously being hidden by other applications. But the HTPC is a computer that's dedicated to being a media source in the home theater, and adding television channels to its DVD video and digital audio repertoire is a great way to increase its value. Lately, high-definition television tuner cards have become available, so an HTPC that can display high-quality DVD playback on a high-definition television can be made even more impressive by adding a high-definition television tuner card.

HDTV

Most major television markets in the United States now have a few digital television stations being broadcast over the air. As the deadline for conversion to digital broadcast looms closer, the number of digital television broadcasts will increase, so investing in HDTV hardware is becoming less of a risk. Though the price of HDTV equipment is still very high, in the future it is expected to drop to levels comparable to standard NTSC television equipment today.

HDTV can arrive in your home in a number of ways. Several stations broadcast HDTV signals over the air, which requires an antenna for proper reception. HDTV reception is not like the fuzzy, ghosted images that plague NTSC reception today. Since HDTV is a digital signal with error detection and correction, it is possible to get a "perfect" picture and perfect sound even if the signal strength is only moderate. A set-top decoder or HDTV set with a built-in decoder is necessary to watch an HDTV broadcast.

Direct broadcast satellite systems in both the United States and Canada have a few high-definition channels in their lineups. These require special satellite receivers to decode the channels and output them to an HDTV-ready television set. The built-in decoder of an HDTV set is not useable with DBS systems, so the set must have component video inputs as almost all of the high-definition receivers output using these connections.

Finally, some cable systems are starting to include high-definition channels. Like the digital satellite systems, a high-definition receiver that connects to the cable is required, and it attaches to the component inputs of the HDTV-ready display.

NOTE *Most high-definition receivers for over-the-air broadcast, digital satellite systems, or digital cable services can output HDTV channels to standard NTSC televisions by down-converting the video to 480i. This makes it possible to watch the high-definition channels without buying an expensive HDTV television, but most of the picture quality is lost when it is converted down to the lower resolution of NTSC.*

HDTV Tuner Cards

An HDTV tuner card for the computer can be a cheaper way to receive HDTV channels. These tuner cards are only able to receive over-the-air broadcasts from an antenna; they cannot receive HDTV channels from digital satellite systems or digital cable services. Since a computer monitor is a high-quality display device, watching HDTV on a computer screen is actually a very good way to view such programming. The only problem is that most computer screens are not large enough for a roomful of viewers—unless the computer screen happens to be a high-definition television connected to an HTPC.

In fact, due to broadcasters' fears about consumers making high-quality copies of high-definition programs, there is currently no recording device that can capture HDTV. Though some products have been announced, and most early adopters of the high-definition technology are getting frustrated waiting for high-definition equipment and programming, there is little on the horizon for the high-definition marketplace until copyright issues are resolved. The only exception to this is to use an HTPC to receive, decode, and record high-definition programming broadcast over the air. This capability is sparking a lot of excitement in the HTPC community for those enthusiasts with access to over-the-air HDTV channels.

For those with access to HDTV channels from a digital satellite service or digital cable service, there isn't much good news about getting those channels to work through the HTPC. The only method for outputting the HDTV video picture at its highest quality is through the component video connections, and there are no television tuner cards or other computer hardware devices that can accept component video inputs. The digital satellite or cable receiver normally has an S-video output that can be connected to the input of the television tuner card (or the video card, in some cases), but this connection only carries the high-definition channel down-converted to NTSC quality. The HDTV industry is still too young and evolving for a wide range of compatible hardware to exist. Ideally, it would be great if the HTPC could accept an analog HDTV video signal via component inputs, or a digital signal via IEEE 1394, but low consumer demand and broadcasters' copyright fears seem to be delaying the introduction of such conveniences.

 **TIP** *Every HDTV tuner card is also an NTSC television tuner card. That is, HDTV tuner cards are all able to tune standard television channels, too. This means that the HTPC only needs one television tuner card. It makes sense to add an HDTV tuner card to an HTPC that is in a region where digital channels are either available or soon to be available over the air.*

NTSC Television

Adding a television tuning card to an HTPC to access standard NTSC channels is relatively inexpensive. Television tuner cards are surprisingly common (how many people really want to watch television in a small window in the corner of their computer screen, anyway?), and since the technology for receiving television signals has existed for so long it is pretty well refined, reliable, and cheap. Television tuner cards are so inexpensive that hobbyists building an HTPC should seriously consider adding one even if they don't think they want to use the system for television.

Common Television Tuner Features

Television tuner cards all seem to have composite and S-video inputs, and some have left and right channel stereo inputs also. This means that the television tuner card provides the HTPC with the capability to capture video from other sources besides broadcast television. Video from camcorders without a digital IEEE 1394 connection is not easily imported to the computer, but with a television tuner card the HTPC can capture this video and store it as digital video.

In home theaters that feature digital satellite service or a digital cable box, the television tuner card can accept analog video from these sources. This is a great convenience since all of the video programming that is shown in the home theater can be routed through the HTPC. The advantage is that the television only has to be connected to one device. All of the video can also be recorded by the HTPC and scaled up to whatever resolution the television can handle. This does not actually improve the picture quality of standard television channels, but when everything is displayed at the same resolution it is easy to jump between DVD, television, VCR, and home movies.

The software that runs modern television tuner cards is very full-featured. Television tuner cards have coaxial cable inputs so you can connect them to either an antenna or a conventional analog cable service. With all those channels, it can be difficult to find a desired program, or even to find something interesting to watch. The software can be programmed to monitor the closed captioning for keywords and then either switch to the channel where the keyword was found or start recording the program. Built-in intelligence like this makes the era of the VCR seem like the Dark Ages! The software also lets you watch television channels in a window on the desktop or makes the television channel take up the whole screen. Some software packages can even replace the desktop wallpaper with the television display. Most software packages also support common features such as recording video or capturing single frames from the video program, scanning channels by displaying a screen filled with thumbnail still images, and timed recording.

Television Tuners and Digital Satellite or Digital Cable Service

Unfortunately, there are some things that television tuner cards will never do. These limits are more a result of security and copyright issues than of hardware limitations, and they may have some bearing on the way you configure your HTPC (or even whether you desire an HTPC at all). The television tuner card will never be able to receive and decode digital satellite or digital cable television channels. These broadcast channels are encrypted with security features so that unauthorized receivers cannot decode and display the video signal. Allowing a computer component access to these signals would compromise the security. Though it would be convenient to be able to watch digital television from satellite or cable without needing the external receiver to change channels, it is almost completely unlikely to ever happen.

The HTPC Project Hardware

For this book, we're assembling two HTPC systems. One system will be a high-end machine, and the other will be low-end, though both will be well within the confines of a reasonable budget. After all, if we had an unlimited amount of money for our HTPC system, we wouldn't need to build a machine to take the place of far more expensive equipment! Chapter 8 provides a full list of all the hardware in each machine, but it is helpful to note here that the first HTPC system will have an AMD Athlon PR2100+ processor and the second will have a Pentium III 450 processor. Neither of these CPUs is cutting edge—in fact, they're both old PCs that were available for the project—but they're both fast enough to build an HTPC system around. This helps to illustrate an important point about getting into the HTPC hobby: It isn't necessary to spend a lot of money to build a great home theater media machine.

HTPC System 1

Since the basis for selecting a video card is the home theater display, this is where we'll start the discussion. The first HTPC system we're building is going to be used with a rear projection, HDTV-ready television. This display has two sets of component inputs that can accept HDTV resolutions up to 1080i, and this is how the HTPC will be connected. Although this display has S-video and composite inputs, using the component inputs will allow us to scale all video up to the high-definition resolution that we want to use.

The ATI All-In-Wonder Radeon series of video cards are widely regarded as the premiere video hardware for DVD playback. The color saturation and adjustments available through the video card drivers are excellent, and the bundled software is full-featured and easy to use. The All-In-Wonder line of video cards also features television tuners, video inputs for video capture, and S/PDIF digital audio output for DVD playback.

With this in mind, we approached ATI for their recommendations on a video card for our HTPC project. ATI generously supplied an ATI All-In-Wonder Radeon 7500 for our first HTPC system. This card sports all of the features of the All-In-Wonder series, plus a radio frequency remote control. Though it includes an S-video output, we are not planning to connect it to the S-video input of the display, but we are planning to use the video input to capture video from a camcorder and VCR. This video card also has a digital audio output, though it is only useful for outputting the audio from DVD playback. The fast processor, 64MB of memory, and very capable 3D graphics processing power of this card will make it a great addition to our high-end HTPC.

One point to note about the ATI Radeon 7500 series of video cards (see Figure 4-5) is that they have a small cooling fan on the video chip. The ATI Radeon 7200 video card has no fan, and though it is not available in an All-In-Wonder package, it is suitable for HTPC systems that are connected to high-definition displays through a VGA-to-component transcoder. The cooling fan on the ATI Radeon 7500 is barely audible, but for those HTPC hobbyists with very sensitive ears, the ATI Radeon 7200 is worth considering.

Figure 4-5. The ATI All-In-Wonder Radeon 7500 supplied by ATI for this project

The great thing about the ATI All-In-Wonder Radeon 7500 is that the price is very reasonable for a full-featured multimedia video card. ATI also manufactures an All-In-Wonder Radeon 8500DV with a faster video chip, better 3D graphics processor, and an IEEE 1394 digital video input for transferring video from a digital camcorder. Though the 8500 is the top-of-the-line offering from ATI suitable for an HTPC, it also has a top-of-the-line price tag. However, since it fulfills many roles (video card, television tuner card, IEEE 1394 video input, and digital audio output), it may be very attractive for those HTPC hobbyists in need of its full set of features.

Keeping in mind that this video card will be used to output HDTV resolutions through a transcoder, we checked the PowerStrip release notes file to make sure that the ATI 7500 video chipset is supported by this software. PowerStrip is the only way to set the video card output resolution and refresh rate to the HDTV-compatible modes, since the Windows drivers that come with the hardware do not support these modes.

We also acquired a VGA-to-component transcoder to connect the VGA output of the video card to the component inputs of the display. There are only a few brands from which to choose, so we picked the Audio Authority model 9A60 (see Figure 4-6). As mentioned previously in this chapter, a transcoder is a pretty simple-looking device. The model 9A60 is a small white box with a VGA input at one end and the three RCA-type connectors for component video output at the other end, plus a power cord. All of the resolution and frequency is set by the computer's video card and passed through to the high-definition television. The transcoder was supplied with a VGA cable, and we supplied our own shielded component video cable.

Figure 4-6. The Audio Authority model 9A60 VGA-to-component video transcoder

TIP *We looked and looked, but we could not find a VGA-to-component video transcoder at any local retail computer stores, electronics stores, specialized electronics stores, computer wholesalers, flea markets, pet stores, or even in the classified ads. It seems that the only way to get one is to order it from a Web site. Keep this in mind as you plan your HTPC system: One of the key items may take 4–6 weeks to arrive!*

HTPC System 2

The display we are using for our second HTPC system is a 32-inch direct-view picture tube television. This set happens to be an HDTV-ready television, but we are not going to build our second HTPC to use any high-definition resolutions. This system will be connected with an S-video cable to the display. PowerStrip will not be needed on this system, but the transcoder from the first system will still allow us to compare the picture quality of the S-video to the component video, as the component video inputs on the television will accept an NTSC (480i) video signal.

Since we are not going to build the second HTPC with a transcoder, we need a video card that has an S-video output. This presented a significant challenge, as we wanted to use the NVIDIA GeForce4 MX chipset, which is offered by several video card manufacturers (NVIDIA do not manufacture their own video cards—they just design the chipset and license it to other hardware vendors), but not all of them include an S-video output on the card. We were eventually able to find an adaptor with the required video output connection.

The GeForce4 MX video card includes the VPE feature that NVIDIA. VPE is essentially an MPEG-2 decoder built into the video card processor. This is meant to save the main system processor a lot of work to decode the MPEG-2 video stream from the DVD or other digital video source. This is one of the main features that made us eager to try this video card in one of our HTPC systems. The GeForce4 is also a top-notch 3D gaming card, though we did not purchase the fastest version of this video card since we are mainly focused on multimedia performance and not solely gaming performance.

The GeForce4 MX does not have many of the other features of the ATI video card that we are using in our first HTPC system, though it is priced quite a bit lower, so for our purposes it is a good choice. The GeForce4 MX has no video input, no digital audio output, and no remote controller, so we will be adding these features with additional hardware.

Figure 4-7. The GeForce4 MX 440 video card used in our second HTPC system

The first HTPC system that we're assembling has a television tuner built into the video card, but this second one doesn't. For this reason, we're adding a television tuner adapter card to the system in order to get television stations from over-the-air and cable broadcasts. We were very interested to try out the newest HDTV tuner cards, so we asked around to a few manufacturers to see what they recommended, and Hauppauge sent us their WinTV-HD hardware (see Figure 4-8). This card has all the features of a regular NTSC television tuner card (coaxial cable input, S-video and composite video inputs, and great software), plus it has a connector for a digital HDTV antenna. Keep in mind that this second HTPC system is meant for S-video output, which won't be able to display HDTV at its proper high resolution, so we'll have to borrow the VGA-to-component transcoder from the first system or connect a PC monitor to see the high-definition modes that this HDTV tuner card can decode.

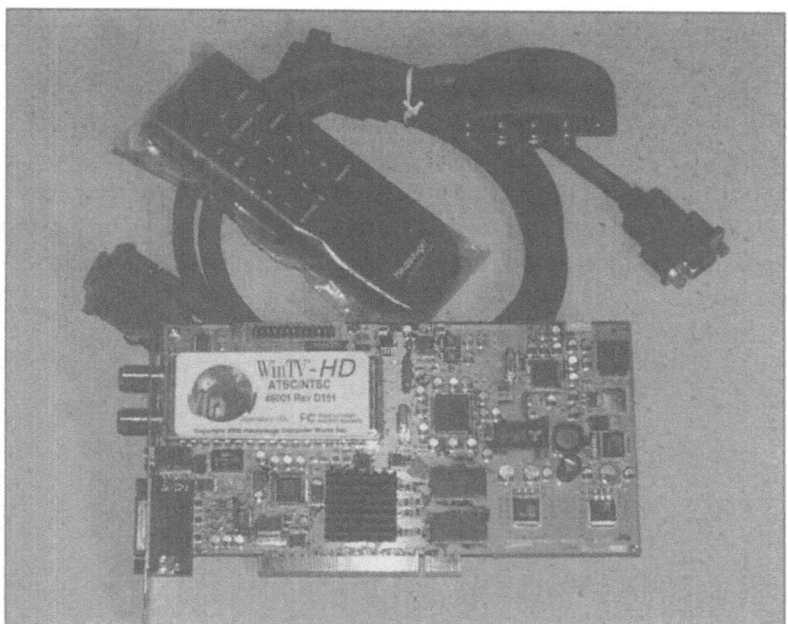

*Figure 4-8. The Hauppauge WinTV-HD HDTV tuner card used in
our second HTPC system*

Neither of the video cards selected for our HTPC systems is expensive, and neither is a top-of-the-line model. The reason for this is indicative of the state of the video card market: A lot of effort is spent to develop and market the best 3D gaming video card, and not much attention is paid to multimedia functions such as DVD playback. Though this seems unfair to the growing HTPC hobbyist community, it is actually an advantage to us. While the game players are spending top dollar to be at the cutting edge, those who simply want great digital video performance have a wide range of medium- and low-cost video cards from which to choose. Though features that improve computer games are not necessarily the same features desired in a HTPC video card, the general performance improvements are a benefit. Additionally, the inclusion of hardware features to improve MPEG video playback indicates that the manufacturers are starting to realize that the HTPC has a big future in the home theater.

With the video card selections for our two HTPC systems made, we can move on to the issues surrounding audio performance and sound cards.

Summary

The video card is perhaps the most critical component of your HTPC. With the proper card you can ensure that the HTPC will be the master of DVD playback, home video editing, and even cutting-edge gaming. Still, there are some trade-offs, and currently there are choices to be made between all-inclusive packages (ATI Radeon 7500/8500) and hot gaming video cards (NVIDIA's cards). In the next chapter, we look specifically at audio cards and explore what to look for in your HTPC's audio setup.

CHAPTER 5

Home Theater
PC Audio Cards

How to best bring the miracle of sound into the home is a contentious and hotly debated subject. For some audio purists, nothing less than thousands of dollars worth of vacuum tubes and power supplies is sufficient to reproduce sound with acceptable quality. Entire books have been written on this subject—indeed, industries have been created and lifetimes have been spent in search of the ultimate electronics to make the home sound system as good as a live performance. The variety of manufacturers, technologies (both high and low tech), and personal tastes makes any discussion of consumer sound systems a risky invitation for conflict.

There is a way through the melee, however. Since this book is concerned with home theater, it is appropriate to limit the discussion of technologies and devices to home theater sound, such as surround sound formats or basic stereo formats. Further, since this book's primary topic is home theater PCs, we may further narrow the discussion to include only such formats and technologies that affect the HTPC. Excluded from this text is any description or discussion comparing audio amplifiers, receivers, speakers (except those meant to be connected directly to the HTPC), and other accessories such as wire, cables, or equalizers. The focus of this chapter is the hardware that makes the HTPC work best with all that other stuff.

Choosing a Sound Card

In the previous chapter, we explained that selection of a video card is best done after selection of a display device, and there is a similar guiding principle for audio hardware. The sound card must suit the intended purpose of the HTPC and be compatible with the other audio components of the home theater. It is essential that you have a good understanding of the different types of sound cards available, their relative qualities, and their capability to connect to the rest of the audio system in the home theater before you select hardware.

DVD Video

One of the most common uses for the HTPC system is to play movies from DVDs. (Actually, it is so common that it is practically unheard of for an HTPC not to be able to do so!) The sound from a DVD is encoded as a digital stream with one or more channels of audio, so the HTPC sound components should be compatible with this digital format. The simplest solution is to find a sound card that can pass the digital audio stream directly out to a digital surround sound receiver for decoding and playback through speakers connected to the receiver. This method requires a sound card with a digital audio output—an S/PDIF port—that is either a coaxial wire or an optical cable connector. Using this hardware, the software DVD player can send the digital audio stream to the external decoder in the receiver through the digital audio output. Most of the current audio cards on the market have an S/PDIF output.

For those home theaters not already equipped with an external digital audio receiver, it is pretty easy to find sound cards that can decode the Dolby Digital or DTS audio formats with software and output surround sound to speakers connected to multiple sets of analog connectors. There are a wide range of speaker sets available that are designed specifically for use with PC sound cards, though many of these speaker sets are intended more for computer games than for DVD movies. Some of the available speaker sets also include an external digital audio decoder, which is a great way to add digital surround sound capabilities to a home theater system without spending a lot of money.

 **TIP** *Sound cards with 5.1 analog outputs for "Dolby Digital Ready" audio receivers are available. A Dolby Digital Ready receiver has analog connectors for the 5.1 audio channels output by a separate device, such as an HTPC, that are just amplified and played through the speakers connected to the receiver. This may be an economical alternative to upgrading to a digital audio receiver.*

For home theater systems being installed from scratch, the merits of choosing an external digital receiver for decoding digital audio and powering speakers versus simply connecting a speaker set to the HTPC are pretty balanced. If the HTPC is the center of the home theater and all video and audio sources feed into it, then there are no issues with connecting speakers directly to it. However, there are at least two reasons to prefer a separate, external digital audio receiver. First, the speakers available for connecting directly to a PC are not as powerful or available in as wide a variety as those for a traditional audio receiver. For small home theaters this is not a concern, but for larger rooms or for those enthusiasts with a favorite brand of speaker, this restriction may be unappealing. Second, when you add an HTPC to an existing home theater environment, you may already have a digital audio receiver to which most audio and video sources are already connected. Even if your existing home theater only has an analog audio receiver (that is, a receiver without S/PDIF inputs and without a built-in Dolby Digital or DTS audio decoder), you may prefer to replace the receiver with an upgraded model and keep the existing speakers. These issues can only be resolved with careful consideration on the part of the individual building the home theater system, but the decision will impact the selection of audio hardware for the HTPC. Figure 5-1 shows a diagram of audio connections with and without an external audio receiver.

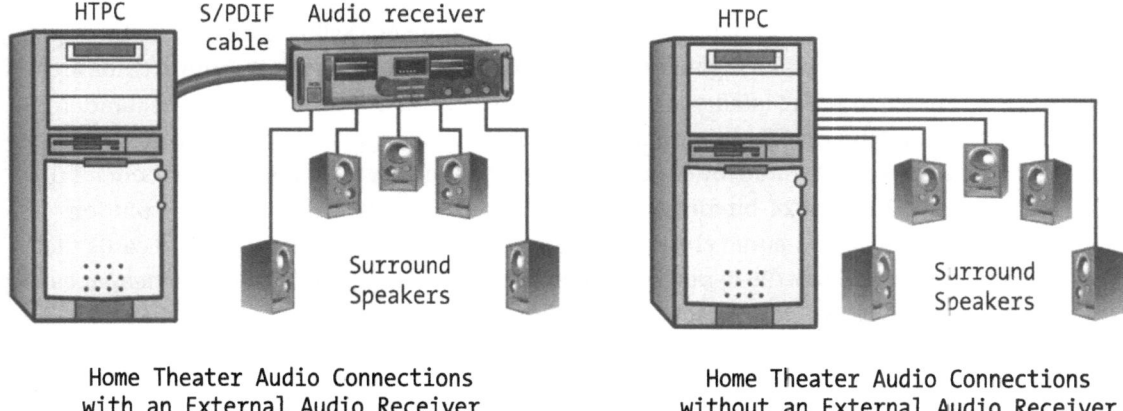

Figure 5-1. Audio connections with and without an external audio receiver

High-End Sound Cards: DVD-Audio, Super Audio CD, and Other Future Audio Formats

The best solution for integrating leading-edge audio formats with the HTPC is to add a sound card that can match the high fidelity of these audio sources. Unfortunately, there are no software applications, codecs, or even down-conversion capabilities for the HTPC to play DVD-Audio or Super Audio CD (SACD) media in its own DVD drive. An external player is needed to play back these formats, and the external player can only be connected by an analog stereo connection. The HPTC needs audio hardware capable of matching the high-quality sound output from the player in order to get the best possible audio signal. Most common PC sound cards are not able to match this quality, so some knowledge of the specifications of DVD-Audio, SACD, and sound cards is crucial to selecting the right hardware.

NOTE *The S/PDIF digital audio output has a maximum rate of 96 KHz at 24-bit resolution. It is not possible to use the digital audio connection to get the full quality of DVD-Audio or SACD players, which can output up to 192 KHz at 24-bit resolution. These components must be connected with analog lines from the player to the HTPC and from the HTPC to the audio receiver in order to avoid downsampling.*

The new audio formats of DVD-Audio and SACD allow for sound to be digitally encoded at a higher quality than CD audio. Since most PC sound cards are matched to the quality of CD audio, they fall short of the newer sound standards. For reference, CD audio specifies that sound is sampled at 44.1 KHz in 16-bit (16/44) stereo. DVD-Audio, by comparison, specifies a range of sampling frequencies up to 192 KHz at 24-bit for stereo audio channels and 96 KHz at 24-bit resolution (24/96) for 5.1 audio channels. There is now a good selection of sound cards that can process 24/96 digital information, but the majority of older and cheaper cards simply down-convert it to 16/44 information.

TIP *For more information about sound sampling and digital sound formats, refer to Chapter 3.*

It is obvious that the sound signal stored on a DVD-Audio disc is much higher resolution than that of CD audio, which should mean that the sound quality is also much higher. In practice, the difference in quality to the listener is subjective; most people can tell the difference between CD audio and DVD-Audio, but not everyone will feel the need to spend more money for the newer format. Those that do will probably want to connect a DVD-Audio player directly to an audio receiver or amplifier instead of an HTPC in order to minimize the degradation caused by multiple connections and the longer path from player to speaker. However, some may want to use the HTPC for mixing or recording, or may have speakers connected to the HTPC, in which case it is important to include audio hardware that is capable of digitizing analog sound at a higher quality than CD audio.

The digital encoding on an SACD disc uses a different method than CD audio or DVD-Audio, so it is difficult to make a comparison between the sound quality of these formats. Most subjective comparisons seem to indicate that SACD is equal to or better than DVD-Audio. Since the only way to connect an SACD player to an HTPC is through the analog stereo connections, there is no compatibility issue except to find a sound card that can digitize analog sound at a high sampling frequency and resolution.

The best sound card for use with a high-quality sound source such as DVD-Audio or SACD is one capable of digitizing sound at 96 KHz at 24-bit stereo. Though DVD-Audio can be encoded at up to 192 KHz, the capabilities of the best current sound cards are limited to 96 KHz. Such a high sampling frequency means a lot of information being stored on the hard drive of the HTPC when sound is recorded, and it also requires a lot more processing power to handle. Sound cards in this range generally have one or more stereo inputs and often include digital audio outputs in addition to analog outputs.

TIP *Popular sound cards that are capable of handling 44.1 KHz at 16-bit stereo sound may also be used with DVD-Audio or SACD players, but they cannot record or mix the sound at the same high quality of more expensive sound cards. That is, they only record at CD quality, so some of the richness of DVD-Audio or SACD sound is lost.*

Connecting the analog outputs of a DVD-Audio or SACD player to the analog inputs of an HTPC sound card is not an ideal method of capturing sound. The digital audio information on the disc is converted to an analog signal by the player, then redigitized by the HTPC for mixing or storage, after which it must be reconverted back to analog in order to be played through speakers. It would be preferable to be able to play a DVD-Audio or SACD disc in the DVD drive of an HTPC so that the digital audio signal is only converted to analog once when it is finally sent to speakers. There is some hope that a DVD-Audio or SACD codec will be released for the PC to enable this feature, but manufacturers and content publishers are reluctant to allow this because it has the potential to allow consumers to make perfect digital copies of discs. The widespread copyright violations caused by the ability to copy or convert CD audio to other formats has made the industry very hesitant to lose control of another digital format.

In the future, a DVD-Audio and SACD codec may be available for the HTPC, or an application that plays these audio formats could be released. As with any other future audio format, it is impossible to predict whether current PC hardware will work with the new formats. Manufacturers may implement some form of digital copy protection on DVD drives that prevent consumers from making copies of discs, and software to use the discs may only work with the new drives. There is a risk, then, that the hardware available today could be obsolete in the future. The HTPC offers some protection from such obsolescence in that it is cheaper to replace a DVD drive than to replace a DVD-Audio or SACD player (and hopefully one PC DVD drive can handle both formats!), but there is no way to be perfectly compatible with all future technologies.

Midrange Sound Cards: CD Audio and Other Stereo Formats

Aside from DVD-Audio and Video, and SACD, the quality of most PC sound cards is suitable for any sound source to which the HTPC is likely to connect. CD audio is ubiquitous and almost every sound card has an internal connector to receive audio from the CD drive in a PC. Most audio formats that preceded CD audio are analog and can be converted to a digital format by the sound card. There are always issues about how much sound is lost and how noticeable the reduction of quality is, but for most people, CD-quality audio is sufficient for processing sound from home movies, CDs, cassette tapes, and other formats.

It is important to select a sound card with at least one "line-level" input—usually labeled "line in." There is a difference between the microphone input and a line-level input, and you must take care not to confuse the two. The microphone input of a sound card works with very low voltages and the relatively high voltage from a CD player or portable stereo can damage the audio hardware. The "phono" output from a record player is also unsuitable for connecting to the line-level input. The line-level input is an analog input for stereo sound that can be used to connect any sound source with a line-level output—often labeled "line out." You can also connect a headphone jack to the line-level input, though you must take care to keep the volume control from the sound source turned down low enough to prevent damage to the input.

Once a sound source is connected to the line-level input, the HTPC can digitize and record any audio signal that is played by the source. The quality of the digitization can be specified, usually in predefined increments from 8 KHz up to 44 KHz and at either 8-bit or 16-bit resolution for mono or stereo. It is important to realize that the HTPC has no way to determine the quality of sound being played into the line-level input since it is an analog input—the user must decide what quality is appropriate for digitizing. In the past, limited hard disk drive space and processor performance prompted users to digitize sound with as low quality as was appropriate for the source (e.g., speech, AM radio, or microphone-quality sound was digitized at less than 44 KHz and 16-bit stereo). Modern HTPCs have much more disk space and faster processors than in the past, and with the recent developments in digital compression, it is just as easy to digitize all audio at the highest quality of which the sound card is capable.

There are now a few hardware manufacturers with lines of midrange sound cards that have S/PDIF inputs. These are either coaxial or optical ports that can accept a digital sound stream from a source such as a MiniDisc player or a digital audio receiver. This allows for higher quality sound, and since it does not have to be converted from analog to digital for storage, it loses none of its quality when it is imported into the HTPC. Some of these sound cards with digital inputs have no analog input port, so in some cases, multiple sound cards may be needed to provide a full range of functionality.

An HTPC is a great way to integrate sound and video from multiple sources, but unfortunately most average sound cards have only one line-level input. Most common sound cards for the PC platform seem to be marketed to gamers, who are less interested in the number of audio inputs than home theater enthusiasts. This leaves few options except to switch connections each time a different audio source is desired, use an external audio switch box, or upgrade to a more costly sound card with more inputs.

Every sound card has, at the least, outputs for connecting to PC speakers. The speaker output can be used as a line-level out for connecting to an external audio receiver, though many sound cards have a line-out connector in addition to the speaker output. Audio hardware that supports any kind of 3D sound format, either a proprietary game format or the more standard Dolby Digital 5.1, has additional outputs for connecting extra speakers to provide rear channel audio. The outputs of most medium- and low-cost sound cards are ministereo jacks, which require an adapter to connect to the left and right channel of the RCA-type jacks used on audio receivers.

 **NOTE** *Fortunately, it is becoming more common to include an S/PDIF output on even low-cost sound cards. All sounds generated by the sound card or passed into it from an external source should be output through the S/PDIF cable to a digital audio receiver, which can decode mono, stereo, or surround sound formats.*

Sound Cards for Computer Games

There are some special audio hardware issues for those HTPC hobbyists who are considering building a system primarily for playing computer games on their big-screen display. For some obscure reason, when surround sound was introduced to PC games, game developers and audio hardware manufacturers decided not to use home theater audio formats. It was perhaps the licensing costs of Dolby Digital 5.1 surround sound, or the fact that it was not a clear industry standard at first that prompted the PC gaming industry to invent multiple, proprietary surround sound formats. The result of this is a confusing medley of surround sound formats and computer games that support some, one, or none of them.

Any home theater configuration should be able to support PC games with stereo, Dolby Pro Logic, or Dolby Digital 5.1 surround sound. Games may also support EAX or A3D, which are two competing surround sound formats developed specifically for the PC. EAX is published by Creative Labs and is supported by most of their current sound hardware. It is a sound-processing technology that adds atmosphere and other effects to games, music, or any audio track. A3D, published by Aureal, was a full surround sound format with dynamic positioning and effects that required a special microprocessor to do all the calculations for the complex sound interactions. Aureal is no longer around, but many of the games that support A3D are still popular. In order to get the benefit of either EAX or A3D sound, the HPTC must have a sound card that supports the format.

It seems that in order to achieve maximum compatibility, computer games should support Dolby Digital 5.1 surround sound, and this is beginning to sink in with game developers and audio hardware manufacturers (see Figure 5-2). The new generation of sound cards are capable of not only passing the digital audio 5.1 surround sound from a DVD movie to an external decoder, but also encoding a Dolby Digital 5.1 surround sound signal in real time for games or other audio effects.

Figure 5-2. Dolby Digital 5.1 is now the de facto industry standard and is used frequently in games.

Sound cards from Creative Labs seem to be the hardware of choice for PC gamers. The EAX sound standard adds a great amount of environmental realism to the virtual worlds inside the computer, and the newest Sound Blaster Live! sound cards support Dolby Digital 5.1 pass-through and real-time dynamic surround sound effects. Though the Creative Labs sound cards have some shortcomings for DVD video playback, they are continuously popular with game developers and game players.

AC '97

In order to lower the cost of common PC components such as sound cards, modems, and network cards, Intel published the Audio Codec '97 (AC '97) and Modem Codec '97 (MC '97), along with the Digital Controller (DC '97) specification. These specifications allowed hardware manufacturers to design cheap audio hardware systems that work with the system CPU to deliver the functionality of a sound card, modem, or network card. The specified audio quality is 16-bit stereo input and output at up to 48 KHz, and recent versions of the AC '97 specification include an optional S/PDIF output. In the past few years, AC '97 audio hardware has been added to several motherboards and is also available from sound cards.

The cost of AC '97 audio hardware is very attractive, and it is well suited for most typical PC uses. However, anyone considering using it in an HTPC should note that it has some limitations. First, since it is limited to a maximum 16-bit sampling rate for input and output, it is not capable of reproducing the optimum sound quality for DVD movies. Second, since the AC '97 specification is meant to lower costs of computer systems, it is not optimized for sound quality and some home theater enthusiasts are bound to find it inadequate when connected to an expensive sound system. Third, the AC '97 sound hardware relies on the system CPU for some processing of sound effects, so the performance of the HTPC is affected, though this is really only an issue for slower processors. Despite these limitations, there are undoubtedly some areas in which an AC '97–equipped HTPC is ample, and the economy of this audio hardware is almost unbeatable.

Special Considerations

Sound cards are available with a wide variety of features, for a range of prices, and with different levels of quality. Selecting the best card for an HTPC system begins with deciding what the primary purpose of the system will be: playing back DVD movies, recording and editing audio, gaming, or listening to music. The next step is to examine the short list of suitable sound cards to decide which features, including the "undocumented" ones, will affect the performance of the hardware.

Though most PC hardware components are generally reliable and economical, there are some special considerations to bear in mind when you select audio hardware.

Digital Audio Coaxial Output Line Voltage

Many home theater enthusiasts building an HTPC will want to connect the system to their existing digital audio receiver through the sound card's S/PDIF output. This is almost always the preferred method of creating a high-quality link between the HTPC and the rest of the home theater audio system. However, while researching this topic, we found a discussion on the AV Science Forum (http://www.avsforum.com) indicating that there are some sound cards with digital audio coaxial outputs that use a higher voltage than the specification requires. This high voltage can damage a digital audio receiver, so it is important to know that the voltages are compatible.

The early versions of the Creative Labs Sound Blaster Live! II had an S/PDIF coaxial output that was meant for use with a proprietary Dolby Digital 5.1 decoder and the line output at 5 volts instead of the standard 0.5 volts. Connecting this output to a digital audio receiver that is expecting 0.5 volts could cause damage to the hardware. The newer Sound Blaster Live! 5.1 cards do not output such a high voltage through the S/PDIF line, though they are apparently still above the 0.5 volt specification. Creative Labs offers add-on hardware for these sound cards that includes an optical S/PDIF output, as does Hoontec (http://www.hoontech.com/english/index.html), which is a safer method of connecting the sound card to the digital audio receiver. As far as we could tell, none of the other Creative Labs sound cards, or any other manufacturer's audio hardware, had this out-of-specification voltage problem.

NOTE *Creative Labs built in the extra voltage to support their external speaker systems. Two Sound Blaster Live! II versions output the proper spec for an external decoder, the rest do not (Live! Value II's [4830 and 4832]). You can find more information on the AV Science Forum Web site (http://www.avsforum.com).*

When 24/96 Is Not Equal to 24/96

The digital audio tracks on a DVD are stored at a sampling rate of up to 96 kHz and 24-bit resolution, which is commonly referred to as 24/96. Ideally, a sound card that can pass the 24/96 digital audio through to an external receiver, or process the 24/96 audio stream and output it to the appropriate speakers, is desirable. It is important to check the specifications of the sound cards you are considering for your HTPC to make sure that they can handle this data without down-sampling before outputting to speakers or an external decoder.

During our research we discovered that the Creative Labs Sound Blaster Audigy and Extigy series of audio hardware down-samples the 24/96 digital audio stream to 16-bit at 48 KHz for internal processing, including pass-through output. Though it is up-sampled for the digital audio outputs, it still loses some quality by being converted down and then back up. This is a little difficult to discover from any of the Creative Labs literature, but independent testing at the Tom's Hardware Guide Web site (http://www.tomshardware.com) reveals the limitation of the Creative Labs hardware. Although the Audigy and Extigy are completely compatible with any 24/96 input and output equipment, the sound quality is compromised by the internal conversion and processing. Of course, to get a better sound card for the PC, you have to pay a lot more money than you do for the economically priced Creative Labs hardware.

External Audio Hardware

As the demand for high-quality audio for the PC platform increases, some manufacturers have begun to offer sound cards that aren't really sound cards—not in the traditional sense of a PC adapter card, anyway. Critics of the PC often claim that the inside of a computer case is full of stray electrical signals and magnetic fields caused by all the unshielded wiring, power supplies, fans, and electronic components. This is the worst possible environment for audio hardware, which ideally should be isolated from any external interference to prevent distortion, static, pops, hisses, and other sound anomalies. The solution now available on the market is an external sound processor (see Figure 5-3).

Figure 5-3. External audio hardware is basically a sound card in a fancy case.

The external processor is essentially the same hardware as a sound card meant to be installed internally to the PC, but with its own casing and a long wire connecting it to the PC. The external device is removed from the electrically noisy environment of the PC case, and all of the inputs and outputs are connected to the external hardware to prevent interference to them, too. The external audio hardware is commonly connected to a USB port, though some actually work on a COM or parallel port. You can expect to see IEEE 1394 versions available if this trend catches on.

Since the audio hardware does not live inside the PC, it cannot use the PC's CPU to assist with any processing. This means that the external hardware is both more capable and more expensive. The Creative Labs Sound Blaster Extigy has a built-in Dolby Digital 5.1 surround sound decoder for very clean audio from DVD movies. The external audio hardware is also perfectly suited for use with multiple HTPCs, since it can be easily moved from one unit to the next, or even with laptop computers. If the HTPC is often moved in and out of the home theater, an external sound device is much easier to connect than all those inputs, outputs, and speakers.

Integrated Sound Hardware

Several motherboard manufacturers offer PC motherboards with audio hardware built into the system board. There seem to be only two types of sound available in an integrated board: Creative Labs Sound Blaster or some version of AC '97 hardware. Currently, the motherboards with the Creative Labs Sound Blaster all feature variations of common Sound Blaster models such as the Sound Blaster Live! or the older Sound Blaster Pro. There seem to be an endless variety of Sound Blaster chipsets, so that the Sound Blaster versions available on motherboards are not the same as the ones available as sound cards, but the quality and features are mostly the same. Generally, this is a less expensive alternative to buying a separate sound card, so for HTPCs that will use a Sound Blaster sound card, finding an integrated motherboard with a Sound Blaster chip should lower the cost of the system.

Before you buy a motherboard with integrated audio, you should do some research. It is sometimes difficult to find the correct sound drivers for the obscure audio hardware that motherboard manufacturers dig up. Integrating sound hardware on a motherboard is almost always a result of trying to lower costs, and there seem to be a lot of motherboards with an audio chip that is used nowhere else in the world. Selecting an AC '97–compliant sound system integrated on a motherboard is a safe way to avoid driver problems. Another issue is with a specific motherboard chipset: The VIA KT133 chipset on some Gigabyte motherboards with onboard audio have severe sound distortion issues under certain operating systems. Windows 95/98/ME work fine with this hardware, but Windows 2000 and XP do not. (There is a more detailed discussion of PC operating systems for HTPCs in Chapter 8.) Though this is an older example of a Gigabyte motherboard, some people have complained about less severe occurrences of this problem on new motherboards from other manufacturers.

Remote Controls

One great feature that some sound card manufacturers are starting to add to their high-end audio hardware is an infrared (IR) receiver for a remote control (see Figure 5-4). This makes it very convenient to use the HTPC from the couch without having to drag a keyboard and mouse cord across the floor. Separate IR receivers are available for the PC, but adding one to the audio hardware saves some cost and adds a lot of value to an HTPC. The Creative Labs Sound Blaster Audigy and Extigy include an IR remote control with certain versions of these sound cards, making them quite attractive to HTPC enthusiasts.

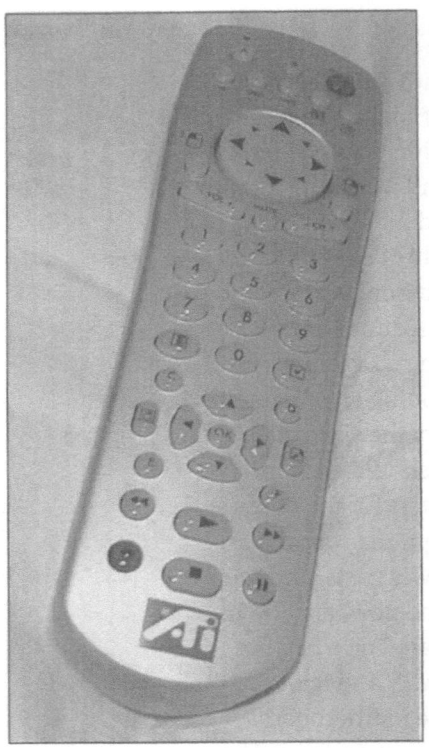

Figure 5-4. What's a home theater system without a remote control?

You can program a remote control IR receiver with PC software to do much more than control the sound card functions. You can use the remote to switch video modes, play DVD movies, and tune the channels on the television tuner card in addition to raising and lowering the volume or jumping through a list of MP3 song titles. For a more detailed discussion of controlling the HTPC remotely, please refer to Chapter 7.

MIDI Connections and Synthesized Music

Most sound cards include a Musical Instrument Digital Interface (MIDI) connector for attaching MIDI devices such as electronic instruments and MIDI sequencers. The Creative Labs series of sound cards also uses the MIDI connector as a game control connector, so an adapter is required to use it with MIDI devices. An HTPC with a high-end sound card is an excellent mixing and recording device, and the addition of the MIDI port makes it a great machine for casual or serious musicians.

In the past few years, music on the PC has become mostly a digitized format. That is, music is stored, compressed, mixed, or played back as a digital representation of the analog waveform that is the sound. In previous years, however, it was much more common for music on the PC to be synthesized. Synthesized music is created by playing digitized representations of instruments at the pitch and volume denoted by a musical score. Instead of playing back a digitized copy of the original, the computer played the music like a musician, using the instrument sounds stored in its memory. The stored instrument sounds were based on the MIDI specification of which instruments were required. Though this method of creating music on the computer is now relatively rare, there are still some uses for it.

The quality of synthesized music and sound created by a PC depends on the quality of the MIDI instruments in the audio hardware. Cheaper sound cards use an FM synthesizer to approximate the sound of a piano, guitar, flute, and so forth. The FM synthesizer generates a sound wave that is close to the wave produced by the actual instrument, but the FM synthesizer generates a consistent and steady sound without the variation and character of a real instrument. Better quality music is produced by storing actual digitized samples of the original instruments and playing them back at the correct pitch. A high-quality MIDI score may be a very convincing reproduction of an orchestra, a big band, a trio, or any instrument.

How important is good MIDI instrumentation? MIDI sound and music is common in PC computer games, so game players who like to listen to the in-game music that keeps pace with the action and story will benefit from the more realistic sounds of audio hardware with a good MIDI instrumentation. Also, anyone who likes to compose music may enjoy better quality instruments instead of FM-synthesized notes.

TIP *The number of simultaneous notes that a sound card can synthesize determines the quality of the musical score, especially for orchestral pieces with multiple instruments. Creative Labs makes it pretty easy to figure out how many notes can be produced at once with Sound Blaster 16, Sound Blaster AWE 32, and Sound Blaster 128.*

Connecting Audio from the HTPC to the Home Theater

Connecting the HTPC to the rest of the home theater is pretty simple. The most important issue is to determine whether the HTPC will output sound through an S/PDIF digital audio port to a digital audio receiver, or if analog stereo or surround sound connections will be used. This decision depends on the available audio components in the home theater and the audio hardware installed in the HTPC. The purpose of this chapter has been to make this decision easy by selecting a sound card that is most suitable for the home theater into which is it going.

Connecting the HTPC to a digital audio receiver via a digital audio cable is the best way to get high-quality sound for all HTPC features. The digital audio cable may be a 75 ohm coaxial cable or an optical fiber-optic cable. Coaxial cables have RCA-type connectors at either end and simply push onto the connector on the back of the digital audio receiver. Most sound cards do not have an RCA-type connector for the coaxial digital audio cable, so an adapter is required. The Creative Labs sound cards simply require a mono miniplug (1/8 inch, 3.5 mm) to RCA-type converter, which connects to the other end of the coaxial cable. It is a good idea to use a shielded cable to prevent interference, even though the cable carries a digital signal. Any audible pops, scratching noises, or dropped sound could be attributable to electrical interference if a shielded cable is not used.

If the sound card in the HTPC features an optical digital audio connector, and the digital audio receiver also has this port, then it is preferable to use an optical link cable (sometimes called a Toslink cable). The sound quality is exactly the same between the coaxial cable and the optical cable, since the same digital information is being sent, but the optical cable is not prone to electrical interference and, as mentioned earlier in this chapter, it will not damage the audio equipment if the voltage output by the audio card is out of specification.

Analog connections are pretty simple for anyone who has set up an audio receiver, CD player, or VHS deck. Most PC sound cards have outputs in the form of ministereo plugs (1/8 inch, 3.5 mm) for connecting to PC speakers or headphones. In order to connect these analog outputs to an audio receiver, a cable that converts the ministereo to the left and right RCA-type plugs is needed. The left and right plugs are usually color-coded red and white, or red and black. To output sound from the HTPC to an audio receiver, you should connect the line out from the sound card to the inputs on the receiver. It is also possible to use the headphone output, if no line out is present, but you should take care to turn down any volume control before making the connection.

CAUTION *It is possible to connect the line out to an audio receiver and to connect the line in from the same receiver, but you should take care to prevent feedback from causing distorted sound or even damage to the audio hardware. When sound is being played out to the receiver, the line-in control should be muted. When sound is being recorded from the receiver, the line-out should be muted.*

If your HTPC is going to be connected to a PC speaker set, either a pair of stereo speakers or a full surround sound set, then the connections will depend on the speaker set and the audio hardware. Some speaker sets have a built-in digital audio decoder, so that only a single digital audio connection is required from the S/PDIF port on the sound card to the S/PDIF input on the decoder. Some speaker sets have an analog input for each speaker in the surround sound set, so that a separate wire must be run to each speaker. Often the speaker inputs are all on one piece, such as the center channel speaker or the subwoofer, so that all the wires run from the sound card to just one speaker component.

NOTE *When you connect a sound card to a surround sound speaker set, you'll often use special attachments to split one output from the back of the sound card to the various inputs on the speakers. These special cables and attachments are included with the sound card or with the speaker set, but it may appear at first as if there aren't enough outputs on the sound card to match the number of speakers.*

The HTPC Project Hardware

Our two HTPC project machines are going to feature the capability to output Dolby Digital 5.1 and DTS 5.1 surround sound for DVD movies to an external digital audio receiver. This feature is becoming common on even low-priced audio hardware such as the AC '97–compatible sound systems. We have found very nice sound cards for both our economical HTPC system and our high-end system, and even the hardware for our high-end system is reasonably priced. As the audio potential of the HTPC is developed and explored, it becomes more and more attractive to build one.

HTPC System 1

Although both of our HTPC project machines will feature digital audio output, we decided that our first system would have a true 24/96 sound card capable of processing audio without down-converting and up-converting. We wanted a sound card with both analog and digital outputs, and with RCA-type connectors for use with our existing home theater audio equipment. Sound cards with the ministereo plugs require a special adapter cable to convert the ministereo jack to the left and right audio inputs and outputs of other audio devices. We also wanted audio hardware with optical and coaxial digital audio outputs in order to compare the two cables to find out if there is any difference in audio quality.

The M-Audio Delta series of sound cards for the PC are highly regarded by the HTPC community for their excellent sound quality and compatibility with PC software. We approached Midiman, the makers of the M-Audio hardware, and asked them for suggestions about sound cards for an HTPC system. They generously provided us with an M-Audio Delta Dio 2496 sound card (see Figure 5-5). This component features true 24/96 digital processing for all audio signals, optical digital audio input and output, coaxial digital audio input and output, and RCA-type jacks for analog stereo input and output.

Figure 5-5. The Midiman M-Audio Delta Dio 2496 sound card

Some further research into the M-Audio line of sound cards showed us that another Midiman sound card, the M-Audio Audiophile 2496, is also a very popular sound card in the HTPC community. This card has the same true 24/96 digital audio processing capabilities of the Delta Dio 2496, but it lacks the optical digital audio connections. The Audiophile 2496 is slightly cheaper than the Delta Dio 2496, so if coaxial digital audio outputs are sufficient (and there should be no difference in audio quality between coaxial and optical connections, if the coaxial cable is properly shielded and free of interference), then the Audiophile is a great way to save some of the expense of audio hardware.

You can find more information about the software configuration and performance of this sound card in Chapter 12.

HTPC System 2

The audio hardware we have selected for our second HTPC system is the Creative Labs Sound Blaster Live! sound card (see Figure 5-6). This sound card is very economical and very popular with computer game players. It is also suitable for use in an HTPC because of its coaxial digital audio output, and it even has the capability to do Dolby Digital 5.1 decoding and analog output to a set of surround sound computer speakers.

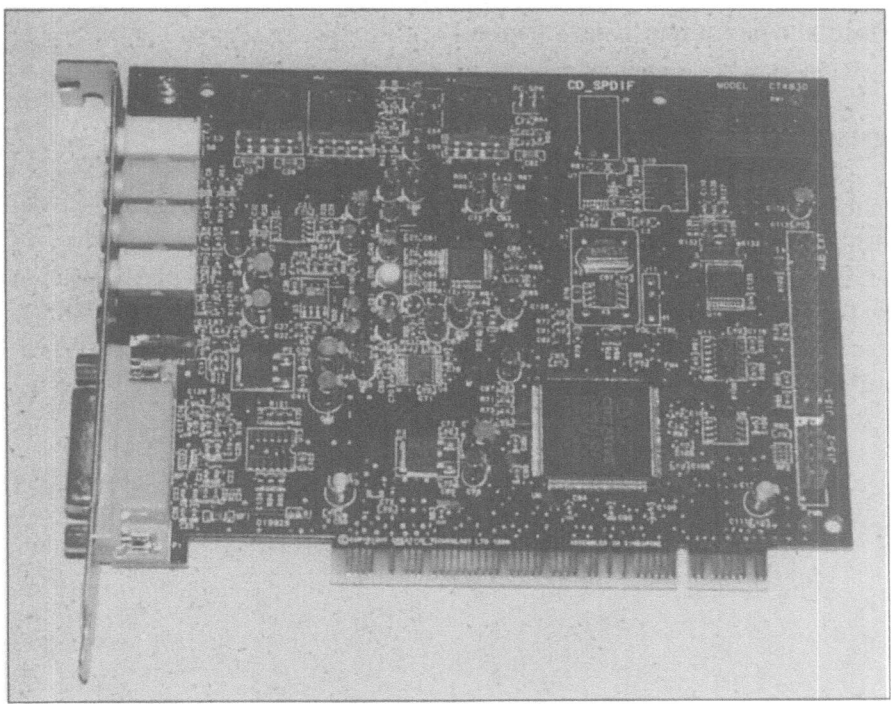

Figure 5-6. The Creative Labs Sound Blaster Live! sound card

This sound card does not have the capability to process 24/96 digital audio, as it is limited to 16-bit resolution at 48 KHz sampling rate. This card does have some excellent sound effects for PC games and music, though. The slight loss of sound quality for DVD movie playback could be counterbalanced by the added value for music and gaming, so we will occasionally swap the sound cards between our two project HTPC systems for comparative testing.

Our HTPC systems have two of the most important components selected so far, but they are not yet ready for use. We need to select a few more pieces, put them all together, and then configure all the software before we can kick back and watch a few DVD movies or enjoy our CD collection. For the results of our sound card tests and performance, see Chapter 12.

Summary

The choice of which sound card is best for your HTPC depends largely on what applications you'll be taxing your HTPC with. Your decision will be different depending on whether you're more concerned with gaming, MP3 playback, or Dolby Digital home theater surround sound. In the next chapter, you'll examine video capture devices, from capturing home movies to setting up your very own digital video recorder (DVR) on your HTPC.

CHAPTER 6
Video Capture Devices

AN HTPC IS, of course, an excellent device for viewing DVDs, maximizing picture quality, and ensuring spectacular sound. These elements are the backbone for HTPC use, but there are other equally impressive uses for the machine that until recently weren't an option. You can use HTPCs as digital video recorders (DVRs) to capture video signals from cable, analog, or satellite. In short, you can use the HTPC much like a super-VCR that can capture hundreds of hours of programming without the bother of swapping tapes.

You can also use the HTPC to capture homemade videos (or even commercial video work). Once you've converted the video to digital information on the HTPC, you can manipulate and professionally edit it to look as good as any Hollywood flick. Ultimately, the HTPC can be a one-stop appliance that plays DVDs, VCDs, CDs, and MP3s; routes satellite and cable signals; archives and displays family photos; and acts as an uber-VCR that can capture hundreds of hours of high-quality video. In short, if you're interested in recording shows or importing home videos for editing on your computer, a video capture device is required, whether it be a FireWire card for capturing digital video from camcorders or a USB video capture device for converting analog video to digital. We explain just what these devices do and how to manipulate them for your needs.

This chapter will look at the various ways to capture, manipulate, edit, and reuse video sources that flow into your HTPC.

Digital Video Recorders

In recent years there has been an explosion of digital video recorders (DVRs) available to the North American public. These include systems such as TiVo, ReplayTV, UltimateTV, and in Canada Bell Expressvu's personal video recorder (PVR). DVRs are versatile video recording devices that use the raw power of today's computers to capture video and save it in a digital format. As you might expect, you can manipulate, search, and save video that's stored digitally much easier than you can with video that's stored on tape.

 **NOTE** *Digital information has the added bonus of not degrading over time the way in which analog videotapes will. For audio/video aficionados, the high quality and fidelity of both the visual and aural aspects of their favorite programming is of paramount importance. Over time, videotapes will degrade noticeably, even if they haven't been used! This degradation is a primary reason for switching to DVRs, so that favorite television shows or home movies can be saved, manipulated, and moved easily with no adverse effect on the quality of the picture or sound.*

Although you have several commercial DVR options, you must also consider the HTPC as a receptacle for digital video as well as a high-performance playback device. In fact, with the recent proliferation of DVD recording devices available for PCs (and a few stand-alone units that act like VCRs), recorded television shows and home videos can be permanently recorded and stored on DVD-R media, and used and reused ad nauseam with no degradation in quality.

What Makes a DVR a DVR?

A DVR is quite simply a device that records video and audio information digitally rather than by the old-fashioned means of recording it on magnetic tape as analog information. Technically, a DVR could be any device that records video signals digitally (digital camcorders are an example of this), but for the purposes of this book we count DVRs only as devices that are solely dedicated to recording video digitally for playback at a later date.

All of the three current commercial DVRs available (TiVo, UltimateTV, and ReplayTV) have the same basic architecture. These machines are essentially glorified computers: Each has a CPU, memory (RAM), one or more hard drives, and an MPEG-2 encoder and decoder. As the video information comes into the DVR (from television, for example), the MPEG-2 encoder compresses the signal and information so that it can be stored digitally (as 1s and 0s) on the hard drive that is contained within the unit. The bigger the DVR's hard drive, the more programming can be stored on the DVR—in fact, there is no logical limit to how much information can be stored in this manner. If the DVR is attached to a redundant array of independent disks (multiple hard disk drives), literally hundreds (if not thousands) of hours can be recorded.

NOTE *Most commercial DVRs come with 30 hours of available recording time, but if you swap a larger hard drive into these units, you can increase that time greatly. On a 30-hour TiVo, putting in one 80GB hard drive to replace the existing hard drive can increase the available recording time from 30 hours to nearly 70. We don't, however, recommend modifying a commercial DVR. After all, doing so voids the warranty and you risk damaging both yourself and the equipment.*

In summary, a DVR is a computer masquerading as a VCR. The DVR runs on some sort of operating system (OS) such as Linux (TiVo runs on a modified Linux OS), but it works behind the scenes so that all the consumer sees is an efficient menu system and a product that's chock-full of previously unheard-of features.

DVR Features/Benefits

As we mentioned previously, DVRs have features that clearly set them apart from tape-based video recorders such as VHS and Betamax. DVRs are most definitely the recording medium of the future, so let's have a look at just what they offer.

Recording Television Programs

Like VCRs, DVRs can record television programs from any sort of input, including antenna, cable, and satellite. Commercial DVRs, however, are tied to satellite or digital cable services and must be used in conjunction with them in order for the features (such as a dynamic onscreen guide) to work. Recording a television show on a DVR is considerably easier than the VCR alternative.

Recording Made Easy

Because the programming guide appears onscreen and shows many hours of programming over numerous channels at a glance, it's easy to pick out programming to record simply by looking at the guide (see Figure 6-1). When you see a program you want to record, you need only move the cursor over the listing and press a single button. The program will then be added to the DVR's "to-do" list and will be recorded.

Figure 6-1. A TiVo control screen in action

With a VCR, you must manually enter a program and include the date, the time, and the channel that the program will appear on. You also have to make sure that you have a tape with enough space free in the VCR before you set it up to record the program at a later time. With the DVR, it's a one-button process in most cases.

Recording While Watching Something Else

While this concept isn't new, the DVR takes it to a new level. Since a DVR stores recorded programs digitally, those programs are very accessible and can be watched at the same time that another program is being recorded. In fact, if the DVR has a dual LNB input (two satellite inputs), you can actually record two shows at once (off of different channels) while you watch a *third* show that had been previously recorded!

With the commercial DVRs (and even with most HTPC DVR software), this recording/playback is seamless and works through a series of menus. The end user never knows about how much data is flowing around inside the machine. The ability to watch a previously recorded show while a completely different show is being recorded simultaneously shows the raw power and awesome versatility of the DVR in the home entertainment environment.

Season's Pass

All of the commercial DVRs are capable of capturing all episodes of any show. On the TiVo this is called a "Season's Pass," and it enables TiVo users to get all of the episodes of any show automatically. For example, if you are a big fan of *The Simpsons*, you could tell the DVR to capture each and every *first-run* episode of *The Simpsons* and save them forever. Or, you could tell the DVR to capture *all* episodes of *The Simpsons* off of any channel, but not to duplicate them.

There are many other variables you can alter when you program the DVR to record an entire season of a show. For example, you can tell it to capture only five episodes at once and to only save them as long as there is enough space on the DVR's hard drive. Or, you can tell it to save the shows until you decide to delete them. Needless to say, those who have several shows they simply must watch can use the DVR to capture the entire season of each show so that they can watch their favorite shows at their leisure.

TIP *Television shows that have been recorded to a DVR are not confined to the DVR forever. In fact, they can be dumped out to either DVD-R or VHS videotape so that they can be viewed on someone else's entertainment system. Of course, dumping shows onto DVD-R or VHS is also a practical way to free up space on the DVR.*

Pausing Live Television

One of the much-ballyhooed features of TiVo, ReplayTV, and UltimateTV is the ability to pause live television. Although it appears that live television can be paused, it's more of a parlor trick than *really* pausing live television. This works because the DVRs keep a running buffer of the channel that's currently selected. The size of this buffer depends on the amount of recording time available in the unit, but usually it's between 15 minutes and 1 hour. When the user presses the Pause button, the live programming is paused, but since the signal is still coming into the DVR, the show is actually being recorded as time passes. When the user resumes playback, the playback is slightly behind the actual broadcast.

NOTE *The SONICblue ReplayTV has a version that can record a whopping 320 hours of programming. This unit can pause live television and buffer a single channel for an incredible 40 hours. Therefore, with this system you could pause a show in the morning just before going to work and come back to it the next morning and continue watching it without a hitch.*

The applications for pausing live television are many. In today's busy world, with phones and doorbells ringing seemingly every few minutes, having the ability to pause a television program is very useful. Since the buffer is always on, DVRs also allow users to quickly rewind to view a scene that happened a few seconds or minutes ago, and they allow users to view these scenes in slow motion or frame by frame—an excellent application for sports lovers. Bart has often found that he'll be watching television and something of interest to his wife will appear. He can call her into the television room and quickly zip back and show her the scene rather than having to describe it to her after the fact.

Active Program Guide

Because most DVRs work with satellite systems such as DIRECTV, the programming guide they use appears onscreen and is dynamically updated so that the information is completely up-to-the-minute accurate. As we mentioned in the "Recording Made Easy" section, picking programs to record using the active program guide is very simple, but an active program guide also allows you to browse through the full range of channels to see both what is currently playing and what is upcoming on each of the channels. Figure 6-2 shows an example of an active program guide from ATI.

NOTE *Many cable channels now have a similar guide structure, although they are not always as flexible or powerful as those with the digital satellite systems. However, that is largely a matter of personal opinion.*

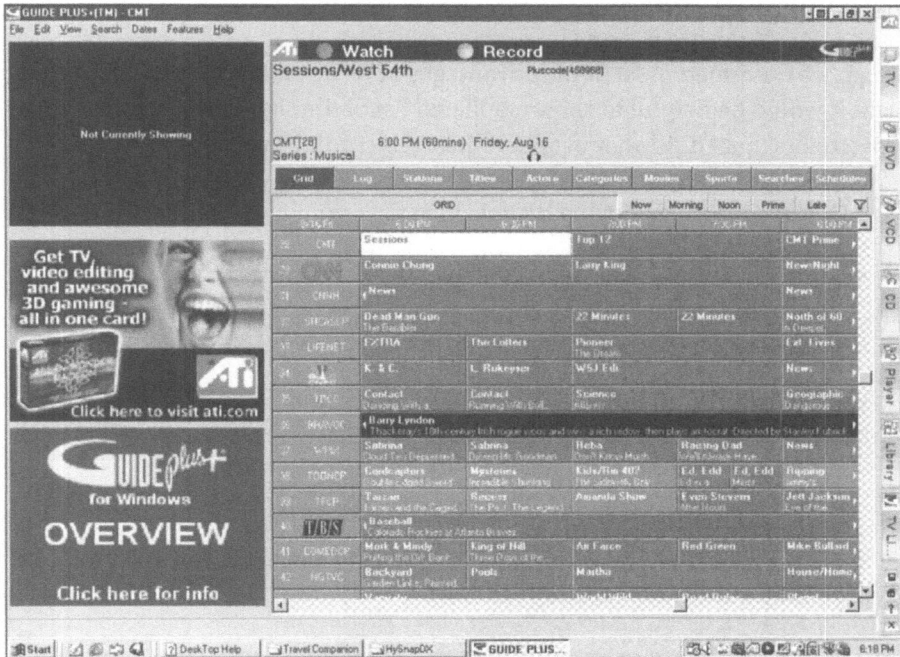

Figure 6-2. ATI's GUIDE Plus+

An active program guide is also valuable when you use the DVR to record future broadcasts. Because the program guide keeps at least 2 full weeks of complete listings on hand at all times, it's easy to tell the DVR to record a football game that won't happen until 10 days from now. It should also be noted that there are now some open source standards being implemented in the way the guide is transmitted using XML by the broadcaster, rather than the service that you have subscribed to. The implications of this include more compatibility between systems and nonproprietary technology use.

Finding Programs by Keyword and Preference

Although using the onscreen program guide can be an efficient way of finding programs on a DVR, the fact is that with today's satellite dishes there are literally hundreds of available channels and thousands of programs being run in any given week. For this reason, all DVRs have the option of searching for programming by keyword. Likewise, some DVRs will keep track of what you watch and will then make suggestions as to what you might enjoy watching.

Advantages of DVRs

Although we described most of the advantages of DVRs earlier in this chapter, we thought it would be helpful to show a bulleted list of the significant feature improvements that DVRs offer over tape-based recording systems.

- A DVR records high-quality digital video.

- A DVR's archived video does not break down over time.

- You can use the online programming guides to record shows.

- You can capture all shows in a single season with "Season's Pass"–like features.

- You can "pause" live television with a DVR.

- Since the recorded programming is digital, you can move through the programs quickly and nonsequentially.

- If you're watching a program and stop it 27 minutes into it, the show will restart at the same point 27 minutes into the show no matter *when* you resume watching it.

- You can record one show while you watch another recorded show. If you have dual LNB systems, you can watch a recorded show while you record *two* shows at once!

- You can upgrade most DVRs by simply inserting a larger hard drive if you have a little technical expertise.

The HTPC DVR

Now that you know a little about just what a DVR is capable of, you need to look at the possibility of adding DVR capabilities to your HTPC. Although it's not necessarily as slick as the commercially available DVRs, an HTPC can give you some distinct advantages over its glossy counterparts. Some of the advantages of the HTPC DVR are as follows:

- You can upgrade software in HTPCs as updates become available.

- You can upgrade an HTPC's hardware as needed. For example, if you feel you need another 30 hours of recording capability, simply pop in another hard drive.

- The HTPC DVR eliminates the need for multiple boxes. Because the HTPC is a sound system, a DVD player, a photo reservoir, a DVR, and a home video editing unit, it eliminates the need for a large component rack in the entertainment room.

- Because most of the required hardware for an HTPC DVR is the actual PC, its cost is reduced significantly.

- You don't pay monthly fees for the DVR service in an HTPC.

- You can record HDTV signals when available. The majority of current commercial DVRs don't have HDTV decoders in them.

Required Equipment for an HTPC DVR

Fortunately, most of the equipment you need to make an HTPC a DVR is contained within the PC itself. Still, there are a few extras you must have in place if your HTPC is to function properly as a home-brewed DVR that will offer many years of reliable service.

Powerful PC

As much as we wish that a lower-end PC would be sufficient to make DVR features work well on a PC, the cold, hard truth is that a Pentium III 450 is about the minimum machine necessary to handle the rather heavy task of compressing incoming video. With the ATI All-in-Wonder Radeon 7500 card in a Pentium III 450 running Windows 98 SE, we experienced some difficulties when switching between the various modes—for example, from DVD to television or from television to the player (which plays recorded files). While the Pentium III 450 (which had 256MB of RAM) was acceptable with the 7500, we found that upping the processing power and adding more RAM significantly smoothed out the edges.

Our recommended machine is a 1 GHz Pentium 4 with at least 512MB of RAM. Just a couple of years ago this would have seemed like a very tall order, but prices have fallen so dramatically that finding an inexpensive PC with these attributes is quite easy indeed. Suffice it to say that you should use the fastest PC that you can afford—you won't regret it. When dealing with video capture, editing, and DVR functions, it's always better to have more speed and especially more RAM. If you can afford it, a higher-end Pentium 4 or Athlon will certainly serve you well for years to come.

NOTE *Even if you can't afford a higher-end PC right now, the HTPC is completely upgradeable for when you can afford to make your equipment a little zippier.*

Hard Disk

The amount of recorded video content available to you is mostly dependent on how much hard disk space is at your disposal on the HTPC. Obviously, the larger the hard drive, the more content you'll be able to archive, and just how much you want to save is entirely up to you. Since 80GB and larger drives are under $150.00 (at the time this book was written), it's relatively inexpensive to load up with more than 100GB of hard drive space available purely for digital video recording.

Just how much recording time each gigabyte of storage space will give you depends on a number of things, including the video quality settings and the software you use for compressing the video. The ATI compression software gives roughly 1 hour of recording time for every 3GB of hard drive space with the quality level at 75 percent. Therefore, an 80GB hard drive that's completely dedicated to video storage will yield around 30 hours of content. Of course, if you turn down the quality, you can double these numbers!

Bundled Software

Most television tuner packages and television video cards come with bundled DVR software. How well this software works depends on a number of factors, but as a rule it all requires a faster-than-average PC to really perform exceptionally well. All of these bundled software packages are certainly more than adequate, and we recommend any of them, although we prefer the ATI All-In-Wonder package overall.

TIP *Some of the software packages, such as ATI's, are capable of deinterlacing video, which makes software such as DScaler unnecessary. In fact, DScaler won't work with ATI's chipset, but this is not an issue because of the excellent job the All-In-Wonder does of deinterlacing the television signal. That said, considering that DScaler is freeware, it is an outstanding piece of software that does an excellent job if you need it. After all, the price is right!*

Matrox Marvel G450 eTV

Matrox has a long history of production-solid television-related products. While their 3D cards don't have the same punch as NVIDIA's, if gaming isn't a huge concern then the Matrox card is a winner. The G450 eTV includes a full video-editing suite, DVR software, component and composite outputs, and even picture-in-picture capabilities. To see the specs for the G450 eTV, go to `http://www.matrox.com`.

ATI All-In-Wonder Radeon 7500/8500

As we mentioned previously, the built-in software suite for these cards is excellent. The only caveat is that the DVR software requires a high-end machine to run seamlessly, but still, we are running two of three HTPCs with Radeon 7500s. The All-In-Wonder (see Figure 6-3) also includes MPEG-2 video editing and capture, DVR, desktop television, GUIDE Plus+ programming, complete wireless remote control system, and output to television. To learn more about ATI products, visit the ATI Web site (`http://www.ati.com`).

Figure 6-3. The Radeon All-In-Wonder 7500

NVIDIA Personal Cinema

Personal Cinema is a PCI card that complements an existing NVIDIA video card. This product also includes a television tuner, time-shifting capabilities, digital video recording, DVD playback, remote control, and the Titan TV electronic programming guide. Visit the NVIDIA Web site (`http://www.nvidia.com`) to learn more about Personal Cinema.

Stand-alone DVR/PVR Hardware/Software

While there are distinct advantages to an all-in-one approach to building an HDTV HTPC, and the NVIDIA, ATI, and Matrox options are tempting, there are also other ways to turn your HTPC into a DVR or PVR (as some call them). In this section, we look at several of these products, some of which include the hardware necessary to import television signals, whereas others are only software packages that require the user to already have the input hardware in place.

Hauppauge

Hauppauge offers a great many products that will complement any HTPC, including television tuners, HDTV tuners, digital video editing boards, and DVR boards and software. For DVR we recommend their WinTV-PVR 350 board. This product sells for around $200.00 and includes hardware MPEG-2 encoding *and* decoding, which greatly reduces the stress placed on your HTPC system during recording or playback. To see the extensive line of HTPC-related products at Hauppauge, go to http://www.hauppauge.com.

WinDVR 2

InterVideo's WinDVR 2 (see Figure 6-4) is a very inexpensive software solution that does a commendable job of working as a DVR with your existing television tuner card. WinDVR 2 includes all of the key DVR features, such as the capability to pause live television, perform instant replays, and skip commercials. It also includes a task manager, a sleep timer, and a "video desktop" that enables your background to be television. WinDVR 2 also has a groovy feature called Channel Surfing, where the screen becomes a grid of 16 or more tiny televisions with each one representing a still shot of what's on that channel. InterVideo offers a free trial of WinDVR 2 at http://www.intervideo.com.

Figure 6-4. WinDVR 2 in action

 **NOTE** *As with the other software-based MPEG-2 encoder/decoders, WinDVR 2 is very much dependent on the speed of the computer it's being run on, so again we recommend the use of a high-end PC with plenty of RAM if you want to capture DVD-quality video content. We discovered that a Pentium III 450 with 256MB of RAM could not capture smooth video on the highest setting with WinDVR 2. Although it was able to capture the content, frames were dropped, making for a jerky, unacceptable result. The lower quality settings, however, were able to capture without a drop in frame rate.*

nanoDVR

Nanocosmos offers a higher priced DVR software product that enables high-quality MPEG-2 video capture off of a television signal (or other inputted video signal). nanoDVR also offers support for machines with multiprocessors—a relatively rare hardware configuration. However, for those who are serious about having a powerful DVR, this software can take advantage of the extra horsepower a multiprocessor computer can offer. This software also offers Video CD creation and future versions are planned to have DVD exporting enabled. You can check out this product at http://www.nanocosmos.de.

SnapStream Personal Video Station

SnapStream Personal Video Station is another software DVR alternative for your HTPC. Personal Video Station is a unique piece of software because it can turn your PC into a media server and send television anywhere on your network via Ethernet or a wireless 802.11b network. Best of all, this media server can serve multiple viewers at the same time, so if you're lucky enough to have a 100 Mbps network wired into your home, you can have your HTPC serve programming to multiple locations. As with the other software options, SnapStream's product also includes an integrated program guide for easy recording and allows for content to be burned onto Video CD. For more information about SnapStream Personal Video Station, visit http://www.snapstream.com.

DScaler

Although DScaler isn't true DVR software, because it has some rudimentary PVR functionality and is such a good piece of software—and free—we thought it worth mentioning here. DScaler offers video source deinterlacing, inverse telecine detection, automatic aspect ratio control, and judder elimination. For more information on DScaler or to download it, go to http://deinterlace.sourceforge.net.

Video Editing

When you construct an HTPC, you must ensure that video input is an available feature, because having a video card that enables home movies to be imported into the HTPC opens up an entire world of home movie editing, not to mention exciting digital manipulation of video content. This section of the book discusses importing video content onto the HTPC and some of the options available to you once you've transferred the content. Technology has come far enough that you can make impressive movies complete with professional transitions, alternate sound tracks, and special effects. Once you've completed these files, you can convert them into Web-based movies, make them into Video CDs, copy them back to digital camcorder tape or VHS recorders, and even burn them onto DVD format.

CAUTION *While there are some unscrupulous people who pirate copyrighted material and burn it onto DVD or Video CD to avoid the cost of purchasing the programming, we do not engage in or support this practice. Therefore, this book won't discuss how to manipulate or capture copyrighted material for use on an HTPC.*

Importing Video into the HTPC

There are two basic divisions when it comes to home video editing: digital video and analog video. Since many of you are likely to have reams of analog videotape, we discuss the conversion of analog video to digital as well as the newer digital technologies.

Importing Digital Video

Apple Computer led the way in digital video editing when they started equipping all of their Macintosh computers with an IEEE 1394 FireWire port, which allowed digital camcorders to be connected to the computers with ease. They also included a piece of software called iMovie that allowed quick and easy editing of home-made videos. That was then, and now some years later the PC side of the world has caught up with the digital video trend, and currently many new PCs come with FireWire ports and include video editing software. There are so many, in fact, that we can't discuss them all here, but suffice it to say that most of them are most certainly acceptable for home use. In order to import digital movies to your HTPC, you'll need a few pieces of hardware to ensure an easy transfer of information.

NOTE *Importing digital video (and audio) from a digital camcorder to an HTPC through an IEEE 1394 cable is very simple indeed. Just start the software and connect one end of the cable to the PC and the other end to the camcorder. In general, the software takes care of everything else.*

Digital Camcorder

A few years ago a digital camcorder was a rare commodity, relegated to very high-end equipment from makers such as Sony, Panasonic, and JVC. As with everything in the digital age, times have changed rapidly and now the majority of camcorders sold are of the digital variety. Digital camcorders are superior to their analog counterparts for a number of reasons, including

- Digital camcorders have a much clearer, higher resolution picture.

- Digital camcorders offer many special effects that can be added both during and after recording.

- Digital information doesn't degrade like analog tapes do.

- As a rule, digital camcorders can be made smaller than their analog counterparts. Some even employ minidisk technology instead of tape.

NOTE *To say that digital data doesn't degrade isn't entirely true. The magnetic tape that digital information is stored on does degrade, but there are error correction algorithms that can virtually "fix" many errors that come about due to magnetic tape decay, thus making the digital picture flawless. Analog tape, on the other hand, degrades both with use and over time (just sitting on a shelf). For proof of this, simply take a VHS tape that has something on it that was recorded 5 or more years ago. The quality loss since it was first recorded will likely surprise you.*

If you have purchased a camcorder in the last 3 or 4 years, there's a pretty good chance that it's digital, thus making your video transfer task (from the camcorder to the PC) very easy indeed.

IEEE 1394 FireWire Port

The majority of new camcorders being sold today are of the digital variety. Digital camcorders have become more popular because of the high quality of the images they record and the fantastic flexibility that digital video offers those wanting to edit the video later. Most digital camcorders come with an IEEE 1394 FireWire port (see Figure 6-5), which enables direct and convenient connection to a PC that also has a FireWire port. This ease of connection makes downloading digital video to a PC for editing incredibly simple, and therefore it is our recommendation to use a digital camcorder and a PC with an IEEE 1394 port if at all possible.

Figure 6-5. A FireWire cable attached to a digital camcorder

FireWire is a high-performance serial bus, which, like many of today's computer standards, was invented by Apple Computer. FireWire provides some key features that make it perfect for managing digital video information. First, it's fast. FireWire can handle up to a 400 Mbps theoretical maximum of information traveling two ways. Second, it's hot-pluggable, meaning that devices can be plugged and unplugged from the PC without fear of damaging them (much like USB devices). Finally, FireWire ports can supply power where necessary, making external power supplies unnecessary.

While many new PCs are coming out complete with a FireWire port, it's a safe bet that any PCs more than 1 year old won't have one. Not to worry, you can purchase a FireWire PCI card for under $50.00 and easily install it into most systems. Also, many (if not most) contemporary audio cards (midrange and higher) have FireWire ports built into them already.

NOTE *Mac users who have used iMovie know well how great a FireWire connection to a digital camcorder can be.*

Large Hard Drive

It goes without saying that a large hard drive is necessary whenever video editing/capturing is being considered. Just how much is enough? A good rule of thumb is roughly 1.5MB to 2MB of information for every second of digital quality video. That means a gigabyte of hard drive space will yield about 8 minutes of high-quality digital video (complete with transitions and extra audio). If you're planning to edit very large amounts of video and have it on hand at all times, you may want to consider a RAID for your storage needs. If putting together smaller, 1-hour video segments is more your style, then a 40GB hard drive should suffice.

Transfer Software

There aren't specific pieces of software specifically designed for transferring video from the camcorder to the computer, because virtually all of the video editing software takes care of that on its own. We discuss just what these software packages are shortly.

Analog Video Importing

To manipulate and edit video on an HTPC, you must have the video information in digital format. Unfortunately, many home movie enthusiasts have analog video equipment that is entirely unable to directly interface with an HTPC. Fortunately, there are now myriad products available that can take that crusty old analog video and turn it into the wonder that is digital information. There will, of course, be some quality loss. That is to say that the way the video looks coming off of the analog camcorder into the HTPC is as good as it will ever look, but the upside is that from that point forward the quality will not degrade further. Let's have a look at what you will need to get your analog video into your HTPC.

Camcorder/VCR

Many home movies are on Hi-8 or regular 8mm tapes, and therefore you'll need a camcorder to be able to transfer them into the HTPC. Other camcorders may use VHS, VHS-C and, in rare cases, Betamax. Other home movies may have originally come from Super-8 film (from the 1950s, 1960s, or 1970s) and may now be residing on either VHS tapes or possibly even Laserdisc. In short, no matter which format the original analog video is in, you'll need the appropriate device to output it to the HTPC for conversion into digital video.

Video Capture Card

Many of the video cards we've already discussed are fully capable of capturing analog video. The ATI All-In-Wonder Radeon 7500/8500, the Matrox Marvel G450 eTV, the NVIDIA Personal Cinema, as well as many other cards offer video inputs. In fact, some television tuner cards can be tweaked to input analog video into an HTPC. There are also stand-alone devices for converting analog video to digital—a good example of these is the USB-based Dazzle Video Creator (http://www.dazzle.com/main.html) series of products. These are all excellent for the job and are easy to set up and use, although USB-based units cannot always handle the data stream necessary for the highest quality transfers. Ultimately, the best way to import analog video is directly in through the video card connected to the HTPC.

Editing Video

Once the information has been fully transferred to the HTPC, it's ready to be edited into a fantastic production that will make viewers laugh, cry, and generally be glad you took the time to make it pretty.

Software

Many software packages are available for editing video, and we aren't able to cover every single one in this book, but we want to give you a feel for just what's out there to help you decide what software best suits your needs.

Low-Cost Editors

As we mentioned previously, many, many video editing suites are available for most systems. We'll look at a group of what we consider to be the best for the price. In other words, our concern is getting the most bang for our buck while considering such important factors as ease of use and system requirements.

Pinnacle Systems Studio

This software package is exceptional because it not only includes solid basic editing tools, but it also comes bundled with an IEEE 1394 FireWire PCI card. Pinnacle Systems Studio offers an excellent timeline system that allows you to match up sound and video precisely, and it also allows you to capture individual scenes from inside a longer string of video. Perhaps the one downside to Pinnacle Systems Studio is its lack of glossy effects and transitions, which are ultimately important to the "wow" factor of the finished movie. You can find more information about Pinnacle Systems Studio at http://www.pinnaclesys.com.

Ulead VideoStudio 5/6

Ulead VideoStudio 5 is another solid performer for the price, although it has roughly the opposite pros and cons as Pinnacle Systems Studio. VideoStudio 5 has plenty of cool effects and glossy finishing touches, but the timeline isn't as refined, making it more difficult to precisely line up special audio and transition changes. VideoStudio is the software that comes packaged with ATI's All-In-Wonder Radeon 7500/8500 cards, so if you're planning to get one of these cards, you'll kill two birds with one stone. As a bundled product VideoStudio 5 is an excellent value.

Ulead has recently released VideoStudio 6, which includes a few new features such as MPEG-Direct capture, which lets you grab DVD-ready MPEG video straight from your DV/D8 camcorder or other device, saving you time and hard disk space. If you buy an ATI card, you (at the time this book was written) get version 5, but if you purchase it from Ulead, then version 6 will be what's for sale. For more information, visit http://www.ulead.com.

Windows Movie Maker

Windows Movie Maker is another reasonable tool that comes included with the Windows Me OS. While it doesn't have the panache of most of the other video editing suites, it's free if you're already using the Millennium Edition of Microsoft Windows. For more information, visit http://www.microsoft.com.

Roxio VideoWave 5 (Power Edition)

This video editing software actually straddles the line between the higher cost editors and the lower cost editors, but at around $100.00 (when this was written) it certainly has a very reasonable price for the features it delivers. VideoWave 5 offers a plethora of features including DVD authoring, video capture from digital or analog sources, effects such as sepia tone and mosaic, and picture in picture effects, and it also allows for the creation of DVD menus. This feature set is certainly poised for the explosion of DVD burners that will be hitting the market as the prices continue to fall in the next year or so. Visit the Roxio Web site at http://www.roxio.com to learn more.

VirtualDub

VirtualDub is one of the freeware video editing suites that, like the freeware moniker suggests, is free! Although it isn't as robust or as fancy as Adobe Premiere, VirtualDub does the trick and has a feature set that includes the following:

- Integrated MPEG-1 and Motion-JPEG decoders

- Removal and replacement of audio tracks without touching the video

- Extensive video filter set, including blur, sharpen, emboss, smooth, 3×3 convolution, flip, resize rotate, brightness/contrast, levels, deinterlace, and threshold

- Bilinear and bicubic resampling (no blocky resizes or rotates here)

- Decompression and recompression of both audio and video

- Removal of segments of a video clip and capability to save the rest without recompression

- Capability to adjust the frame rate, decimate frames, and perform 3:2 pull-down removal

- Capability to preview the results with live audio

- Integrated volume meter and histogram for input-level monitoring

- Real-time downsizing, noise reduction, and field swapping

- Verbose monitoring, including compression levels, CPU usage, and free disk space

Again, considering this software is free, it's jam-packed with features that will cost you considerably more elsewhere. To see the full feature list or to get your hands on this software, visit http://www.virtualdub.org/index.

TMPGEnc (Tsunamai MPEG Encoder)

Also freeware, TMPGEnc allows you to convert AVI files to MPEG-1 files (the Video CD format). Using a variety of options in TMPGEnc, you can perform high-quality compression of your video files. TMPGEnc enables you to adjust bit rate, quantize matrix, GOP structure, interlace, and many other parameters. Although it's more for the hardcore video editing aficionado, TMPGEnc is a good example of the many freeware programs out there.

 **NOTE** *There are a plethora of video editing software packages on the Internet just waiting for you, with more being added all the time. Although some of them aren't exactly polished, you'll be surprised at how much you can get for the only the price of the bandwidth to download the software.*

Higher Cost Editors

Those with a real penchant for high-end video editing have several excellent choices. Perhaps the best choice of all is Final Cut Pro from Apple, but since this ultra-high-end software only runs on the Macintosh running OS X, we leave it out of the HTPC discussion. Here's a look at four high-end software packages available for the HTPC.

Adobe Premiere 6.5

This is the granddaddy of PC video editing suites, and its latest incarnation is version 6.5. At around $550.00, this is no inexpensive tool, but it's not a penny-ante video editor either. One of Premiere 6.5's biggest improvements is the inclusion of real-time previews. These allow you to see the changes such as transitions and titles instantly. The feature set of Premiere is complex and the learning curve is much steeper than with other editors, but the payoff is a studio-quality result with many tricks, transitions, and effects that can make a monster movie out of basic home movies, which can then be burned to DVD. For more information on Premiere, visit http://www.adobe.com.

CineStream 3.0

While a capable software suite, CineStream really can't compete with Premiere, and considering the prices are similar, it may not be worth going with the relative unknown over the tried and true. Although CineStream has some very impressive features, such as Event Stream Technology (the ability to put in links to other streaming video inside the finished movie), it doesn't always come together as well as it should. To learn more about CineStream, go to http://www.media100.com.

MediaStudio Pro

This is the higher-end version of the Ulead product that's bundled with the ATI cards. At around $200.00, it's a decent value, and it's reasonably easy to learn. Still, it can't match the awesome power and functionality of Adobe Premiere. One addition to MediaStudio Pro is the inclusion of Video Paint, a tool that allows you to custom paint in animations on a frame-by-frame basis, which can make for some significantly cool effects. If cost is an issue, this is a decent choice over Premiere. Visit http://www.ulead.com for further details.

Vegas Video 2.0

This entry from Sonic Foundry is an adequate video editing suite for the money. It has a relatively easy-to-learn interface and contains editing, transitions, and effect extras, but ultimately it's not up to the Adobe Premiere standard.

Editor Summary

In summary, the low-cost video editing tools are largely equal, and if high-end editing is your bag, we recommend that you open up your wallet and shell out for the established leader in this field, Adobe Premiere 6.5.

Editing Techniques

There are a number of video editing techniques and extras, many of which are proprietary to a specific software vendor. Still, there is a set of basic video editing techniques that you should look for in software that will help you to create the best home movies possible.

Scene Transitions

Scene transitions are perhaps the most impressive and important part of video editing. They take viewers from one scene to another, and if they're implemented properly, they do so smoothly and help the video presentation to flow from scene to scene. Some transitions will sweep the scene away from left to right, whereas others will sweep the screen like a clock, leaving behind the new scene. Still others will take the scene and shrink it into a tiny box until it disappears, again, leaving behind the new scene. When they're used properly, scene transitions *make* a home video, so it's important that the video editing software you use has a decent selection of these.

Audio Layers

Most editing suites have at least one extra audio track for you to add in music or voice-overs, and most have two or more extra tracks. Most software has built-in ripping that enables you to put an audio CD into your HTPC and copy the music directly to the segment of video that you want to attach it to. We suggest that the editing software has at least one extra layer but preferably two or more so that you can add in both sound effects and music as you see fit.

Special Effects

Special effects vary greatly between software packages, but there are a few tried-and-true special effects you'll use frequently. In fact, many of the special effects in software suites are also available right on digital camcorders.

Sepia Tone

Sepia tone is a brownish hue that gives the video a tint much like very old movies or photographs have. If you're looking for a black-and-white (actually brownish) old-time feel to your videos, sepia is the way to create it. Most video suites have a sepia setting, as do many camcorders.

Mosaic

Mosaic is a fairly nonfunctional (for viewing detail) effect that breaks down each area of the screen into a large block. This gives an image that might look complete to someone standing 20 feet away, but close up it's impossible to see any detail in it. Still, it's a cool effect and can be worthwhile to use in home movie creation.

Streaks (or Trails)

This is another common special effect that leaves streaks or trails behind anything that moves in the video. Again, it's not something that you would be likely to use often, but it can be a very effective tool, especially if you're trying to give the impression of speed (for example, with someone running a race or a car driving fast past the camera).

Reverse Video

Higher-end editing suites allow you to tweak the video frame by frame or run certain clips backward instead of forward. Bart used this technique when making the introduction to a recent video of his children and family. By filming a series of events that required animals jumping and objects being thrown, the end result when played backward (Bart had to walk backward when he was filming the shot to make the backward result look like it was running forward) was a comical scene indeed.

Summary

In this chapter we looked at various video capture devices, digital video recorders (DVRs, also known as personal video recorders, or PVRs), commercial services such as TiVo, and importing and editing home videos. We also examined some of the software that can help to make your HTPC a master of video editing, recording, and playback. The next chapter examines the role of remote controls in making the HTPC an easy-to-use home entertainment appliance.

CHAPTER 7

Home Theater Remote Controls

MOST OF THE EFFORT of building and configuring an HTPC is concentrated on selecting the most suitable hardware, installing the correct software, and then spending countless hours perfecting the configuration of the system. Only after this great effort has been expended, the machine is working perfectly (or as well as it can—some hobbyists never stop tinkering!), and everyone has settled into their home theater seating and is waiting for the movie to start, does it become apparent that something is missing. Getting out of your chair to start or stop a movie, or to change channels is so old-fashioned—no serious HTPC owner can truly have the ultimate multimedia experience without a remote control.

Since the HTPC is, at its heart, a personal computer system, the standard way of controlling it is with a keyboard and mouse. Unfortunately, a conventional keyboard has a relatively short cable attaching it to the back of the system, and the mouse cord is barely any longer. The HTPC must also be connected to a display device, so unless the whole home theater room is less than 6 feet long, there is not enough cord to reach from the viewer to the HTPC to the television. It is often desirable to locate the HTPC beside the other audio and visual equipment to which it must connect in the home theater, so the use of a normal keyboard and mouse becomes an exercise (literally) in walking back and forth between the viewing position and the HTPC. In some home theaters, the HTPC is located inside special soundproof cabinetry or in another room entirely, which makes the keyboard and mouse even more inconvenient.

For these reasons it is popular to look for an alternative to the old-fashioned keyboard and mouse controls. The HTPC can be as convenient as any consumer electronics device or even more so. The PC's customization potential applies to all home theater functions, including remote control capabilities. The consumer market even seems to be in tune with the HTPC movement as lots of great control gadgets and devices are showing up. There are many ways to drive the HTPC from the comfort of an easy chair and this chapter examines some of the most popular remote control devices.

Wireless Keyboard and Mouse

The most natural alternative remote controller for a PC is a wireless keyboard and mouse. The advantage of using a wireless keyboard and mouse (see Figure 7-1) is that they provide complete control and access to all features of the HTPC just the same as using a keyboard and mouse connected by a cable. Recently, these devices have become widely available in sets that combine the keyboard and mouse. This is a great advantage to the consumer because buying these devices in a set means that they will not interfere with each other, and the installation of both is usually done simultaneously. Some keyboards even feature a track ball or a directional control to replace the mouse, which saves the need for a separate mouse, though many PC users may prefer the feel of a traditional computer mouse.

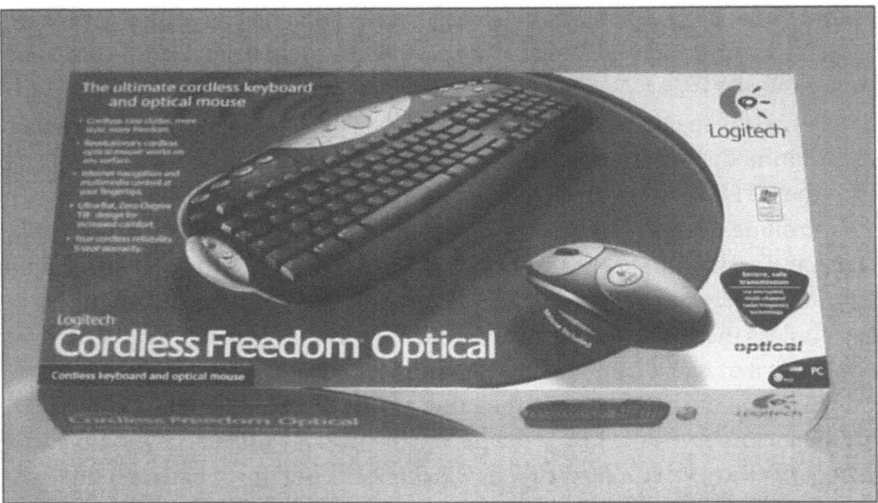

Figure 7-1. A wireless keyboard and mouse set

The distance from which these units will work depends on the brand and model. The manufacturer usually indicates the effective range on the packaging. Two types of wireless devices are available: those that use infrared (IR) light and those that use radio frequency (RF). Neither has an advantage for control distance, but the IR devices will not work through walls, whereas RF devices often will. This may have a bearing on home theaters where the HTPC is hidden away behind soundproofing or in an adjacent room, but either type is great for allowing the user to sit back on the couch and surf the Web, send e-mail, or watch movies.

Many recent multimedia keyboard models include additional buttons and dials that work with PC software to control volume and other functions. This has the potential to make the HTPC very convenient to operate, as commonly used features such as "play," "stop," "skip ahead," and the sound volume can be accessed without having to use the mouse to minimize the picture and find the appropriate button on the screen. However, some users may find that all of the extra buttons are not useful, as may of them are configured by default to launch into the manufacturer's Web page or a sponsor's online service. For an HTPC configured with only a wireless keyboard and mouse, Play buttons and other controls are usually quite handy, but if another type of remote control is going to be added, then these extra features may be redundant.

In the past few years a new type of computer mouse has been introduced for the PC market. This new type of mouse does not use a small roller ball on the bottom to detect movement, but instead uses an optical sensor and a tiny light source (see Figure 7-2). These new mice are far less prone to clogging with dirt and so they never need to be cleaned and they never stop working due to the buildup of crud on the rollers or on the ball. They also work on almost any surface, including fabric and other soft or nonflat areas. This optical mouse technology is perfect for wireless devices to control an HTPC, since the mouse will most likely be used on a couch, a lap, or the arm of a chair where a roller ball would lose surface contact or pick up lint and dust. The optical mouse generally means that the wireless set will cost a little more, but the greater versatility is worth the price.

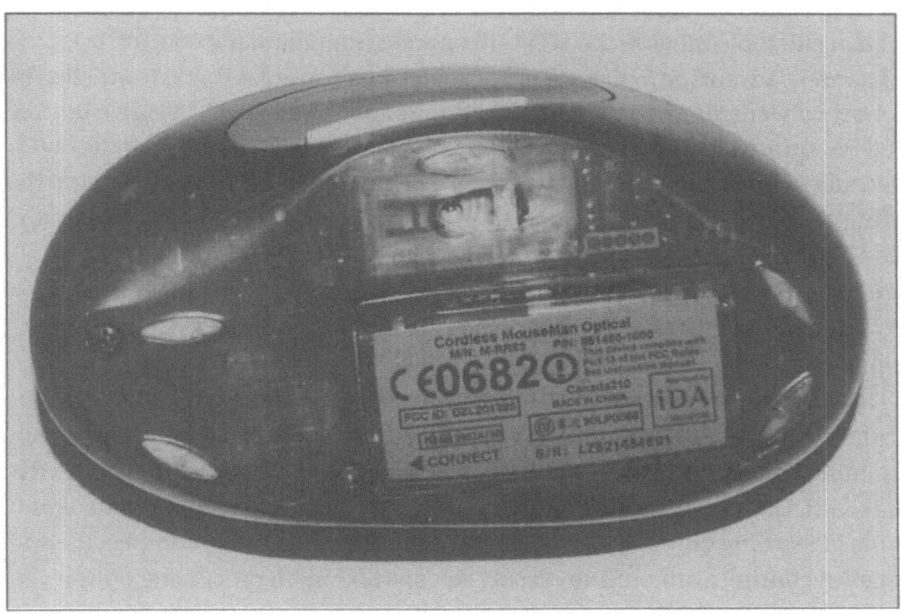

Figure 7-2. The underside of a wireless optical mouse

The wireless keyboard and mouse provide the most control over the HTPC, but they have some disadvantages. A keyboard and mouse set is much larger than a conventional remote control. The set cannot be operated with one hand, and it usually takes several mouse movements and clicks to start up a movie, play an audio CD, or start up the television tuner. Though the wireless keyboard and mouse make it more convenient to control the HTPC, they do not make it simpler. In a home theater used by more than one member of the household, the HTPC may be too complicated to appeal to everyone trying to simply watch a movie. Fortunately, there is a remote control solution to this problem.

Universal Remote Control with an IR Receiver Connected to the HTPC

Universal remote controls have been available for years, and they are a popular way to reduce the number of remote controls needed to operate home theater equipment. These remotes can learn the IR codes to operate any television, VCR, audio receiver, or other piece of consumer electronic equipment with an IR receiver. Some universal remote controls even have codes for popular brands of equipment preprogrammed so that they only need to be told what command set to use. Anyone who has spent time programming a universal remote control to reduce the clutter of remotes in his or her home theater will be pleased to know that he or she can configure the HTPC to operate from the same control.

The great advantage to using a universal remote control is that it is the simplest and most convenient method of sending commands to an HTPC. A single button on the remote can cause the HTPC to switch to a new video mode, start the DVD player, and play the movie in full-screen size. Other buttons can pause or stop the movie, increase or decrease the volume, switch to another application to play an audio CD or an MP3 track, or even record a television program. Compared to a mouse and keyboard, the remote control is far easier to use. It is much easier to teach someone how to play a movie on an HTPC if they only have to press one button!

The universal remote control programmed to work with the HTPC can also run other home theater equipment. This is a great relief for those who suffer from the remote control clutter caused by collecting a different control for each device in the room. Universal remote controls vary in complexity, from the simple unit capable of learning only a few other device command sets to the complex (and expensive) controls with built-in display screens and more processing power than computers had a decade ago. Any type of remote can work, but the more commands it can store, the more functionality it can bring out of the HTPC.

In order to work with an IR remote control, an HTPC must have an IR receiver connected to it. Different types of receivers are available, but the most suitable are the ones that connect to a USB port or a serial port. Since serial ports are older technology they can be a little finicky to configure, and if the HTPC already has devices connected to the serial port (most PCs have only two), then a USB version is recommended. Many PC IR receivers seem to come bundled with a remote control, so it may be a challenge to find one without a controller if you already have a universal remote control.

TIP *Though any IR receiver should work with any universal remote control, there have been some reports of receivers that cannot capture all commands from some remotes. When you select an IR receiver, try to find one that is advertised for use with HTPC systems, or at least for use with multimedia computers.*

The IR receiver will have software drivers so that the computer system can recognize it and receive information from it, but additional software is required to convert the IR commands into instructions that start or stop applications or trigger functions in them. Many IR receiver/remote control sets include an application to do this, but there are also software packages available to enhance the features of the remote control.

One of the best software applications for mapping remote control commands to HTPC functions is called Girder, which is available for free from http://www.girder.nl. Not only can you use this application to connect remote control buttons to computer events, but you can also use it to map any input from any device, including the keyboard, the mouse, and the remote control. Girder also makes it possible to run multiple commands with one button, such as a macro that sets a screen resolution, starts the DVD player, and turns up the volume. Some expensive consumer remote controls can run macros, but this depends on the remote being able to send a series of uninterrupted signals to one or many devices. With Girder software, the remote just has to send one command to the HTPC, which can then run a preprogrammed series of commands. Like any powerful application, Girder takes time to learn and configure, but once it is set up, it makes the HTPC as simple to use as a VCR.

 **TIP** *If you have a Palm Pilot or a similar handheld computing device, you can use an IR booster kit to turn your handheld into a powerful universal remote control. The IR transceiver in most handheld devices generates a signal barely strong enough to communicate beyond a yard, so a booster is required. These kits also come with software to let you program buttons and command macros to control a range of devices suitable for use with an HTPC. Life as a universal remote control is a great retirement for an otherwise outdated gadget! For more information, check out the Pacific Neo-Tek Web site (*http://www.pacificneotek.com/products.htm*).*

Though the universal remote control is the best solution for the problem of operating a complicated HTPC, it does have some limitations. The commands and macros take some time to configure in the remote control and in the HTPC software. The time it takes to set them all up is easily recovered by the simplicity and convenience of using the remote control, but whenever you desire a new feature, you must program it into the system. The versatility of a remote control is also limited by the fact that the only features you may access are the ones already programmed. It is possible to control the mouse pointer with a remote, but it is not very easy to use a computer application in this manner. If the HTPC is used for video editing, computer gaming, or even just typing e-mail, a keyboard and mouse will quickly become the preferred method of input.

PC Remote Control

As the multimedia capabilities of the PC platform grow more powerful and the HTPC becomes a home theater machine of choice, more devices dedicated to increasing its power and convenience will come to market. It is now possible to buy remote controls for the PC that look like the remote controls that come with televisions, audio receivers, or DVD players. These remotes are quite convenient to use since they have built-in mouse cursor controls, making it possible to move the mouse pointer around the screen. This makes it possible to use almost every application installed on the PC, though keyboard commands are still difficult or impossible to invoke with a small, handheld remote control. Compared to a universal remote control that is meant for use with typical consumer electronic equipment, the PC remote is more versatile for use with an HTPC.

One great advantage that a PC remote offers over a universal remote is the potential to use RF instead of IR light. The RF signal can pass through walls and other solid objects that block an IR signal, which means you can locate the HTPC in a separate room or behind soundproof materials. Keeping sound levels down is one of the critical factors in building a successful HTPC, and being able to locate the unit away from the home theater area is one possible method of reducing noise. One other advantage of using an RF remote is that it does not have to be pointed at the equipment to work, though only a very hard-core couch potato may appreciate the effort saved from not pointing a remote!

Choosing an RF remote does have one important limitation that may make it unappealing for some home theaters. Since almost every other device in the home theater uses IR signals, the RF remote cannot be programmed for use with anything else besides the HTPC. Selecting an IR device allows for the potential use of a universal remote in the future without having to upgrade to a new receiver or remote control.

A novel way around this problem is to use an IR repeater to allow the HTPC to send IR signals to other devices in the home theater. A keen hobbyist may be interested in a device called the UIRT2, for which plans are available at http://www.caseserve.com/ht/UIRT/uirt2.htm. This device can send and receive IR signals, and with Girder software, it can be used to turn on and control other components of the home theater system from the HTPC. It even features wake-on-LAN (WOL) so that it can be controlled from a remote PC on a network.

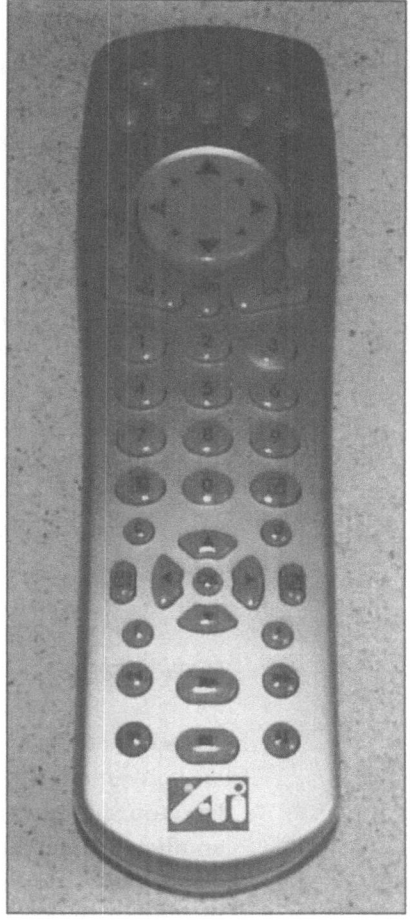

Figure 7-3. The ATI remote wonder, a dedicated PC remote that uses RF signals to control an HTPC

A dedicated PC remote also comes with the hardware and software to connect and configure the computer. The hardware includes the IR or RF receiver, which generally plugs into a USB or serial port. The software includes the drivers to let the HTPC recognize that a remote control is attached and usually some sort of controller software that can be configured to operate selected applications such as the DVD player or the CD audio player. As mentioned earlier, the excellent free software controller Girder can take the place of the bundled software controller if you desire a more powerful and fully programmable alternative. Figure 7-3 shows the ATI Remote Wonder, an example of a dedicated PC remote.

Desktop Sharing: Remote Access Software

One novel method of remotely controlling an HTPC comes not from the home theater world, but instead from the PC world. The ability to control one computer from another has existed in various forms almost since the first computer networks were built. For the maturing PC platform, you have several options for taking control of a computer connected to a network, and since the HTPC is, at heart, still a PC, these methods are well suited to it.

You access a remote computer by installing the appropriate software on two machines: the one that will be controlled and the one that will be used to control the other. In this discussion, the PC that will be controlled is the HTPC, and the controlling PC is any other PC connected to the HTPC via a computer network, phone line, serial cable, wireless connection, and so on. The software may simply allow the controlling PC to run applications on the HTPC, or it may allow full access to the desktop on the HTPC. There are several commercial software packages that allow different levels of control and that support different connection methods.

NetMeeting

A few free software products with remote access functionality for Windows users are convenient and suitable for HTPCs. Microsoft NetMeeting has a feature called Desktop Sharing that simply allows one computer to control the desktop of another. NetMeeting is a free component of most recent versions of the Windows operating system, and you may upgrade older versions with a free download from the Microsoft Web site (http://www.microsoft.com/windows/netmeeting/). To use NetMeeting to access an HTPC, simply install it and run it once to set it up. In the application is a menu command called Remote Desktop Sharing that configures the HTPC to share its desktop. You can set a username and password for security, or you can leave it accessible to any user of the network. Any other PC on the network can then run NetMeeting and connect to the HTPC to take control of it. A little knowledge of Windows networking is useful here since you must specify the network name of the HTPC, or its IP address, to connect to it.

NetMeeting can be a little tricky to configure on HTPCs running Windows 2000 or Windows XP. The machine will only accept connections if a valid username, password, and workgroup name is supplied. This information must match a user account set up on the HTPC. Also, the machine that is controlling the HTPC must be configured to place secure calls.

NetMeeting and most of the other remote access software for the PC has an impact on the performance of the HTPC. Since the machine has to receive and obey remote commands at the same time that it is trying to perform its home theater duties, it has a lot more to do than just play a movie or audio CD. On HTPC computers that are just barely fast enough for DVD playback, running remote access software may be too much work and the video and audio will sputter and jerk. A remote access application that offers the ability to run applications remotely without having to display the desktop of the HTPC may be a better option when performance is at the borderline.

Another drawback to using a desktop-sharing remote-access application is that most of them convert the desktop down to 16-color or 256-color depth in order to speed up the performance of the remote display. Sending true-color video across a network is not possible with most home LANs, so the color depth must be reduced in order to get acceptable display performance without overwhelming the network. To top it all off, some DVD players won't even work when the HTPC is being controlled by another PC through desktop sharing, though different remote access applications may have different results. All in all, NetMeeting is a great tool for remotely accessing a PC, but even for free it may not be suitable for all intended functions of the HTPC, such as starting and stopping DVD movies.

Virtual Network Computing

Another popular remote access application for PCs is called Virtual Network Computing (VNC). It is available as a free download from http://www.uk.research.att.com/vnc/ for most popular operating systems. VNC allows one computer to control the screen of another, like NetMeeting, but it can work from almost any type of remote system. It also seems to work better with HTPCs because of lower performance impact and less conflict with software DVD players. It is a popular remote access tool for HTPC hobbyists, so it is worth a try for any system that needs to be remotely operated through a computer network.

The real convenience of using a remote access software application is not to start and stop DVD movies, however. The real power is using it in conjunction with an IR or RF remote controller. Media functions can be driven by the small remote control unit, but system configuration and maintenance can be done remotely via NetMeeting or any other desktop sharing application. Since the HTPC is most likely to be located near the home theater display, it will not be in a location convenient for prolonged keyboard and mouse access. Also, depending on the display quality, it may be much easier to read text on the screen of a remote control computer than on the home theater display. Tasks such as installing applications, configuring software, copying files, and other maintenance are much easier and more convenient with remote access software. With remote access software installed, an HTPC doesn't even need a conventional keyboard and mouse connected, which may be important for systems that are meant to fit in with the home theater decor.

The whole concept of using remote access software depends on computer network access. The HTPC can be configured with an ordinary network card, such as a 10/100 Mbps Ethernet card, a wireless network card, a serial cable, or any other form of link supported by the PC platform. Besides allowing the use of remote access software, a LAN connection affords an easy method of accessing the Internet, transferring files to and from the HTPC, or even playing movies or audio files from another PC. Networking an HTPC is a tremendously attractive option, and an HTPC that is part of such a computer LAN is a great candidate for remote access software.

The HTPC Project Hardware

Both of our HTPC project systems will be connected to computer networks, so remote access software will be used on each. In addition to the software control, we are adding wireless keyboard and mouse sets to each machine and a PC remote to our system that features the ATI All-In-Wonder Radeon 7500 video card. Since these machines are destined for the media equipment racks in our home theater rooms, the ability to configure and control them remotely is an important convenience. The low cost of wireless devices such as keyboard and mouse sets makes them almost too tempting to resist for anyone considering an HTPC system.

HTPC System 1

This system is configured with the ATI All-In-Wonder Radeon 7500, which comes with the ATI Remote Wonder RF PC remote control. The remote control is bundled with software that allows full use of the ATI media suite, including their DVD player and television tuner. The RF receiver for this unit plugs into a USB port and, as we discovered, it is very important to follow the installation instructions before jumping in and making this connection. The number of USB ports on this HTPC is an issue, since we also want to connect a USB Webcam. With both USB devices attached, there are no extra ports available for more accessories unless we buy a USB hub to expand the capacity. The Remote Wonder also has a mouse cursor control pad in addition to an array of other typical remote control buttons, so it is an excellent unit for controlling a PC.

This system will also have a Logitech Cordless Freedom Optical keyboard and mouse set, as shown in Figure 7-4. The Logitech set is also an RF device, but it doesn't conflict with the ATI Remote Wonder, though we weren't sure about this until we actually set it up for testing. The RF receiver for the keyboard and mouse set attach to the keyboard and mouse ports of the computer, so we didn't need to use another USB connection. Adding a wireless keyboard and mouse set to an

HTPC that already has a PC remote control and NetMeeting is a little bit of overkill, but the cost of wireless devices has plummeted in the past few years and it is worth the extra convenience.

Figure 7-4. Logitech Cordless Freedom Optical keyboard and mouse set

The Logitech keyboard and mouse set includes an optical mouse, which is great for use in a home theater room where a clean, flat surface is not always available. This mouse works on the arm of a chair, the cushions of a sofa, or even on an arm or a leg. If a keyboard and mouse is to be the primary means of controlling an HTPC, a set with an optical mouse is essential.

The keyboard from the Logitech set has several shortcut buttons and media controls built into it. These are very convenient for controlling the sound volume or pausing the playback of a movie or an audio file. In our system, however, they are somewhat redundant since we can also control these settings with the ATI Remote Wonder, but they are great features for systems without a PC remote.

To add complete remote control versatility and programmability to this HTPC system we will be installing the Girder software. The Girder Web site has a great selection of configuration sets available for downloading, including a configuration for the ATI Remote Wonder. This will save us some time when we set up the system.

HTPC System 2

The only wireless remote control device connected to this system will be an IBM keyboard and mouse set that we found in a clearance bin at an electronics store (see Figure 7-5). The IBM set has a very compact and reliable keyboard with some media controls for volume and playback, and a row of shortcut buttons across the top. Compared to the Logitech set used with the first HTPC system for our project, this keyboard is smaller and less cluttered. Unfortunately, the mouse included with the IBM set has a roller ball to track movement instead of an optical sensor, so it will be a little less convenient to use in the home theater room. It's lucky that DVD cases make such great mouse pads!

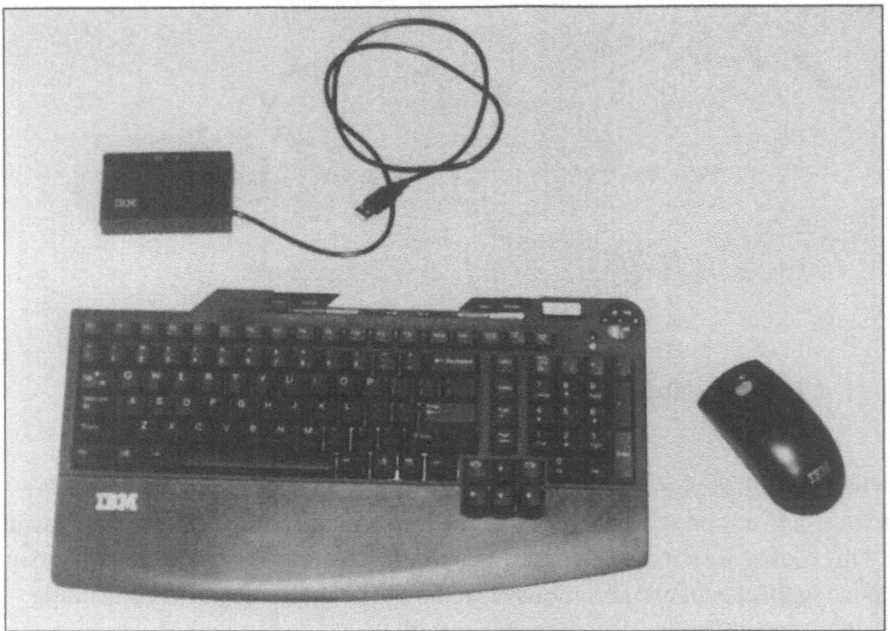

Figure 7-5. IBM keyboard and mouse set

The IBM set is also an RF wireless device, and the sensor connects to a USB port instead of the keyboard and mouse ports on the back of the HTPC. The sensor has buttons to select the wireless channel for the keyboard and for the mouse. We found this more convenient than the Logitech set, which lets the user set the channel in the software driver. When channel conflicts arise, it is almost impossible to use the mouse or keyboard to correct the problem on the computer screen if neither device is working.

Both systems will have Microsoft NetMeeting installed for remote access from other machines. Neither of our HTPC systems will be configured with much disk space, since they participate on a network and can play files from a dedicated file server. Since they are already networked, it is a trivial task to set up NetMeeting to allow us to do maintenance and configuration.

One consideration about remote access software is the location of the other computers on the network. If the HTPC is located in the home theater room, and other systems are located elsewhere, it can be frustrating to have to constantly move back and forth between them. This can happen when the HTPC is being used to generate video, compress audio, download files, install software, or any other task that requires intermittent attention from the user. Using remote access software to keep an eye on the HTPC and occasionally click a button or change a setting is a great convenience.

Another consideration about remote access software is that some of the packages will lock the display resolution and color depth of the HTPC desktop. This is obviously a major problem for a machine that outputs various resolutions and timings to an HDTV display. For both of our HTPC systems, we must remember to shut down NetMeeting's desktop sharing before we try to watch DVD movies.

Summary

Choosing the remote control devices for our project systems is the last major HTPC component selection we will make before assembling the hardware and breathing life into these machines. A PC remote control or a wireless keyboard and mouse may seem like frivolous accessories for a PC, especially to someone who has only had experience with PCs as business tools or game machines. Even many new HTPC enthusiasts wouldn't consider these devices as "major" components. But a few hours experience with a fully functioning HTPC will convince any user of the importance of a convenient way to operate the machine. In fact, without a remote control of some sort, it's really not an HTPC at all!

In the next chapter, the real fun begins. Now that the major components have been selected, it is time to begin assembling and configuring the ultimate home theater machine.

CHAPTER 8

Additional Hardware Requirements and Putting It All Together

VIDEO CARDS, SOUND CARDS, and other media accessories are the major components of a computer system that is destined to be an HTPC. The selection of these parts requires a weighty amount of consideration as they affect the capabilities of the system more than any other individual component. It is these hardware devices that can turn a typical office workhorse PC into a home theater media hub. Upgrading the video and sound hardware of a slightly out-of-date home system can bring it new life as an HTPC by making it a digital audio and video hub with capabilities beyond expensive consumer electronics. As we've explained in the previous chapters, the right video and audio hardware doesn't need to be expensive, but you should take some care to find the right components with the right features for the purposes you intend to fulfill with your HTPC.

Of course, the HTPC is more than just a video card, transcoder, and fancy sound board. This chapter explores the rest of the hardware that goes into an HTPC system and provides some instruction for upgrading or assembling the hardware. The computer operating system (OS) for the HTPC is important for hardware and software compatibility, and is a potentially controversial topic, so this chapter also examines some OS alternatives and their advantages and disadvantages. Finally, an overview of computer networking is appropriate in this topic area since it depends largely on the additional hardware and the OS selected for the system. With the information in this chapter, you should be able to assemble the computer hardware and create a basic HTPC system.

Additional Hardware for the HTPC

After you've selected the video, audio, and other HTPC-specific hardware, you should devote some attention to the more general-purpose components of the PC meant for the home theater. This section provides a general guide for PC hardware such as the central processing unit (CPU), memory, and hard disk drives that are appropriate for use in an HTPC. The requirements for features and performance of these components are mostly the same as those for any other PC system, though a brief explanation of each component and its performance guidelines is useful for new HTPC enthusiasts who are considering assembling a system. Experienced PC hobbyists will be familiar with much of this information, but there are a few details specific to the HTPC that will make this section helpful to them.

The Central Processing Unit

Most PC users know that the *central processing unit* (CPU) is the main processor in the computer system. It is the computer chip that does most of the work, and its performance is the key measurement for the overall performance of the PC. The CPU operates at a specified frequency, referred to as the *clock speed,* where the higher the frequency, the faster and more powerful the CPU. For many computer users, the fastest CPU is always the best because it makes games play better and software run faster.

CPU Performance Range

The performance of CPUs offered for sale by manufacturers is constantly climbing thanks to improvements in design and manufacturing. One of the founders of Intel, Gordon Moore, suggested that the power of state-of-the-art CPUs would double every 18 months—this has come to be known as "Moore's Law." It has continued unbroken for decades, and there seems to be no end in sight. This is great for the computer industry, as better and better products can be sold that entice consumers to spend more and more money. But it may be considered a little unfair to consumers, who watch in amazement as their expensive CPUs become worthless in just a few years.

For this reason, the CPU in an HTPC does not always need to be the newest, fastest, and most expensive unit available. CPUs with enough performance to be used in systems with DVD playback have been available for many years. An HTPC that is going to be used primarily for watching movies or listening to MP3 or CD audio gains no advantage from having a CPU faster than necessary for these tasks. Full-screen software decoding of DVD video is possible with a reasonably fast video card and a 400 MHz CPU. A video card with hardware MPEG-2 decoding features takes more load off of the main system CPU, so that an even slower chip can be used. Of course, it is almost impossible to find a brand-new CPU this slow, but there are plenty of older computers available that would be suitable for use as an HTPC with the right video and sound card upgrades.

Some HTPC tasks will benefit from having the fastest possible CPU. Video encoding and (to a lesser extent) audio encoding need more CPU power than video and audio decoding. An HTPC that will be used to edit home movies, compress video to MPEG or another video format, or compress audio will benefit from a faster CPU. In fact, at standard NTSC resolutions and using one of the newest CPUs, it is now possible to encode video as fast or faster than it is played back. Older systems can take hours to compress a few minutes of video, which makes video editing and rendering a slow and laborious task.

An HTPC with a television tuner card that will be recording video will also benefit from a fast CPU. The software that records from television tuner cards or from the video inputs of a video card can usually do some kind of real-time compression to save disk space, and the faster the CPU, the more compression the software can do. This has the benefit of fitting more video into the disk space available. However, as mentioned in the "Hard Disk Drives" section, hard disk capacity is getting cheaper, and it may be easier to double the drive space than to double the processor performance.

One other consideration for CPU performance is that a faster processor will handle multiple tasks smoothly. If the HTPC is used to record television broadcasts while it also plays back MP3 audio or surfs the Web, there will be a noticeable performance lag on slower systems. Some users also like to run background processes such as SETI@home or the United Devices Cancer Research Project on their HTPC since they leave them on all the time. Any concurrent use of the HTPC for multiple tasks will benefit from having a faster processor.

CPU Brands

There are two popular CPU brands for PC systems commonly available. The products from Intel and from Advanced Micro Devices (AMD) are both suitable for HTPC systems and both manufacturers offer a wide range of CPUs at various points on the price/performance curve. Experienced PC hobbyists may have a preference for one brand over another, but as each is compatible with the hardware and software needed to build an HTPC, there is no overall consensus about which is better.

The available Intel CPUs are the Pentium III and Pentium 4 series, and the Celeron series of lower-cost chips. The Pentium III is still in production (mostly just for mobile processors), but the Pentium 4 is priced so low (at comparable frequencies) that it isn't very likely that buying a new Pentium III CPU would make sense. The Pentium 4 is the premier line of CPUs from Intel, and the top-of-the-line chip represents the fastest available PC processor on the market at the time of this writing.

Intel markets a low-cost line of processors called the Celeron series. These chips are based on the same core technology as the Pentium III, but they have less internal cache memory. They are available at higher frequencies than the Pentium III, though, and for a lower cost. These chips are a popular choice for HTPC enthusiasts on a tight budget.

AMD markets its PC processors as a low-cost alternative to the Intel products. AMD attempts to sell processors with similar power to the Intel chips at lower prices for every available frequency offered by Intel. The premier line of processors from AMD is the Athlon XP series, and the low-cost line of processors with reduced features is the Duron series. As with the Intel products, the frequencies and performance available for the low-cost line are several steps behind the premier series of CPUs.

There are some important differences between the CPUs from these two manufacturers. The Intel Pentium 4 core uses an architecture that allows for higher clock speeds, but it actually executes fewer instructions per clock cycle than previous Intel CPUs such as the Pentium III and the Celeron. The AMD Athlon XP series, by contrast, can execute more instructions per clock cycle than the Pentium 4, but it cannot be manufactured to run at the higher frequencies of the Pentium 4. AMD markets their Athlon XP by giving it a number that represents not the true frequency of the chip, but the frequency of a Pentium 4 at the same performance level. This leaves some doubt about which CPU is actually faster.

To add to the confusion, there are some computer tasks where the higher frequency of the Intel Pentium 4 CPU is an advantage, and there are other tasks where the better performance of the AMD Athlon XP is an advantage. Any task that requires a lot of floating-point math, such as 3D rendering or engineering, is faster on a Pentium 4 CPU than on an Athlon XP CPU. To counter this disadvantage, AMD has added a special set of CPU instructions known as 3DNow! to their CPUs that speeds up 3D rendering for software that supports this special set of instructions. Intel has added a special set of instructions to its Pentium 4 CPU known as SIMD that works to speed up many multimedia tasks such as video encoding and decoding, but like the special AMD set of instructions, it only works with software that supports it. It is beneficial to the HTPC hobbyist to install software that supports the special instruction set for the processor or to select a processor that will achieve a performance benefit with the intended software.

Overall, just about any CPU manufactured in the past few years is suitable for use in an HTPC. Any 400 MHz or faster processor should be able to play back DVD video and MP3 audio. If you are planning to use your HTPC to render and compress video or to compress video as it is captured, you may want to consider buying a faster CPU. Of course, if you are going to use your HTPC to play computer games, you will always benefit from a top-of-the-line processor, but as every PC gamer knows, there is never a CPU fast enough!

Random Access Memory and Motherboards

Personal computers require memory to hold information for the CPU to access. The more memory in a computer, the more applications that it can run at the same time, and the more information those applications can access. Playing media such as DVD video or CD audio doesn't require much memory since the information is read from the disc and played almost immediately, but editing media files such as pictures, video, or audio can use up huge amounts of memory.

There are two basic questions to answer when you're considering the random access memory (RAM) for an HTPC: "What kind of RAM do I need?" and "How much RAM do I need?" The answer to the second question is almost always *as much as possible*, but the answer to the first question is more complicated. The type of RAM you can use depends on the choices you made when you selected the CPU and the motherboard.

When Intel introduced the Pentium 4 processor, it also introduced a new kind of system memory called Rambus RAM. The modules that the Rambus RAM are attached to and installed into PCs are called Rambus dynamic random access memory (RDRAM) modules. At first, the RDRAM was very expensive, so the popularity of Pentium 4 systems was hurt as consumers turned to AMD systems and the cheaper synchronous dynamic random access memory (SDRAM) that would work with these CPUs. Eventually, Intel offered a way to use the cheaper SDRAM with the Pentium 4 processor by introducing a compatible motherboard chipset. The result of all of this is that you can build an HTPC with a Pentium 4 CPU with a motherboard that uses either SDRAM or RDRAM.

The memory issue is more complicated than that, however. When the Pentium 4 and its RDRAM was introduced, the manufacturers of motherboards and CPUs that used the older SDRAM wanted to increase performance to match the RDRAM systems, so double data rate SDRAM (DDR SDRAM) was introduced to increase the speed of the memory for SDRAM systems. This improvement also required a new chipset, so old motherboards that accepted only SDRAM had to be replaced with newer motherboards for DDR SDRAM. The speed of both RDRAM and DDR SDRAM has moved a few more steps beyond the original specification, so now there are a range of motherboards available that support either RDRAM or DDR SDRAM at various maximum clock speeds.

NOTE *RDRAM is only available for Pentium 4 motherboards. AMD does not support RDRAM for any of their CPU products.*

For most HTPC uses, any type of RAM is suitable since the system does not need to be an absolute speed-demon machine. Having more RAM is more important than having fast RAM. When the available RAM in a PC is filled, the OS will swap the least used parts of memory to a swap file on the hard disk drive to make more room. This disk swapping is very slow relative to the speed of RAM, and it causes a big performance drag on the system. An HTPC with 512MB of SDRAM is better than an HTPC with 256MB of DDR SDRAM because the greater amount of RAM will allow for more open applications and less swapping to disk. As with the CPU performance, there are some tasks where faster RAM makes a big difference (video rendering and compression, for instance), but for most HTPC applications, the RAM performance is not a critical issue.

The standard amount of RAM in personal computer systems goes up continuously. Users with systems that are a year or two old are usually dismayed to find that new systems are available with double the amount of memory. Generally speaking, an HTPC that plays movies and music does not need much memory. The smallest amount of RAM that would be advisable is 64MB, though 128MB is probably a better minimum if the system will be used for e-mail and Web surfing. An HTPC that is used to edit digital pictures or audio should have at least 256MB, and for editing video 512MB is a comfortable starting range. The prices of computer memory are relatively low, so building an HTPC with a gigabyte of RAM is not inconceivable if the machine will be busy recording television shows and editing home movies. As with all recommendations in this industry, these figures will seem out-of-date within a year of this writing, and the experiences of each individual user may dictate that more or less RAM is necessary.

 **TIP** *It is a trivial task to add more RAM to an HTPC if you have built the system with the potential for expansion. RAM modules (SDRAM, DDR SDRAM, and RDRAM) come in various capacities (64MB, 128MB, 256MB, 512MB, and so forth), and motherboards come with limited RAM slots, so use the largest capacity module in each slot. In other words, to add 256MB of RAM, buy a 256MB module instead of two 128MB modules. There is usually a small price premium to get a single module instead of two smaller ones, but leaving room for expansion is worth the money.*

Hard Disk Drives

You need to consider a number of issues when you plan the hard disk drive capacity of an HTPC. Hard drive capacity has increased to an amazing size in the past few years, and there is no end in sight to this growth. It may seem like a straightforward idea to throw as much disk space into the HTPC as possible, but this is not always the most efficient or practical solution. Other factors such as disk performance, noise and heat levels, and network capacity have a bearing on the type of hard disk drive suited to the HTPC.

Performance

The performance of the hard disk drive in your HTPC doesn't need to be very high if you'll mainly use the system for playing movies or listening to audio. In fact, if your machine spends all of its time playing DVD video and CD audio, then it barely needs a hard disk drive at all. If you connect your HTPC to a home network, it's possible to build an HTPC that boots remotely from the network so it doesn't need an internal hard disk. The benefit of this is that there's less heat generated inside the system case, so you can have fewer fans, or the fans can run slower and create much less noise than in a traditional PC. A diskless HTPC is an extreme example of a system optimized for low-noise environments, though such a system is not easy to build.

More commonly, the HTPC will have a small hard disk drive onto which the OS and media applications are installed. Ideally, this hard disk drive should be quiet, so a low-performance drive that spins at about 5400 rpm is sufficient. This is fast enough to play back audio or video files, access the Internet, and perform most common HTPC tasks.

A drive in this performance range will have trouble keeping up with a video capture device, however. The resulting video file will have quite a few dropped frames, which will make the video look jumpy and could distort the audio. A 7200 rpm or faster drive would be a better choice for an HTPC system that is used to record video, and it also makes a big difference for systems that do video rendering and compression, since these tasks involve a lot of continuous disk access. The faster a hard disk drive spins, the more noise and heat it generates, so there is a trade-off in performance for noise level.

To counter the increased noise from increased performance, many hard disk drive manufacturers offer products with noise-reducing features. These features include liquid-filled bearings, special casings, and power-reducing spin-down utilities that reduce heating and noise when the drive is not used for a specified time. These features increase the cost of the drives slightly, but some users find them very effective at reducing noise. Our experience is that nothing in the HTPC is as loud as the fans, and reducing heat generation is the most effective way to cut the fan noise, so selecting a slow-spinning hard drive is usually the best way to reduce noise.

Size Requirements

The size of the hard disk drive you need in the HTPC depends on the software you've installed, the tasks for which you'll use the system, and the network connections available. If you don't connect the HTPC to a network, and you use it only to play multimedia content or to access the Internet, then a small drive in the 10GB to 20GB range is sufficient. This allows room for the OS, applications, and some media files such as a collection of compressed audio files or a few video files. If you'll use the system to collect audio files, then a bigger drive in the 60GB range affords plenty of capacity to store hundreds of audio CDs in compressed audio format. If you'll use the machine to store video files, you should consider the highest capacity drives of 100GB and more, as nothing seems to fill up a hard disk drive like home video and downloaded movie trailers. Some applications allow users to store DVD movies on their hard drive, and at 2GB to 4GB each, a medium-sized collection of 40 DVD movies could fill a single drive!

For systems connected to a home network, there are even more possibilities to consider. The HTPC may be a client on the network that plays media files stored on another system. In this case, it is better to add disk storage capacity to the computer that serves files instead of adding it to the HTPC. The file server may be used to store vast quantities of information, including the media files that the HTPC can access and play back in the home theater. This allows for a relatively small capacity and low-performance hard disk drive in the HTPC, so that it remains quiet and unobtrusive in the home theater room. This means that the file server must be left running at all times when the HTPC needs to access media files, and unless a very fast (and therefore very expensive) home networking technology is used, the HTPC would not be able to capture video to the file server and would not have much disk capacity to capture to itself.

The HTPC may also be designated as the media file server for the rest of the PCs on the home network. The HTPC would be configured with a large-capacity high-performance drive, or perhaps more than one. It would be difficult to build such a machine to be quiet enough to live in the home theater room without some kind of special soundproofing, such as a cabinet, closet, or small anteroom. Despite the noise, this arrangement may be quite appealing because the HTPC is the only machine in the household that needs to be left on continuously.

RAID

One hard disk drive technique that is worth considering is *volume striping*, also known as *RAID level zero* (RAID 0). This technique consists of the use of two physical hard disk drives as one drive volume. The drives are set up so that the PC sees only one logical disk drive, and when information is written to the drive, half of it goes to each physical disk. Since the two disks can write the information at the same time, performance is doubled. This goes for reading information also. There is some overhead processing that must be done to keep the two drives synchronized, so the performance gain is actually not quite doubled, but it is significant.

There are two ways to create a striped volume: through software or through hardware. The software method involves configuring two drives in the OS to behave as one drive. The OS must tell the CPU to do some processing each time the striped volume is accessed for reading or writing, so a software RAID 0 does not perform quite as well as a hardware RAID 0 volume. The hardware RAID 0 volume uses a special RAID controller that can be added as a PCI adapter card or can be built into the motherboard to control two or more disk drives. The hardware RAID controller can also be configured to boot the PC since it does not rely on the OS, whereas the software RAID 0 can be accessed only after the OS is started. The versions of the Windows OS that support RAID 0 in software are Windows NT, 2000, and XP.

The advantages to using a striped volume are only really worth considering if you'll use your HTPC system to capture and render a lot of video. Since the striped volume is composed of two or more disk drives, it has the capacity of all of the drives combined—that is, you can use two 20GB drives to create a 40GB striped volume. Video rendering and compression constantly access the disk drive, so the performance gains translate directly into faster file processing.

A striped volume involves some risk to data, however. If any one of the drives that make up the striped volume fails, all of the data in the volume is lost. There are variations of the RAID technique that allow for data recovery, but they all involve losing disk capacity or performance. It is recommended that a striped volume be used only as a temporary capture and processing disk space, not as a long-term storage space.

Other Devices

A number of other components that go into a PC have some effect on the system performance and capabilities. You can add most of these components as upgrades to an existing system, but some (for example, the motherboard) are not convenient or simple procedures to replace. It is worth it to carefully consider these items before you build your HTPC to make sure that you haven't overlooked any detail.

Motherboard for Multiple CPUs

For those rare and uniquely ambitious HTPC hobbyists who plan to work their systems very hard, it is worth considering a multi-CPU motherboard. This allows for two CPUs in the HTPC system, which can increase performance for some types of activities. Among Windows OSs, only Windows NT and its descendant OSs (Windows 2000 and Windows XP) can use multiple CPUs, and only software that is written with multiple concurrent execution paths (threads) will take advantage of both processors. Alternately, if an application is not multithreaded, then multiple CPUs can allow the application to run at full speed on one CPU, while the other CPU handles other system processes or other applications. This could allow video or audio compression to run at full speed in the background while the user surfs the Internet smoothly and without any performance lag. The cost of multiple CPU motherboards is slightly higher than that of conventional motherboards, and obviously it costs twice as much to buy two CPUs than to buy one, but for hard-core HTPC hobbyists, the benefits of faster video rendering or smoother activity could be worth it.

TIP *The cost of two AMD Athlon CPUs for a multiple CPU system is actually more than twice as much as a comparable Intel system. You cannot use the Athlon XP in a multiple CPU computer—instead, you must use the Athlon MP, which costs more than the Athlon XP. In fact, the Athlon MP costs more than a comparable Pentium 4, so for multiple CPU systems, the Intel Pentium 4 seems to be the most cost-effective processor.*

Universal Serial Bus

Most motherboards sold in the past few years have included at least one (usually two) universal serial bus (USB) port. The USB bus is used to connect all types of external devices from keyboards and mice to video capture devices and image scanners. The USB bus is important for an HTPC because this is where an IR or RF receiver for a remote control is connected. Also, a small Webcam for video conferencing may be connected to add even more functionality to the HTPC. The USB bus transfers data at 12 Mbps and can theoretically handle 127 devices at once, though in practice this limit is much lower. In order to connect more devices to the bus after all the ports are used, a USB hub must be attached to the bus, or additional USB controllers may be added to the HTPC with PCI adapter cards.

An upgraded version of USB, called USB 2.0, is now available. This standard theoretically supports data transfer rates up to 480 Mbps and is backward compatible with the USB 1.0/1.1 standard. USB 2.0 is still quite new, but it is expected that there will be many new products and may new categories of USB products made to work with the much faster USB 2.0 specification. If the HTPC is going to be based on a brand-new motherboard, it is probably going to be worth the effort to get a board that supports USB 2.0

Serial and Parallel I/O

In the "old days" of personal computers, before the USB bus and before the IEEE 1394 digital link, the common method of attaching peripherals to a computer was through either the serial port or the parallel port. The parallel port was mainly used for printers, though there were some diskette-type drives and even CD-ROM drives that could attach to the parallel port. The serial port was for modems, a mouse, or any other type of device that wanted to interact with the PC. In these "modern days" of personal computers, almost all new peripherals are made for USB or IEEE 1394 ports, so building an HTPC with a serial or parallel port is not really crucial. Many motherboards still have these old-style connections, but many manufacturers have announced that in the next year or so they will no longer be included. Unless you are going to use your HTPC with a printer that has only a parallel port connection or an external modem that works with the serial port, adding these connectors is probably not worthwhile.

Floppy Diskette Drive

Like the serial and parallel ports, the venerable floppy diskette drive seems doomed to obsolescence. Most PCs still seem to have a diskette drive, but when was the last time it was used for anything? Transferring files via floppy diskette is painfully slow, as the 1.44MB capacity is too small for any media file (except small digital photos, perhaps, but even they can fit just a few per diskette) and too small for any software installation. Occasionally, a device driver could fit onto a diskette, but manufacturers always seem to send CD-ROMs anyway, as they are cheaper to manufacture even for a single, small file. For most HTPC systems, a floppy diskette drive is not necessary.

CD and DVD Drives

Since the most popular use of an HTPC system is to play DVDs, it seems to be a foregone conclusion that a DVD-ROM drive is the best removable media drive to install. For most systems, this is the ideal drive, but there are other possibilities worth considering.

If you're going to use the HTPC to capture and edit home movies, a CD-R drive that can record video to a CD-R disc is a convenient way to preserve or send files off of the system hard disk drive. With the right software, the HTPC can even burn Video CD or SVCD video discs that play in compatible DVD players. Since a CD-R recorder can't read DVD discs, you must install it in addition to a DVD player. It is also getting cheaper to buy DVD recorders, though the format wars haven't (at the time of this writing) settled down, so choosing among DVD-RAM, DVD+RAM, DVD-R, and the other formats is not an easy decision. The advantage of a DVD recorder is that a separate DVD-ROM drive is not needed, so you can build the system with only one removable media drive. There are also combo drives available that do CD-RW and read DVD-ROM.

Computer Networking: Hardware to Connect to a Local Area Network

It is surprisingly inexpensive to add a network card to an HTPC in order to provide the capability of connecting to a local area network (LAN). Unfortunately, it is relatively expensive to buy all the other networking equipment that such a LAN requires. The prices for 10/100 Mbps Ethernet cards are so low that the old 10 Mbps cards have pretty much disappeared. We provide a little more information about networking later in this chapter, but we should mention here that 100 Mbps LAN is about the slowest speed that is convenient for transferring large media files across a network. Trying to send hundreds of megabytes across a 10 Mbps network can take a long time. A gigabyte of data will take around an hour to send at 10 Mbps, depending on the amount of other traffic on the network. Also, 10 Mbps is too slow to play even NTSC-quality video, so networking an HTPC at less than 100 Mbps is not very useful.

Most computer networking hardware currently available is for Ethernet networks and uses unshielded twisted-pair wiring with RJ-45 connectors. For those not technically adept at working with computer networks, what is required is that a 10/100 Ethernet network card with an RJ-45 connector is used in the HTPC. This should provide compatibility with the vast majority of home networking equipment available.

TIP *The RJ-45 connector at the end of the computer network cable looks like an oversized telephone plug. The receptacle on the Ethernet network card, therefore, looks like an oversized telephone jack. There are other (older) types of computer network cabling available, but the type that uses the RJ-45 connector is now the most common.*

Ten years ago it was very rare to see a computer LAN in the home, but with the growing popularity of the PC and the falling costs of LAN hardware, it is now a very attractive convenience to set up a LAN at home. Many new homes are built with network cabling inside the walls, and it is possible to retrofit cabling in older homes or just use a wireless connection. The HTPC is a valuable addition to a home network because of its potential as a media file server or as an unmatched media player for files from another server or from the Internet.

Computer Cases

There seem to be two approaches to selecting the computer case needed for an HTPC. The first approach is to regard the HTPC primarily as a computer. The machine needs no special case since it is plainly a computer, and trying to disguise it or make it look inconspicuous defeats the purpose of having a computer next to the television or video projector in the home theater. Computer cases are available as either tower or desktop models, though most can be arranged either way, so the hobbyist need only select a case that fits the location of the system. Lately, cases have begun showing up in all sorts of colors and with neat transparent panels or glowing lights, which can help the machine fit into the room's decor but can also distract viewers from what they are meant to be watching. A plain beige tower case is the cheapest, simplest and, for many hobbyists, the ideal HTPC covering.

The other approach is to regard the HTPC as one of the audio/video components of the home theater and to try to find a case that fits the style, size, shape, and color of the other devices on the equipment stand. The design of consumer electronics products is anything but utilitarian—matching shades of black, gray, or silver with color-coordinated LED displays make the home theater equipment look purposeful and powerful. A big beige tower case would contrast badly with an otherwise perfectly harmonized set of components.

For appearance-conscious home theater enthusiasts, the world of HTPC cases is becoming friendlier all the time. Several companies make computer cases especially for HTPC systems with great features such as clean face plates and digital alphanumeric displays instead of the typical incongruous power and hard drive activity lights, or a power and reset button beside a row of removable device bay covers. These specialized HTPC cases are usually priced higher than standard PC cases, but they do improve the appearance of the system by quite a margin.

One big problem with all PC cases, including the specialized HTPC cases, is that they tend to be very large compared to an audio receiver or a DVD player. The sizes of the computer motherboard and the adapter cards that must fit inside the case limit the size to which it can be shrunk. The current standard for motherboard size is the ATX form factor, and every computer case that conforms to the standard must be at least large enough for the motherboard and other components that fit inside.

The alternative is to build a system based on the microATX form factor or the FlexATX form factor. The microATX form factor is smaller than the full-size ATX motherboard specification, so the cases meant for these smaller motherboards are smaller. The FlexATX form factor is smaller yet, as it is meant for rack-mounted PC systems. Though these cases are not designed specifically for HTPC use, they do have some advantages when used for this purpose. The smaller case requires a smaller, quieter fan to move enough air through it to cool the system. The smaller case is also more portable, which may not be much of an issue for most HTPC hobbyists, but it is also more likely to fit into a cabinet or stand meant for other consumer electronics components. Unfortunately, the selection of microATX and FlexATX motherboards is rather limited, and few of them seem to have a proper Accelerated Graphics Port (AGP) video card slot, so their appeal may be limited for those hobbyists looking to put a cutting-edge video card into their system.

TIP *The world of specialized HTPC computer cases is so new that most of the current manufacturers are not well known in North America, and more and more are available all the time. The best way to find out what is out there is to do a Web search on the topic "HTPC case."*

Cooling

The issue of cooling the components inside a computer case is usually dealt with by suggesting additional fans to draw air in or more fans to blow air out. Unfortunately, adding fans to an HTPC system is not really desirable, as the system is meant to be as quiet as possible. Adding one fan may not seem like much of a noise increase, especially to computer operators used to sitting in an office with air conditioning and other noises constantly drowning out the hum of the PC fan, but in a quiet home theater one fan can be annoying. Even the power supply fan that most PCs have can be heard quite easily during quiet sections of a movie or audio track. The goal is to not only avoid adding fans, but also reduce the noise coming from the existing fans.

Heat is generated by the components inside the computer case. The most prolific heat generators are the power supply, the CPU, the hard disk drive, and the video card. All CPUs and many video cards available today have a heat sink and small fan attached to help dissipate the unwanted heat. Choosing a video card with no heat sink fan can easily eliminate one source of noise from the system, though it is not always possible to get the desired video performance this way. Removing or disabling the CPU fan or the power supply fan is not an option, since the computer will quickly overheat and become unstable, or even sustain damage.

It is possible to run the HTPC with power-saving features that slow down the CPU fan. This can reduce the noise volume substantially, so it is important to select a motherboard that allows you to set the fan speed or that can automatically slow down the CPU fan when the system is not working hard and generating a lot of extra heat. It is also possible to get quieter power supply fans that use special rotor bearings or spin at a lower rate to reduce noise. Some HTPC hobbyists have built custom wiring in the power supply to provide a lower voltage to the fan to slow it down, though this is not recommended as there is a potential for unchecked heat buildup if the fan is not blowing the amount of air called for in the design specification.

A more unconventional way to cool an HTPC is to add a water cooling kit to the PC case. This is similar to the water pump in a fish tank: It circulates water to special heat sinks that fit onto the CPU, hard disks, and other heat-generating components. The water is then passed through a radiator to cool it down again. With no fans, this method can yield a system that is almost silent, though care must be taken to find a quiet water pump. There are even systems that go one step further and add refrigeration to the case, though these are meant more for hobbyists trying to over-clock their systems than for home theater enthusiasts trying to watch a DVD movie.

Perhaps the ultimate solution is to build an enclosure for the HTPC that allows for air to circulate (perhaps from another room) but does not allow sound to escape into the home theater. Any heavyweight HTPC with multiple hard disk drives and a powerful video card will not survive without an additional case fan (or fans), which will make the machine seem deafening compared to the quiet sections of movies or audio programs. Some hobbyists have experimented with putting the HTPC in an adjoining room and controlling it with an RF remote control or a keyboard and mouse. Some have cabinets with the front fully enclosed by glass and the back open for cooling and connecting the wires. An even more drastic solution is a *hushbox*, an enclosure for the HTPC that is soundproofed with foam or thick material, but keep in mind that the HTPC does require fresh air circulation, and any openings for air will admit the fan noise into the home theater room. Cooling an HTPC is a fine balance between air circulation and noise generation.

Assembling an HTPC: A Few Key Procedures

Those with experience building PCs know that the topic of hardware assembly is so big that more than a few large volumes are already dedicated to the subject. It is not our intention in this chapter to cover the basics of putting a computer together, since that could easily be a book on its own. Some hardware assembly procedures are particularly relevant to HTPC systems, however. These procedures are either very common when building an HTPC, such as upgrading a video card, or very proprietary to an HTPC, such as connecting an optical digital audio cable. Most of these procedures are simple and quick to perform, but having them explained and illustrated can help to bolster the confidence of any hobbyist faced with a new task.

Unlike most other electronic equipment, the PC is meant to be opened up and modified by the user. This does not mean that the inside of a computer system is always a friendly or accident-proof environment, though. These procedures require due care and constant attention to detail. It is possible to damage components inside a computer case with an insignificant spark from a static electricity discharge or by installing the components incorrectly. Any mistakes or malfunctions caused by the user accessing hardware inside the computer case are generally not covered by any manufacturer's warranty. If you decided to proceed with these hardware upgrades, you must do so at your own risk.

The general guiding principal of working on computer hardware is to proceed slowly and carefully. It is worth taking extra time to think through a procedure before performing it because doing so often means doing it right the first time. Also, it is important to pay attention to small details as the work progresses. The tasks explained in this chapter are fairly simple, but they do involve several steps, and making a small mistake early on can result in your having to undo everything in order to correct it.

TIP *Personally, we find installing new hardware very exciting because we're always thrilled with the expectation of a substantial performance gain. We also find it intimidating, because we're never sure if our expensive new toy works until we've installed and configured it. This makes it tempting to rush through the procedure to get to the results, but we've done this enough to know that rushing is the worst way to work. At the very least, we recommend reading through all the manuals and enclosed literature that accompany new hardware. This forces you to know what to expect, and it can often provide valuable information that would otherwise cause problems. You'll find that taking the time to read the manual will usually make the actual installation process go faster.*

It is important that you have all the tools and equipment necessary for the hardware upgrade on hand before starting. There is not much required, but having the proper tools in front of you saves you frustration and time during the work. Here's our recommended list of equipment for simple HTPC hardware procedures:

- **Screwdriver:** You'll use this tool to open and refasten the case cover.

- **Needle-nose pliers or large tweezers:** You'll use this tool to retrieve screws dropped inside the case.

- **Flashlight or adjustable desk lamp:** A hands-free flashlight or lamp makes it easier to see small details inside the shadowy corners of the computer case.

- **Scissors or sharp knife:** This tool should actually never even come close to the HTPC case, but it is handy for opening hardware packaging.

After you have tinkered around inside the guts of computer systems for a few years, you will invariably have a collection of extra screws, mounting rails, wires, and other small bits that seem to have no use until they go missing. A few clean glass jars (or any other transparent container) with lids make great storage containers for these bits. Saving the small items can really save you time down the road when you try to install a hard disk drive, a DVD drive, or another item that came with no mounting screws or data cable.

Installing or Upgrading an AGP Video Card

The procedure for installing an AGP video card is pretty straightforward and simple, but for anyone who has never opened a computer case, it can be intimidating. Upgrading a video card is a popular way to improve the performance of an HTPC or to begin to turn a conventional office machine into an HTPC. It is an essential process that every HTPC hobbyist should feel comfortable doing, and after one or two journeys into the inner space of a computer case, almost everyone will. In this hobby, most participants already know their way around, but as the hobby grows and entices more and more participants, there are eventually going to be some who did not start out as computer experts. Fortunately, installing or upgrading a video card is the sort of easy task that almost anyone can do.

Before you begin any hardware procedure on a computer, it is important that you double-check that the hardware to be installed is compatible with the computer. For AGP video cards, this means checking that the AGP version of the video card is supported by the AGP slot on the computer motherboard. The motherboard manual, or the manual that came with the system, should list the features of the system near the beginning of the booklet. The first version of AGP (AGP 1.0, also referred to as AGP 1X/2X) featured a 3.3 volt bus. The next version (AGP 2.0, or AGP 1X/2X/4X) used a lower voltage of 1.5 volts. The AGP 2.0 slot has an extra tab, and the video cards have an extra notch along the connector edge. The AGP Pro slot has an extra length of connectors but is backward compatible with AGP 2.0 video cards. The AGP Pro slot usually has a paper or plastic cover over the extra length to prevent AGP 2.0 video cards from being inserted incorrectly. Some AGP video cards will work in either an AGP 1.0 or an AGP 2.0 slot. The latest development, AGP 3.0, has now been implemented on some video cards and motherboards, and it allows for speeds of 1X/2X/4X/8X.

It's important to check the specifications of the video card you're installing, and the slot on the motherboard, to see that they're meant for each other. In the absence of the proper manuals, it may be possible to determine the compatibility from the labeling printed on the motherboard and video card or from the relative size and shape of the slot and connector. The risk is that some AGP 2.0 video cards that can only work at 1.5 volts will fit into an AGP 1.0 slot running at 3.3 volts, which could cause damage to the video card and the motherboard. Usually, when you install something, if your computer doesn't boot up right away normally, you should turn it off immediately to prevent damage. In cases like this, you should undo the procedure or at least review it to find the problem.

Installing the Hardware

When you have the required tools at hand, you have turned off and disconnected the HTPC from the power cable, and you have the new AGP video card standing by for installation, follow these steps for upgrading the video card:

1. Check that the HTPC is powered off and disconnected from the power cable. We can't emphasize this enough!

2. Lay the HTPC flat so that the case cover is on top, as shown in Figure 8-1. It's easier to work inside the computer if the open part is facing up.

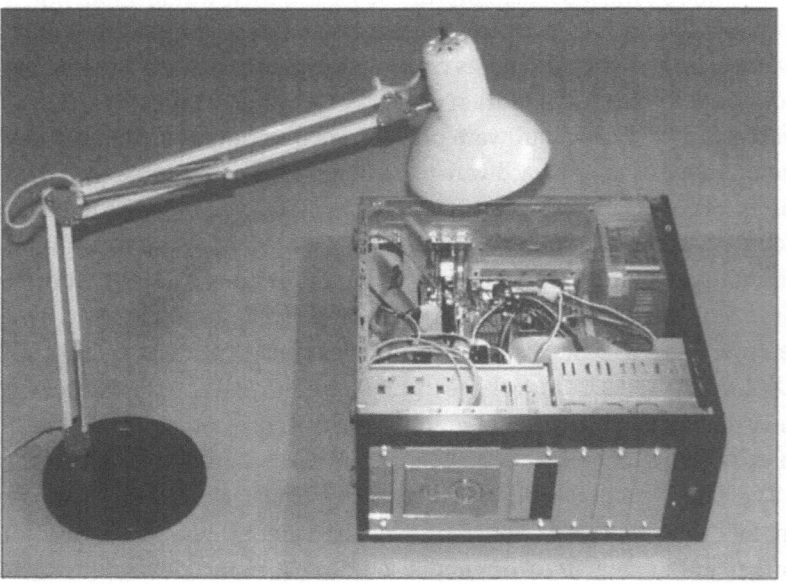

Figure 8-1. Lay the case flat to allow easy access and good lighting.

3. Remove the screws holding the case cover onto the case. There are many styles of cases and coverings, so you may have to check all around it to find the correct screws to remove. Generally, the screws are at the back (see Figure 8-2), the bottom, or sometimes the bottom sides of the case.

Figure 8-2. Look for the case-cover screws at the back of the case.

4. After you remove the screws, gently push the case cover until it slides off. Ground yourself by touching either the bare steel within the case or a static strip.

5. Find the AGP video card or the empty AGP slot on the motherboard (see Figure 8-3). Chances are that you already have an AGP video card in the system if it has an AGP port, but some systems have built-in video or a PCI video card that could have an empty AGP slot.

Figure 8-3. An AGP video card slot

6. Remove the existing AGP video card or disable the built-in video feature of the motherboard. Removing an AGP card is usually a simple process that consists of unscrewing the mounting screw from the bracket at the back of the case, as shown in Figure 8-4. Some AGP cards are fastened with an extra plastic collar around the slot, so check for more screws securing the video card where it attaches to the motherboard. The flashlight or desk lamp will come in handy now.

7. If the motherboard in the HTPC features a built-in video chip that uses an internal AGP bus, it must be disabled. Finding a motherboard with a built-in AGP video chip and an empty AGP slot is relatively rare; usually a built-in AGP video chip means that there is no AGP slot. For systems like this, it may still be possible to disable the AGP video and install a PCI video card. In many systems, as soon as an AGP card is detected in the slot, the onboard AGP shuts down.

Figure 8-4. Remove the screw from the mounting bracket.

 **NOTE** *Though a PC can have only one AGP video card, it supports multiple PCI video cards. Most recent versions of the Windows OS can detect and configure multiple video cards quite conveniently. They also support one AGP video card and one or more PCI video cards, so it is not strictly necessary to disable an onboard AGP video chip in order to use a PCI video card.*

8. Disable the built-in AGP video card either by setting a jumper on the motherboard or by changing an option in the system BIOS configuration. Either way, consult the motherboard or system documentation to find out how.

9. Insert the new AGP video card into the AGP slot. The connector may be a very tight fit, and sometimes the mounting bracket that faces the back of the case is tricky to push in. The best method is to keep the card as straight as possible, line the bracket up with the empty gap on the back of the case, and push it straight into the slot, as shown in Figure 8-5.

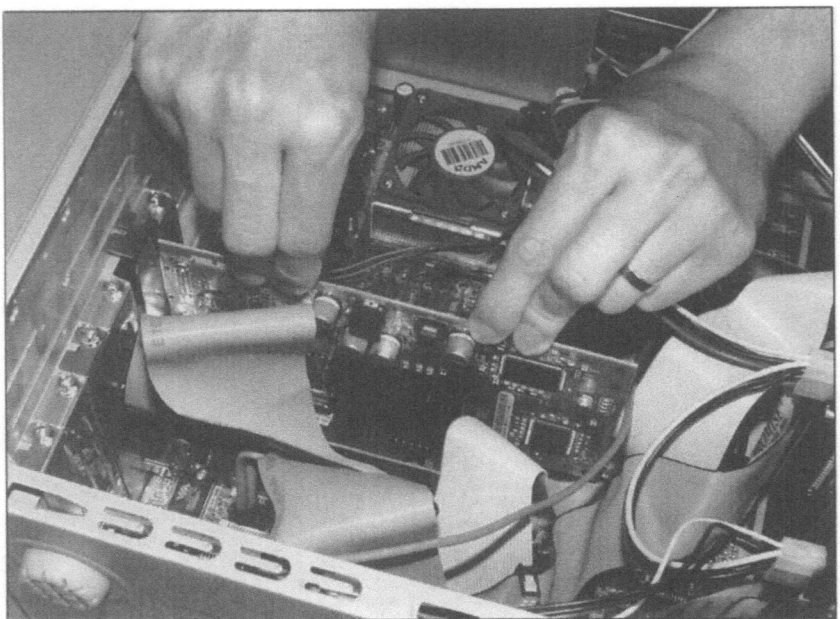

Figure 8-5. To insert the AGP video card, start with the card in this position and push straight down.

10. The video card should sit in the AGP slot with the metal connectors all hidden inside the slot, and the mounting bracket at the back of the case should be seated flush against the case. Put a screw into the appropriate hole to attach the mounting bracket to the case.

11. Replace the case cover and put the screws back in to hold the cover in place. Most experienced PC technicians leave all but one or two screws off in order to facilitate faster access next time, which is a helpful technique if you plan to access the inside of the HTPC again soon.

12. Some technicians also prefer to leave the case cover off until they boot the PC and confirm that the new hardware is working. If you feel doubtful about the installation of the hardware, and you don't mind booting the computer with the case off, this could save a little time if there's a problem with the new video card.

13. Finally, plug the power cable back into the HTPC and reconnect it to the monitor, the sound system, and whatever else it connects to. The machine is now ready for you to turn on and configure with the new hardware.

Configuring the Hardware

When you turn the computer on for the first time after you upgrade the AGP video card, it should boot up normally at first. If you see the display showing the normal boot information from the motherboard BIOS and then the OS, then the video card is installed properly. Alternately, if you see no image on the display, and if you hear a series of beeps, then the new video card is not working properly. In this situation, it is important to power down the computer right away and unplug it from the power cable.

Some common problems that cause the video card to not work are easy to fix. It is possible that the card is not seated properly in the AGP slot: If it was not pushed down all the way into the slot, or if it was misaligned in an AGP Pro slot, it will not work. You can fix this by opening the case up again, removing the new video card, and reinstalling it. Some motherboards may flex when the card pushes into the AGP slot, preventing it from seating fully into the slot. Some video cards may fit very tightly into the AGP slot and require very firm pressure to install. You can overcome this by gently and slowly rocking the card along the direction of the slot as you apply pressure to seat it. This situation can be very precarious, as too much force can cause damage to the slot or the motherboard, so double-check that the card is meant for the AGP slot and is aligned properly.

Some video card problems aren't easy to fix and require replacement of the card. If the card doesn't work after you've tried a few times to reseat it, or if it looks like it's seated properly but still doesn't work, then you should return or exchange the card. If the voltage of the AGP slot doesn't match the card, then the system will either refuse to boot up or be very unstable. In this case also, you must return the card or exchange it for a compatible model.

If the system starts up normally and loads the OS, then you must configure the OS for the new video card hardware. All versions of the Windows OS since Windows 95 are capable of detecting new video hardware and prompting for the installation of video drivers. These are normally provided on a CD-ROM, which you can insert when the OS prompts for it. After the drivers are installed, Windows will need to reboot to load the new video driver.

The OS drivers are not the end of the software configuration of new video hardware. Often, video cards are supplied with a suite of utilities and applications that provide extra settings and features for the new hardware. You also install these utilities and applications from the CD-ROM that came with the hardware. If these extra software accessories do not include DirectX drivers, then it is a good idea to reinstall DirectX after you install the other utilities. DirectX is a hardware application program interface (API) that allows software to use the system hardware directly, which improves performance for computer games and other video or audio applications such as DVD movie players or MP3 players. The DirectX API is available from the Microsoft Web site (http://www.microsoft.com) as a free download.

Connecting a VGA-to-Component Transcoder

Compared to installing a video card, connecting a transcoder is a breeze. There are no screwdrivers, case covers, or hardware drivers involved, and you can do the whole procedure in less than a minute. There are some tricky connections, however, and the whole procedure can take a lot longer than a minute if you don't approach it with the same care as a video card upgrade.

The key to making the connection from the VGA output of a video card to the component input of a television is to start with the HTPC system set to the right screen resolution and timing. The high-definition television specification allows for several different resolutions, but only one of them has foolproof compatibility between the HTPC and the high-definition display. Before you try to connect a transcoder for the first time, you should set the HTPC to display 640×480 at 60 Hz. This is not an interlaced video mode, so this will only work with display devices that are capable of showing a progressive-scan picture. In other words, this mode will not work with a standard NTSC television.

NOTE *Some standard NTSC televisions have component inputs, but they can accept only an NTSC signal. The display device must be an HDTV-compatible device in order to work with a VGA-to-component transcoder. It is possible to output an NTSC signal through a transcoder (the HTPC must be set to display 640×480 interlaced video), but most video card drivers do not allow interlaced video modes at this resolution.*

It is easiest to have a PC monitor hooked up to the HTPC when you are first configuring it for use with the transcoder. When the video mode is set to 640×480 at 60 Hz, you can disconnect the monitor and connect the transcoder. Technically, it is always best to power down equipment before you make any connection, so you should shut down the HTPC before switching to the transcoder. You use a VGA extender cable to connect the output of the video card to the VGA input of the transcoder, as shown in Figure 8-6.

Figure 8-6. The VGA cable connects to one end of the transcoder.

The next tricky part is connecting the three-part component cable from the output of the transcoder to the input of the television. One of the cables carries a black-and-white version of the video signal, and the other two cables carry color information. The three connectors on the transcoder and on the television may be labeled as Y-Pb-Pr, or they may be color-coded green-blue-red or yellow-blue-red. The difficulty comes when one device is labeled and the other is color-coded. The Y label corresponds to the green connector, the Pb to the blue connector, and the Pr to the red one.

If the connectors are not properly arranged, the resulting video image will have inaccurate color, or no picture at all. If the color is wrong, the display will show red and yellow shades where blue and green should be. In this case, the Pb and Pr cables are reversed, and you can switch them to correct the problem. If there is no picture, then the Y cable is connected improperly.

CAUTION *It is also possible to make the connections one at a time while the television is turned on, though this is not really a good idea unless you have already confirmed that the video signal being output by the HTPC is compatible with the display device.*

When you have completed the connections, you should plug the transcoder into the power supply, and you should plug the power supply into the wall outlet. You should turn on the television and set it to display the picture from the component inputs used by the transcoder. Finally, you can turn on and boot up the HTPC.

The boot screen and introduction screens of the Windows OS should display normally on the television, as they are not high-resolution video modes. When the OS is finished booting and the desktop is displayed, the HTPC will kick over into the 480p mode that it was set to before connecting the transcoder. This mode should display clearly on the HTPC, but if the picture is distorted or completely obscured, or if the television picture goes black or the set makes any unusual noises, you should turn it off immediately.

In the case of problems displaying the 480p mode, you may reconnect the computer monitor to confirm that the proper video mode is being output. If the video mode is correct, then the display device is not compatible with a progressive-scan video picture and should probably be used with an S-video cable instead of a transcoder.

Some transcoder models feature small dials to control the picture center on the display screen. Since the video utilities for HTPC systems also allow this control, it is not necessary to adjust this dial frequently. You can set it to a fairly centered location and then fine-tune it with the HTPC software. Each video mode will probably require adjusting, so preserving the adjustments in software is much more convenient than playing with the transcoder dial after every mode switch.

Installing or Upgrading a Sound Card

The process of installing or upgrading a sound card in an HTPC is very similar to the process of upgrading an AGP video card. Sound cards that fit inside the HTPC case are made for the PCI bus slots on the motherboard. PCI slots look different from the AGP slot, and since there are usually five or more of them, it is not necessary to remove any existing adapter cards from the system unless an existing sound card is no longer desired. Like the video hardware, some motherboards feature built-in sound hardware that can be disabled. Since the Windows OSs can support more than one sound card, the built-in sound hardware can also be left active in addition to the new sound card.

The PCI bus does not have the compatibility issues that the AGP bus slot has, so the only real requirement you need to check before starting is that there is at least one free PCI slot in the system. You can determine this by looking at the back of the case where the metal mounting brackets cover the adapter slot openings. Most computer systems manufactured in the past few years have motherboards with four or five PCI slots, so if there are fewer than four mounting brackets with connectors on them, then there is probably at least one free PCI slot. This method is a general appraisal, however, as there are many types of PCI adapter cards that do not have connectors on the mounting bracket. Ultimately, the only way to know for sure is to open the case and look inside.

 **TIP** *The steps for installing a PCI sound card are generally the same as those for installing any PCI adapter card.*

Installing the Hardware

Gather the required tools, turn off the HTPC, and disconnect the HTPC from the power cable. When you have the sound card ready for installation, follow these steps:

1. Check that the HTPC is powered off and disconnected from the power cable. We can't emphasize this enough!

2. Lay the HTPC flat so that the case cover is on top, as shown in Figure 8-7. It is easier to work inside the computer if the open part is facing up.

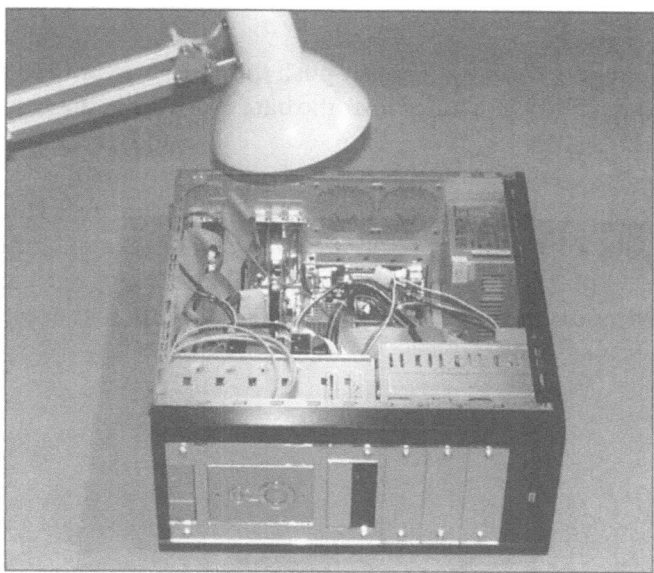

Figure 8-7. Lay the case flat to allow easy access and good lighting.

3. Remove the screws holding the case cover onto the case. There are many styles of cases and coverings, so you may have to check all around it to find the correct screws to remove. Generally, the screws are at the back (see Figure 8-8), the bottom, or sometimes the bottom sides of the case.

Figure 8-8. Look for the case-cover screws at the back of the case.

4. After you remove the screws, gently push the case cover until it slides off. Ground yourself by touching either the bare steel within the case or a static strip.

5. Find an empty PCI slot on the motherboard (see Figure 8-9). The best slot for a sound card is at the very bottom of the case or the slot farthest from the power supply. The sound card is susceptible to interference from other devices in the system, so try to isolate it as far from the rest of the components as practical.

Figure 8-9. A PCI adapter card slot

6. Remove the existing sound card or disable the built-in audio hardware
    of the motherboard if desired. Removing a PCI card is usually a simple
    process that consists of unscrewing the mounting screw from the bracket
    at the back of the case. The PCI slots can be quite sticky, so you may need
    to use moderate force to remove the old sound card.

7. Disable the built-in audio hardware either by setting a jumper on the
    motherboard or by changing an option in the system BIOS configuration.
    Either way, consult the motherboard or system documentation to find out
    how. If the setting is in the BIOS, you can adjust it when you boot the
    system.

8. Insert the new sound card into the PCI slot. The connector may be a very
    tight fit, and sometimes the mounting bracket that faces the back of the
    case is tricky to push in. The best method is to keep the card as straight as
    possible, line the bracket up with the empty gap on the back of the case,
    and push it straight into the slot, as shown in Figure 8-10.

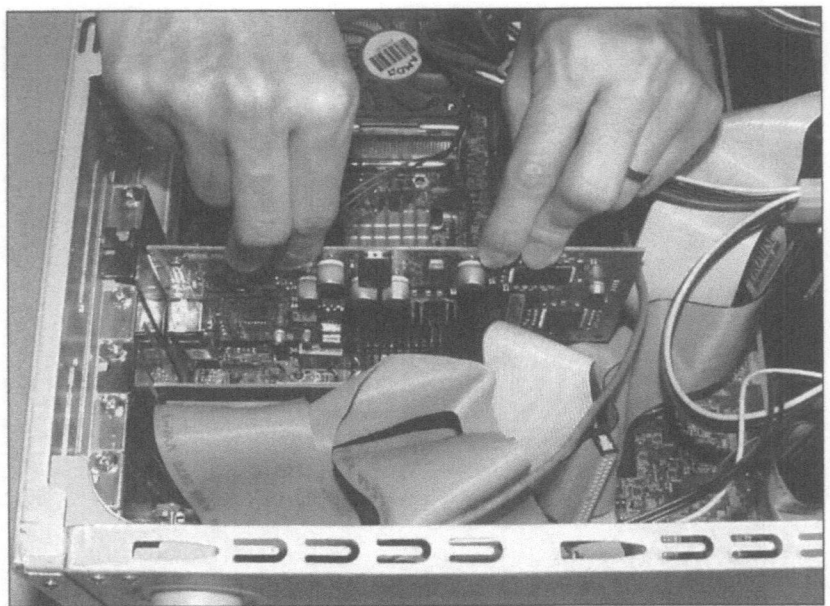

Figure 8-10. To insert the PCI video card, start with the card in this position and push straight down.

9. The PCI adapter card should sit in the slot with the metal connectors all pushed inside the slot, and the mounting bracket at the back of the case should be seated flush against the case.

10. The sound card requires an analog connection to the CD or DVD drive in the system in order to play audio CDs in the conventional manner. The CD or DVD drive actually decodes the digital audio and sends it via a three- or four-wire connector to the sound card. The cable (see Figure 8-11) is usually included with the CD or DVD drive, and the connector fits into a jack on the sound card and into a similar jack on the back of the drive. The audio information on a CD may also be sent digitally to the CPU and decoded for the output via the sound card. For this process, the analog audio connection is not required, but it is usually a good idea to connect it anyway.

11. Screw in the sound card, replace the case cover, and put the screws back in to hold the cover in place, or leave the case open until you confirm that the new hardware is successfully installed.

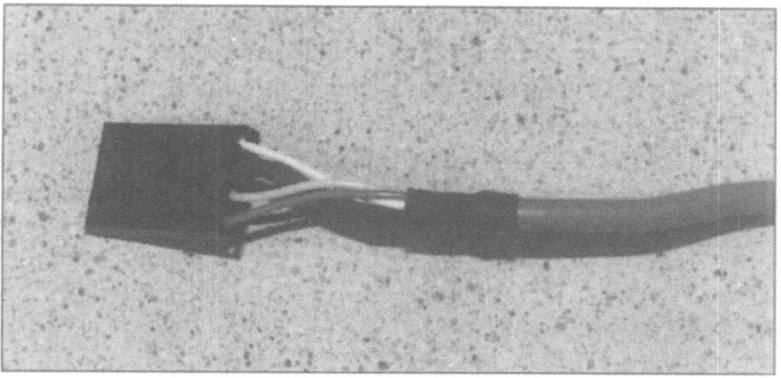

Figure 8-11. The analog audio connector cable that connects the CD or DVD drive to the sound card

12. Finally, plug the power cable back into the HTPC and reconnect it to the monitor, the sound system, and whatever else it connects to. The machine is now ready for you to turn on and configure with the new hardware.

Configuring the Hardware

If the new sound card has a hardware failure, the HTPC will beep or display an error message, and it will likely not boot into the OS depending on the severity of the problem. If the card is working properly, then there will be no indication of it until the OS starts up and detects new hardware. Insert the CD-ROM included with the sound card when you are prompted by Windows to load the new audio drivers. In many cases, Windows will already have a driver that works properly with the audio hardware, but installing the manufacturer's software and utilities is a good idea in order to gain access to all the features of the new hardware. As with video card configuration, the extra features are usually installed from the CD-ROM disc after the basic drivers have loaded.

Some common problems that cause a PCI adapter card to not work are easy to fix. It is possible that the card is not seated properly in the slot, if it was not pushed down all the way or if one end is seated higher than the other. You can fix this by opening the case up and reseating the card. Some motherboards may flex when the card pushes into the PCI slot, preventing it from seating properly. Some audio cards may fit very tightly into the PCI slot and require firm pressure to install. You can overcome this by gently and slowly rocking the card along the direction of the slot as you apply pressure to seat it.

Connecting a Sound Card to an Audio Receiver

There isn't much to explain about connecting a sound card output to an audio receiver. Anyone who has hooked up a VCR to a stereo system or connected a television to an audio receiver already has the basic skills required. There are a few points you should consider when you make this connection, though, and you have a few different methods from which to choose.

Analog Sound Connections

The left and right stereo connectors that are common on the back of audio receivers are not common on the back of computer sound cards, so making an analog connection requires a special adapter cable. This cable has a ministereo plug at one end and branches to the left and right RCA-type connectors at the other end. The ministereo plug goes into the sound card analog output, and the RCA-type connectors go into the audio receiver inputs. This is perhaps the simplest step in setting up an HTPC.

The length and quality of the analog audio cable used to make this connection may have some impact on the quality of sound that you hear. A long cable that passes near high voltages in other electronic components or power cables can suffer noticeable signal degradation. Some HTPC hobbyists recommend using shielded cables to make any analog audio connection. If the sound quality is not as good as it should be, a set of shielded cables is worth considering as a possible solution, though rerouting the analog audio cable is a cheaper first step.

Most sound cards have more than one ministereo jack on the rear mounting bracket, and the small labels can be difficult to read (see Figure 8-12). A flashlight is very handy for finding the correct audio output jack. Quite a few of the newest sound cards feature multiple audio output jacks for multichannel sound, so depending on the audio mode configured for the HTPC, the output jacks on the back may have different functions at different times. There is usually one jack that is always the left and right stereo channels, though. This is the best output jack to use for an analog connection to the audio receiver.

Audio receivers vary from simple models with one auxiliary sound input to complicated systems with audio inputs for every type of sound device known to mankind. Most midlevel and higher audio receivers are also video receivers that are capable of receiving several video sources and switching the audio and video synchronously for output. We have yet to see an audio receiver with an input labeled "HTPC," however, so you must choose one of the other inputs as the HTPC connection. Usually, an "AUX" or a "Line" (which may be numbered) is fine. The only input that you can't use is one meant for phonograph turntables (vinyl record players), which is usually labeled "PHONO."

Figure 8-12. The microscopic line-out label on the back of a sound card

Some audio receivers have multichannel analog inputs for surround sound audio channels. These receivers are usually marked "5.1 surround sound ready" or "AC-3 ready," which means they are ready for the analog sound channels after they have been decoded from digital audio by a DVD player or other external decoder. Audio receivers like this were popular when DVD players first appeared, but the cost of digital decoder chips is now so low that most manufacturers just build them into their audio receivers. However, these types of audio receivers are pretty handy for use with an HTPC that can output multichannel surround sound through analog connectors. Standard RCA-type connectors are used to make the connection from the HTPC to the audio receiver. The sound card usually includes the adapter cables that split the miniplug signal from each jack into the surround sound channels with RCA-type connectors.

Digital Sound Connections

You can connect the digital audio output (S/PDIF) from an HTPC to an audio receiver with either a coaxial digital audio cable or a fiber-optic cable (also known as a Toslink cable). Most low and midrange sound cards that have a digital audio output use a miniplug to output the digital signal. This requires a special adapter cable to convert the miniplug on the sound card to the more common RCA-type connector on the back of the digital audio receiver. There are some sound cards with out-of-specification voltage levels on the digital audio output jack—Chapter 5 provides more information about this problem.

The optical digital audio connection is just as easy to make as the coaxial connection. For sound cards with an optical output, a fiber-optic cable with the proper digital audio plugs at both ends can fit into the output jack on the HTPC and into the input on the back of the audio receiver. Fiber-optic cables are immune to electrical interference, but they are generally more expensive than coaxial cables, and they are more susceptible to breaking if bent or twisted.

Installing USB Devices

The USB was developed to make it easy to connect peripheral devices to a computer. Before the USB was available, most peripherals connected through the printer port (also known as a *parallel port* or *LPT port*) or through one of the serial ports (also known as *COM ports*). The ports could move information at different speeds and in different formats, so they had to be manually configured for each type of device. These ports were also based on old standards that have become inadequately slow for modern types of peripheral hardware. Most devices could not share a port with other devices, so each required its own dedicated resources from the computer.

The alternative is the USB, which solves the problems of the older ports. USB devices are self-configuring, which means that they report their settings to the computer when they are attached. The USB bus is also capable of much higher speeds than the old parallel ports or serial ports, and the bus supports up to 127 devices concurrently (though in practice, this many devices could hardly be attached, and if they were attached, they would overload the data capacity of the bus). USB is a great upgrade for the PC industry because it has made using peripherals so easy that many new categories of devices have been developed just because of the bus.

The USB connector on the back of the HTPC is a wide, flat socket. Most computer systems equipped with USB ports have two or four sockets. Typical USB devices that are likely to be used with an HTPC are IR or RF receivers, keyboards, mice, and Webcams. These peripherals usually have a USB cable that is permanently attached, though many USB devices have a detachable cable. The socket on the USB device for a detachable cable does not look the same as the socket on the back of the computer case. The peripheral socket is smaller and square. Since the USB bus carries power for small devices, the USB cable has two differently shaped plugs to prevent it from being used to link two separate computers, which would cause a short-circuit and probably damage the systems.

Most manufacturers include explicit instructions for installing their USB peripherals on a computer system. Generally, you must install the required software before you plug in the USB device for the first time. The PC will detect the device and attempt to load a driver for it, and if no driver can be found, the device will be disabled. In some cases, you must delete the faulty configuration information from the OS before you can correctly install the device. It is much simpler to load the drivers first so that the proper configuration information is used. It is important to read and follow the installation instructions for USB devices, no matter how simple and straightforward they seem.

Operating Systems

Firstly, we must admit up front that we prefer to use Microsoft Windows as the OS for our HTPC computers. There are so many compelling reasons to argue for and against Microsoft Windows, or for and against any other OS, that discussing OSs is becoming as difficult as discussing religion. We wish to avoid a debate on the topic, so we will only say that you can use any OS as the basis for an HTPC, and there are some better and some worse than Microsoft Windows. However, this is our project and we are going to cover just Windows in this section, which deals with computer OSs.

Two basic flavors of Windows are suitable for use in an HTPC. The original Windows was barely more than a shell that ran on top of the antiquated disk operating system (DOS) that has been around since the first day that PCs were developed. This original Windows has evolved through many generations, but it was not a real OS until Windows 95 was introduced. Since then, there have been upgrades and improvements to it, and the result is the most recent incarnation of Windows Me. This version has support for a wide variety of hardware and can run well on slower PCs with small amounts of RAM. The prior version, Windows 98, is perhaps more suitable for PCs that were manufactured before the year 2000. Though Windows Me is a favorite of many PC hobbyists, it is based on an archaic DOS architecture and is the last in the line of Windows 95–based OSs.

The other line of Windows OSs started with the introduction of Windows NT 3.1 (no, there was no version 1.0, 2.0, or 3.0—the first version was numbered to match the existing version of DOS-based Windows so that it would not seem like it was behind the times). Windows NT 4.0 followed quickly afterward, then Windows 2000, and now Windows XP. Though the names do not seem to be related, the OS line is a continuation of the Windows NT architecture. This OS is not a DOS-based system—it is a completely new technology ("NT") for the modern age of PCs and it has some great advantages in stability and security over the older Windows 95 line of OSs.

In this book we could not possibly explain every difference between versions of Windows OSs, nor could we provide installation instructions for them. There are many good support Web sites and books available for those who feel adventurous enough to configure their own HTPC OS. Some components of the various Windows versions have a bearing on their capability to serve in an HTPC, though, and a brief explanation of these features is helpful when selecting a flavor of Windows or any other OS.

Windows 98 and Windows Me

From the old DOS-based line of Windows OSs, there are really only two that are worth considering for use with an HTPC. Windows 95 was introduced before the days of USB, IEEE 1394, AGP video ports, and other key PC technologies. It does not support most of them, and it supports others relatively poorly through third-party software or patches. Windows 95 is no longer supported by Microsoft as of November 2001. New versions of Windows software are not certified to run on Windows 95, and some key software technologies such as DirectX updates are no longer available for it. Without a current version of DirectX, most media applications such as DVD players or audio encoders cannot run. This means that Windows 98 and Windows Me are the only real choices for this line of OSs.

Windows 98 has some advantages over other versions of the Windows OS for an HTPC. It uses the least amount of hard disk drive space, which makes it suitable for simple HTPC systems that are meant for playing media from a network file server, or from a DVD or CD drive. Windows 98 requires the least amount of RAM and has the lowest required minimum processor power. For minimalist HTPC systems, this is an efficient and functional OS. Windows 98 supports USB, AGP video, and most other recent PC technologies. Perhaps the most enticing thing about this version of Windows is that due to its immense popularity, virtually all PC hardware is supplied with drivers for Windows 98.

Windows Me was introduced in September 2000 as the last in the line of the Windows 95 family of OSs. It uses a little more disk space and requires a little more processing power than Windows 98. However, it has some nice advantages over previous versions, such as the video editing application Microsoft Movie Maker and its built-in support for more audio and video media formats.

Windows 98 and Windows Me have some limitations for use in an HTPC. They both use a file system called the file allocation table (FAT) or a variation of it called FAT32. The largest file size that can exist on a FAT32 file system is 4GB. This may seem huge, but HTPCs that record video can easily exceed this limit with only a few minutes of uncompressed NTSC-quality video. Some video capture applications will automatically split captured video into two 4GB files, but this is somewhat inconvenient when you are switching from one application to another, or when you are compressing, editing, copying, or otherwise manipulating the files.

Windows 98 and Windows Me also have some arcane limitations on the number of applications that can be opened and the number of windows that can be displayed. These limits are rarely an issue, but the overall poor memory management that results from the outdated DOS architecture is a crippling limitation of this Windows 95 family of OSs.

Windows 2000 and Windows XP

In the Windows NT line of OSs, there are just two choices for use in an HTPC system. The old Windows NT had poor support for most media hardware and software. The only version of the indispensable DirectX that works under Windows NT is version 3.0, which is included but not upgradeable. Windows NT 4.0 is being retired by Microsoft, and it will no longer be supported after June 30, 2003. Windows NT was never really marketed by Microsoft as a home OS—it was meant for offices and workstations where computer games, television tuner cards, and camcorders dare not go. The real selection in this line of Windows OSs is between Windows 2000 and Windows XP.

The Windows NT family is the real darling OS of Microsoft. Originally developed to provide a secure and robust OS for professional uses, it is now marketed to home users and office workers alike. To suit these different environments (and budgets) Microsoft provides different subversions of Windows 2000 and Windows XP. Windows 2000 is available in Professional, Server, Advanced Server, and Data Center editions. Windows XP comes in Home and Professional editions. There are small differences in features and capabilities of these subversions, but in general the least expensive package is suitable for building an HTPC.

Windows 2000 Professional and Windows XP Home editions are more expensive than Windows 98 or Windows Me, but they have some important advantages. Windows 2000 and Windows XP are built on the NT architecture, which features improved memory management, stability, security, and support for larger hard disk drive volumes. Since an HTPC is a system that will be running constantly and needs to perform flawlessly, selecting a more robust OS is important. For an HTPC that sits in a home theater room that may be accessed by many members of a household, the security of the Windows NT family of OSs is much better than Windows 98 or Windows Me.

Windows 2000 Professional is a popular choice among PC power-users. It features the solid reliability of Windows NT with the great flexibility of the most recent version of DirectX. It is the first Windows NT family member that can play computer games and DVD movies, and that supports USB and other key PC technologies. Its popularity means that it has wide support for most PC hardware, and it can do anything that Windows 98 or Windows Me can do, although it requires a faster CPU and more memory.

Windows XP is an update to Windows 2000 that adds a slick new user interface and more support for media files of all types. It has all the elements of Windows 2000, plus some new ones. The Microsoft Movie Maker application from Windows Me is included, along with the latest version of the Windows Media Player. A great new feature is the ability to switch users while leaving applications open. An HTPC is a great machine to share for e-mail, Web surfing, and other Internet applications, and the ability to leave one person's applications running while another logs in is a great convenience. The added protection of strong security between accounts, even when multiple users are logged in, is a bonus that makes a Windows XP machine suitable for sharing between parents and children or roommates.

Networking an HTPC

The personal computer continues to grow in popularity with the home user, and as it does hardware gets cheaper, better, and more practical for home use. Networking used to be a topic for corporate and professional environments, but in the last few years a lot of equipment has been marketed to home users and the number of households with some type of computer network is rising. The HTPC is a great addition to any home network, as it can act as a file server for media files, a client to play media files from another server, or even as a participant in a multi-player gaming environment. This section gives a quick overview of the required hardware and software for connecting an HTPC to a computer network.

Network Hardware

To connect an HTPC to an existing computer network (known as a local area network, or LAN) the hardware requirements are quite simple. The HTPC needs to have a network adapter card or a network adapter built into the motherboard, and a network cable to connect it to the rest of the LAN. A few different types of LAN hardware are available, so the adapter card must be compatible with the network in use. The most common networking hardware for home users is called *Ethernet*, and it is usually carried on unshielded twisted-pair wiring that looks like it has oversized phone plugs at each end. The HTPC requires an Ethernet adapter card to connect to an Ethernet network.

Cabling

The cabling used by Ethernet networks is categorized by the amount of information it can carry. The slowest twisted-pair cabling for Ethernet is rated at 10 Mbps capacity and is usually marked as category 3 or category 4 (cat-3 or cat-4). Faster networking is available with cat-5 cable, which supports up to 100 Mbps data transfer rate. More exotic cat-5E and fiber-optic cable is available, but the costs start to get prohibitive above 100 Mbps for both cabling and the other hardware required. Generally, cat-5 cable for a 100 Mbps LAN is sufficient for home use. Since 10 Mbps or 100 Mbps networking will run fine over cat-5 cable, this is the best choice.

Ethernet Cards

Ethernet adapter cards for home use are available at most computer stores, and since Ethernet over unshielded twisted-pair cabling is so common, it is almost impossible to buy the wrong network card. The only choice to be made is whether to get a 10 Mbps or 100 Mbps speed adapter. Fortunately, the cost of a 10/100 Mbps adapter that is compatible with both LAN speeds is relatively low, so this is usually the best alternative.

If the LAN does not exist already, then there is one extra (and relatively expensive) item to acquire in order to set up the network. Each client computer on the network needs its own LAN adapter card and network cable, but the cables must all connect together somehow. This connection is made with a hub or switch, which is a small device with four or more jacks for the network cables from each PC. The hub or switch must be compatible with the speed of the network cards attached—a 10 Mbps hub or switch will work with 10 Mbps LAN adapter cards, but not with 100 Mbps adapter cards. This is why 10/100 Mbps adapter cards are so practical. You can use them with a 10 Mbps hub until you replace it with a faster 100 Mbps hub. Hubs or switches come in different shapes, sizes, and capacities, and with different features, so some consideration of desired network performance versus cost is helpful to select the best device for a home LAN.

Cross-Over

If you have a small network of only two computers, you can use a cross-over cable instead of a hub to link the machines directly to each other. A cross-over cable looks like a normal Ethernet cable, but the wires are crossed at one end to allow two computers to communicate directly instead of through a hub. You can find cross-over cables at most major computer stores, or you can have them custom made at a local PC shop. A cross-over cable has the advantage of being somewhat cheaper, as a hub is not required, but it is extremely limited in expandability. Without a hub, a PC needs a LAN adapter card and a cross-over cable for each computer to which a connection is desired.

Wireless

Wireless networking is also becoming very popular, especially at home where network cabling does not already exist inside the walls. Wireless networks require a wireless LAN adapter card for each client PC and a wireless hub to connect more than one computer to the network. Wireless networking is easy to install and very convenient for mobile PCs or for any PC that gets moved around from time to time.

The disadvantages of wireless networking are rather critical, however. Wireless networks are much slower than conventional cabled connections. A typical 11 Mbps wireless network is about nine times slower than a 100 Mbps LAN, which is too slow for playing video at a decent quality over the network. An HTPC with a wireless network connection may be sufficient for Web surfing or playing MP3 music from another computer, but it is not capable of playing video files across the wireless connection. The speed of wireless networks also drops off with distance and interference. If the HTPC is not close enough to the wireless hub to get the full performance, the network connection may be even slower than 11 Mbps. A 10 Mbps conventional network connection suffers from the same low bandwidth problems as a wireless connection, but it can reach much further distances and does not experience as much signal degradation or interference.

To connect the computers on a LAN to the Internet, only one connection is required, as all of the PCs can share a single access. This can be through a dial-up modem, a broadband connection such as a cable modem or DSL modem, or any other Internet connection method. The PC that hosts the connection needs to have special software installed to share it out with the rest of the clients on the LAN. An alternative to this arrangement is to use a hub with a built-in Internet router. The hub is connected to the dial-up or broadband modem and the computers connected to the hub can all access the Internet through it. Routers are more expensive than plain hubs, but they are very convenient and often provide great security, as there is no PC connected directly to the Internet.

Network Software

The Windows OS provides the software necessary to connect the computers on a LAN to each other and to the Internet. A software driver for the LAN adapter card is required, but many adapter cards are automatically recognized by Windows. Computer networking is a huge subject, and a complex one, but we will simplify it by explaining that there are two software components that make it work: the networking utilities and the applications that use the networking utilities.

Networking utilities are the protocols that the PC uses to communicate on the LAN. The most common protocol in current use is the *transmission control protocol/Internet protocol* (TCP/IP, sometimes referred to as just IP). This is the "language" of the Internet, so it is used worldwide and it has been adapted for use on small LANs in order to make them compatible with the Internet. When Windows detects a LAN adapter card, it automatically installs the TCP/IP protocol and configures it with default settings that work for most situations.

The default TCP/IP settings may not be appropriate for a small home LAN, however. The TCP/IP protocol depends on each computer on the network having a unique address to identify it. This address is composed of four numbers, each in the range of 0 to 255. The IP address of a computer can be set automatically if the LAN is configured with a special service called *dynamic host control protocol* (DHCP). One (and only one) machine on the LAN is set up as the DHCP server, and it gives all of the other PCs an IP address. Unfortunately, most people setting up a LAN at home for the first time will not have the ability to create a DHCP server, and none of the PCs on the LAN will get IP addresses, so they will not be able to connect to anything on the network.

TIP *An IP address looks like this example: 127.0.0.1. This is actually a special address that points to the local machine—trying to connect to this address will cause a PC to connect to itself.*

Instead of using the default Windows TCP/IP settings, it will be necessary to configure each PC with an IP address manually. Remember that the TCP/IP protocol is used worldwide for every computer on the Internet and that each computer must have its own address. Any IP address selected randomly for use on a home LAN is likely to be used already somewhere else on the Internet. If the home LAN is not connected to the Internet, this doesn't really matter, but if it is, there can be conflicts and big problems with the LAN, and some potential security issues. For this reason, the TCP/IP protocol specification reserves a few certain ranges of addresses for use on private networks. Addresses in these ranges are not used by any computer anywhere on the Internet, so they will not conflict with the PCs in a private network.

For this reason, when you set the IP address of LAN clients manually, it is strongly recommended that you use addresses in the range from 192.168.0.1 to 192.168.255.254. Each computer connected to the LAN must have a unique address, and they do not have to be numbered contiguously or in order. When you set the IP address, the client PC must also have a *subnet mask* specified. This mask lets the computer know the range of other addresses to which it may connect. Typically, the subnet mask is set to 255.255.255.0, which means that the computer can see all the other addresses where the first three numbers match. In other words, a computer with an IP address of 192.168.0.1 can see all the addresses in the range 192.168.0.1 to 192.168.0.254.

After you have determined and set the address of the HTPC, you have some other numbers to configure, depending on the way you have configured Internet access. The PC on the LAN that hosts the Internet connection becomes the gateway to the Internet for the other LAN clients. Each client must be configured with the IP address of the gateway in order to find the route to the Internet. Sometimes it is also necessary to configure the address of the domain name server (DNS) and the secondary DNS. One important step is to confirm that the NetBIOS protocol is piggybacked onto the TCP/IP protocol. There is usually a setting somewhere in the Windows Networking configuration utility in the Control Panel that allows the user to turn this on, though in recent versions of Windows it is on by default. Without this setting, the HTPC will connect to the Internet, but it will not be able to see the other computers on the LAN.

NOTE *NetBIOS was the default networking protocol for Microsoft Windows PCs—that is, until the rising popularity of the Internet made TCP/IP the preferred protocol for most users.*

You can avoid much of the complexity of configuring an IP network with a home router. This device, mentioned previously as a feature of some hubs, is also available as a stand-alone unit without the hub features. The home router acts as a DHPC server, so that the default Windows TCP/IP configuration works correctly, and there is no manual intervention required. For most home users, the cost of a router is worth the savings in time and frustration when setting up a LAN.

After the networking utilities are set up, the software that uses the utilities to communicate on the network is comparatively easy to install. Windows comes with a feature called Network Neighborhood that allows the HTPC user to browse through the shared files and printers on the other computers attached to the LAN. To share a folder so that other computers can see it, you use the Sharing tab in the Folder Properties window. Options on this tab control the shared status and shared security of the folder.

NOTE *It is easy to share files across the network, either by copying them to the local machine or accessing them directly on the remote machine. It is not, however, possible to share applications this way. An application must be installed on each PC that will use it—it cannot be shared by simply accessing the folder from another PC.*

Connecting to the Internet is as easy as starting a Web browser or e-mail application. Since the PC is always connected to the LAN, the Internet application will simply access the LAN for an Internet connection. If the HTPC has previously been used with a dial-up connection, it may be necessary to change the settings in the Internet Control Panel utility to tell the machine to access the Internet through the LAN.

Network Security

Recently, there has been a lot of discussion about computer security, and you should not connect an HTPC to a LAN without first considering the potential for security problems. A LAN that is not connected to the Internet is relatively secure, as the only way that settings can be changed, new software added, or files accessed is through one of the other PCs on the LAN. When you connect the HTPC to the Internet, the number of computers that can potentially access the HTPC is suddenly vastly increased, and you must take precautions to prevent problems.

The easiest way to implement strong security for a home LAN that is connected to the Internet is to use a home router for Internet access. These devices are configured to be very secure by default, and since they are meant for home users who may not have the expertise of corporate and professional network technicians, they are made to be simple to use and configure. Generally, any unauthorized attempt to access the LAN behind a router is stopped at the router and no PC on the LAN is ever in danger. The PCs on the LAN still have full access to the Internet and behave as if no router existed at all.

If a router is not practical, then some other sort of protective barrier is recommended. Computer professionals call this barrier a *firewall*. One of the best firewalls available is Zone Alarm. This is a free utility for Windows PCs that monitors all incoming and outgoing network traffic and lets the user control what is allowed and what is blocked. Zone Alarm can be run on the PC that is a gateway to the Internet for the other machines on the LAN, or it can be run on every PC, including the HTPC. Generally, protecting the gateway PC is sufficient to ensure security from hackers.

Hackers are not the only problem with PC security, though. Viruses and Trojan applications can infect an HTPC when they arrive hidden in software downloaded from the Internet. Antivirus software has become almost mandatory for any Internet-connected computer, and keeping the antivirus software up-to-date is just as important as putting it on the HTPC in the first place. This protective software can affect the performance of an HTPC, so many users opt to keep it disabled and only run it at regular intervals. This is a balance between security and performance that must be determined for each HTPC system. Machines that are used to run a lot of downloaded software should be scanned more frequently.

The HTPC Project Hardware

For this book, we are assembling two HTPC machines. The first is a high-end machine with a fast processor and a striped disk volume across two physical hard disk drives. The second is a low-end machine with an older processor and less expensive components. Comparing these two machines reveals a lot about the hardware requirements of the HTPC hobby, as even the low-end system is quite capable of stunning DVD playback, which has become the benchmark of HTPC performance.

HTPC System 1

The CPU in this machine is an AMD Athlon XP 2100+. This machine is often used for video capture, editing, and rendering, so high performance is required for more than just playing DVD movies. Rendering video is the process of taking raw digital video information and compressing it with a codec such as MPEG-2 into a smaller file size that saves space without losing too much quality. This process takes a lot of processing power, so a faster CPU means faster rendering and more work can be done.

There is 512MB of 333 MHz DDR SDRAM in this HTPC system, which is way more than is necessary for media playback, but for video editing this is just barely a comfortable amount. This machine is also used for computer games occasionally, and this amount of RAM is quite suitable for this purpose, too.

A major hardware advantage that this system has over other fast PCs is the use of two hard disk drives in a RAID 0 striped volume. There are two 7200 rpm 40GB hard disks that provide almost twice the performance of a single 80GB drive with the same capacity. An ATA RAID controller adapter card is used to control the drives so that the HTPC can boot from the striped volume. Volume striping improves performance for video capturing, editing, and rendering, and it also improves performance for digital VCR functions such as recording television shows. Having two drives increases the noise and heat generated, but this machine will be enclosed in a sound barrier, so this is not expected to be an issue.

This system has four USB 1.1 ports and two USB 2.0 ports, which is important because we expect to use a USB Webcam and RF receiver in two ports, which leaves enough free ports for future upgrades. This HTPC lives on a LAN, so a 10/100 Mbps LAN adapter card allows us to connect at 100 Mbps to our 100 Mbps hub and Internet router. Since there is another PC with a CD-R drive on the LAN, the HTPC does not need a CD burner, but it does have a DVD drive for playing movies.

The high-end HTPC system is enclosed in a black tower case with brushed aluminum faceplates, as shown in Figure 8-13. We decided that this HTPC did not require a snazzy home theater case since it would be mostly hidden behind the sound barrier, but the black case was chosen to match the color of the television and the other components. The black case necessitated a DVD drive and floppy diskette drive with black facing, which cost a little more, but makes the system look well coordinated.

Figure 8-13. HTPC System 1's case

This system has Windows XP Home edition installed. We decided to upgrade to this newest version of Windows to get the stability of the Windows NT family of OSs and the latest multimedia features available. Windows XP has great support for multiple users, and since this system will sit in a home theater room, more than one family member will use it for e-mail and Web surfing.

Finally, though this system has access to the Internet, the access is through a home router, so we do not require any firewall software on the HTPC. An antivirus package is used to scan it regularly, but we disable the antivirus software during HTPC use in order to reduce performance impact while editing video or watching DVD movies.

HTPC System 2

The CPU in our second HTPC system is an Intel Pentium III running at 450 MHz. This is an older PC that is being recycled into a great HTPC system. It will be used to play DVD movies, audio CDs, and MP3 music, along with prerendered home movies and video clips downloaded from the Internet. The Pentium III 450 is well suited to these tasks.

This machine has 256MB of RAM and a single 10GB hard disk drive, which is used to hold current media only. Since this machine is connected to a LAN, it does not need to store a lot of media files locally—it can access them on other PCs. The single hard disk drive reduces the amount of noise and heat from this system, so it can live comfortably in the home theater room without any special noise barrier.

This system has a DVD drive for movie playback. Though the processor is comfortably powerful enough to play back DVD video, the video card features MPEG-2 hardware decoding that will assist the CPU and make the system more than adequate for smooth DVD performance.

Since this is our low-cost HTPC, we chose to keep the computer case that came with this hardware (see Figure 8-14). One advantage of using an older system to build an HTPC is that the case can be painted, decorated, and customized to suit our home theater room without concern for its expense.

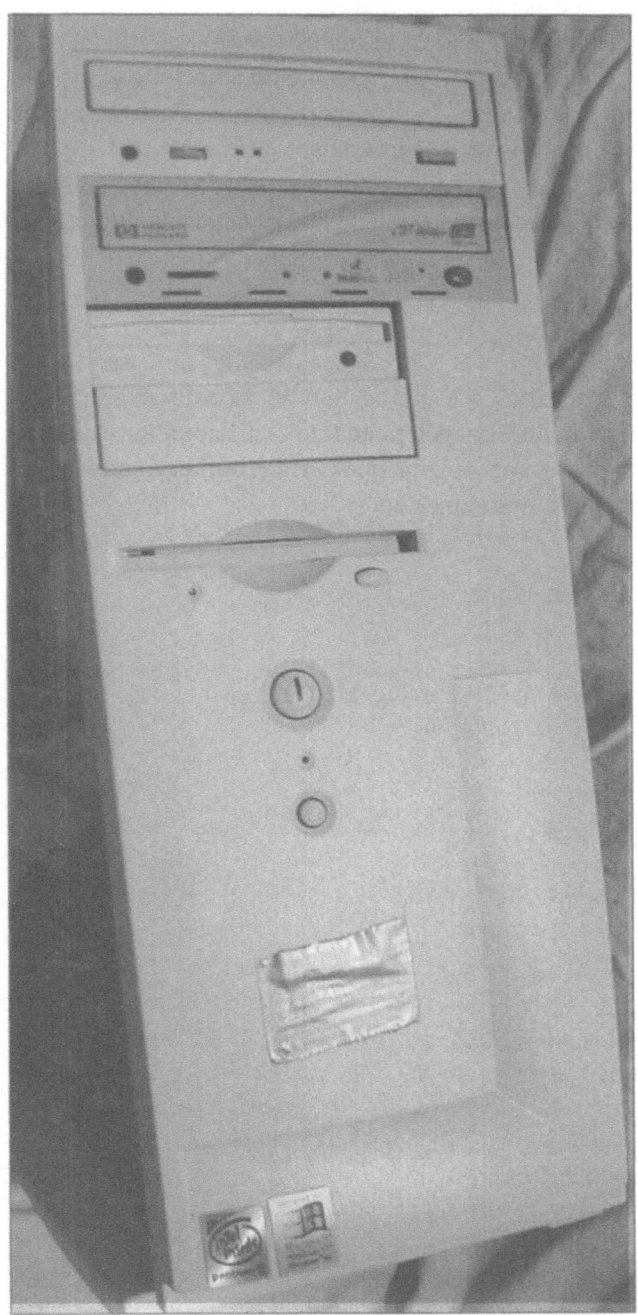

Figure 8-14. HTPC System 2's case

We have selected Windows 98 as the OS for this HTPC. This version of Windows permits the best performance on PCs in this age group and still allows for networking and Internet access. We are trying to build this machine to be as simple and efficient as possible, and Windows 98 requires the least disk space and offers great compatibility for the hardware in this system.

With our systems selected and assembled, we are now ready to move into the next phase of building our HTPC machines: installing and configuring the software.

Summary

In this chapter we looked at how to pull everything together in order to end up with a functioning HTPC that can do what you need it to. In Chapter 9 we discuss the software you'll need for every aspect of your HTPC, from bundled software to the freeware utilities that can make your box sing.

Software and Other Solutions

CHAPTER 9

The Software

ASSEMBLING THE COMPONENTS of an HTPC is a real art form. Selecting the perfect video card or finding the best sound card for the system can make it perform better, improve the picture quality, or boost the realism of the audio track, all of which can make the home theater more like a movie theater. HTPC hobbyists spend a lot of time deciding what hardware to use, finding out where it is available, and configuring it for optimum performance. However, after all this work, the project is still only half done.

Finding and configuring the correct software is just as important as using the most appropriate hardware for the HTPC system. Using the right application can add to the performance and convenience of the machine, so selecting software is more than just picking the right DVD player, it is also knowing about and selecting the software that will add functionality and features to the home theater. Without the right software, all that fancy HTPC hardware has nothing to do.

In our discussion of HTPC operating systems (OSs), we chose to limit ourselves to Microsoft Windows and its variants. Likewise, in our discussion of software applications, we only review Windows software. This is not meant as an endorsement of the Windows OS in general or specifically for use with HTPC systems. Other OSs, such as Linux, are capable of serving in a multimedia PC and can be the software basis of a great HTPC. We are limiting this chapter to Windows software because it is the OS with which we are most familiar and with which we have found most readers are comfortable.

Some of the software that any HTPC will need is available for free or is included with the Microsoft Windows OS, but most of the specialized software is available for purchase. Since the HTPC hobby is still relatively new, many of these software packages are not available at retail stores or computer shops, so they must be downloaded or ordered from online retailers. This is actually a great way to buy software, as shopping online provides two advantages over a brick-and-mortar store. First, there is often a "shareware" version of the software available for you to try out before you decide to buy the full version. Second, you can usually download the full version immediately after you purchase it, which means it is available to use almost instantly.

It is important to state that the authors of HTPC software (and all software) work very hard to provide a product that benefits users, so supporting them by purchasing their software is the best way to show gratitude and encourage new features and fixes in the applications. You should use shareware only to evaluate a product, and you should use full versions of software only if you are the licensed purchaser. This keeps the industry going, drives innovation, and holds prices down. After you add up the cost of hardware, buying a few HTPC applications is a minor expense that is well worth making your HTPC the best it can be.

Utilities

The first category of software that is required for an HTPC is the collection of applications that allow the user to configure the machine. These applications do not play audio or video files; rather, they control the way these files are played. PC users often have a set of favorite utilities for tweaking and configuring the PC for optimal disk performance, game performance, or memory settings. These PC utilities are helpful for configuring an HTPC, but this section describes some special utility applications that are meant for use with an HTPC.

Video Utilities

HTPC video utilities are mostly concerned with providing the best possible picture quality for high-definition television displays. The high cost of HDTV video sources and the lack of available material have left a gaping void that the HTPC is quickly filling. The HTPC can up-convert conventional NTSC video to HDTV resolutions, and it can display over-the-air HDTV signals with a high-definition television tuner card, which makes it the most cost-effective HDTV video source. Outputting HDTV-quality video is not completely straightforward, however, and up-converting NTSC video to HDTV is even more complicated. A few software utilities are available for the HTPC that make these tasks easier.

For those HTPC hobbyists who do not have an HDTV display, or who are not concerned with using the HTPC with a high-definition television set, these video utilities are not necessary. A video card with a composite or S-video output will already provide the best quality picture for a standard NTSC television. It is possible to use these utilities to configure color and brightness, or to make other adjustments, but the resolution and quality of the picture is determined by the NTSC hardware in the video card.

PowerStrip

The world of computers and the world of televisions have only recently come together, and many compatibility problems are still lingering. PowerStrip is a software utility that can set the display mode on a computer to any resolution and timing that you want, which makes it easy to synchronize the video output signal from an HTPC to the HDTV display.

Custom Resolutions

NTSC television sets are always showing the same video mode, no matter how good or bad the quality of the video signal. The vertical resolution of an NTSC television picture is set at 525 lines, though only about 480 lines are actually visible. The refresh rate, or display frequency, of NTSC video is about 30 complete frames per second. Like all analog video formats, the actual resolution of the picture may be lower than the standard indicates. VHS is usually considered to be about 240 lines, and S-VHS (S-video) is about 400 lines. This is only a relative measurement, however, as the NTSC television does not change video modes—it is always outputting 525 lines. The horizontal resolution depends on the signal bandwidth available and is not usually specified. An experienced eye can quickly tell the difference between various types of NTSC video sources.

Computer displays can switch among many different resolutions, which are specified as the number of vertical lines by the number of horizontal lines. The resolution of a computer display is selected by the user, and the number of display resolutions available depends on the quality of the hardware in use. The display mode can be set to a number of different refresh rates and may be interlaced or progressively scanned, though most computer hardware and software is configured for progressive-scan images. Since the computer display mode is known, there is no guessing about the actual quality of the picture.

Mixing analog television and digital computer video formats is not a straightforward process. A computer can output standard NTSC video only with special hardware. Many video cards include an S-video or composite output connector (for more information, see Chapter 4) that converts the computer display to an NTSC-compatible signal. This usually limits the display modes of the computer, since higher resolution modes do not convert easily to the lower NTSC mode.

....

Enter HDTV

The introduction of high-definition television in North America has moved the television industry a little closer to the display modes of the computer industry. The resolution of HDTV modes is measured the same way as computer display modes, and HDTV displays can switch between different resolutions. Though not all HDTV-compatible displays support all of the official Advanced Television Systems Committee (ATSC) resolutions for digital television, most sets support at least one or two modes above 480p.

Mixing digital television and digital computer video formats is not much easier than analog television, though. You'll still need special hardware to convert the VGA output signal from a computer to the component input of an HDTV. In Chapter 4 we described a VGA-to-component transcoder, which is necessary to connect the HTPC to an HDTV display. Making this connection is not the end of the challenge, though. The display modes for high-definition television are not the modes that computer users will find familiar, since HDTV is meant for a different picture aspect ratio than most computer displays use. Even after you've connected the transcoder, you still must configure the HTPC to send a compatible video signal to the HDTV.

The 480p mode is the lowest common denominator mode for HDTV displays and computer video output. For the computer, this is a 640×480 at 60 Hz display mode. Actually, most HDTV displays are compatible with NTSC, which would be equivalent to 640×480 at 60 Hz interlace display mode, but few modern computer display adapters can be set to interlaced timing for such a low resolution. Other HDTV modes, such as 960×540 at 60 Hz not interlaced, 1280×720 at 60 Hz not interlaced, or 1920×1080 at 30 Hz interlaced, are not typical options supported by the display drivers for PC video cards. To use an HTPC at anything above 480p, you will need a special display utility that can set the PC video card to match the HDTV modes.

Fortunately, there is just such a utility available: PowerStrip. The basic purpose of PowerStrip is to set the video display to an HDTV-compatible mode. PowerStrip allows you to override the display properties of the video card and set any custom resolution and refresh timing that you desire. This makes it possible to use the HTPC to output the high-definition television modes such as 540p, 720p, and 1080i for compatible television sets, giving the HTPC excellent picture quality for DVD movies, television, or any other type of video. For more information about setting up PowerStrip with custom resolutions and timings for HDTV displays, see Chapter 10.

....

More Than Custom Resolutions

PowerStrip does a lot more than just allow you to set custom resolutions and timings. It provides controls for color adjustment, hardware performance, video processor and memory clock speed, and multiple monitor support for any version of the Windows OS. You can program this software to automatically adjust the display mode when specific applications start up, and it lets you adjust brightness and color settings with the keyboard or remote control while applications are running. It is a great do-it-all video utility.

You can download PowerStrip as shareware from the PowerStrip Web site at `http://www.entechtaiwan.com/ps.htm`, and you can purchase it online by running the application and selecting Online Services from the menu. You should install and evaluate this software as shareware on your HTPC before you buy it, as it is only useful if it supports the video card chipset in your machine. In fact, it is worth downloading this software to check the list of supported video cards before you choose video hardware just to make sure that the new video card will work with PowerStrip. At the time of this writing, registering PowerStrip costs $29.95 for use on one to four HTPCs.

YXY Aspect Ratio Controller

The introduction of HDTV to North America is an exciting development for home theater enthusiasts, but it has been slow and confusing, and it has not solved all of the problems that the analog NTSC format has. One major problem is that the new digital video formats are meant for use with display devices with a different picture aspect ratio than the current NTSC televisions. This means that the HDTV picture is wider than the NTSC picture, so it does not fit into an older television set display area.

To fit the whole HDTV picture onto an NTSC television, the sides of the picture must be clipped off or the size must be reduced to leave a blank area at the top and bottom of the screen. Similarly, for a conventional NTSC program on a new HDTV set, the top and bottom must be clipped or the picture size must be reduced to leave the sides blank. To add to the confusion, many HDTV-compatible sets are available with the NTSC aspect ratio of 4:3, but they display the HDTV picture either by shrinking the picture and leaving blank space or by stretching and distorting the picture. Since NTSC and HDTV video will coexist for many years into the future, this compromise will continue to confuse and frustrate users.

If you add the wide variation of compatible resolutions and timings for HDTV sets provided by PowerStrip to the equation, suddenly it becomes obvious that there are many different picture aspect ratios available for use with the HTPC. This can be a problem if the preferred display mode for a given video card and HDTV causes picture distortion. Some software DVD players try to fix the distortion, but they do not have enough settings to correct for unusual display modes.

To overcome this problem, Jim Ferguson has written the freeware application YXY Aspect Ratio Controller. This utility enables you to set the aspect ratio of the video overlay used by most video cards to display DVD, television, or other video. You can set the exact dimensions and location of the overlay picture, even if the dimensions are bigger than the screen size. This allows you to correct any distortion caused by an unusual aspect ratio, such as a 4:3-shaped HDTV displaying a 16:9 video mode.

You can download YXY Aspect Ratio Controller from the Keohi HDTV Web site at http://www.keohi.com/keohihdtv/htpc/yxy/yxy.html. This Web site also features great information about HDTV topics, including a general overview of HTPCs.

DScaler

Standard NTSC video can look worse on an HDTV than on an NTSC television set. NTSC video is interlaced, which means that each complete frame is made from two sets of alternating lines of the picture. If the video features a lot of movement, then some objects on the screen will move in the time it takes to draw the second set of lines. On a standard interlaced display such as an NTSC television, this is not a problem, since only half of the lines are displayed at one time. However, a progressively scanned display device such as an HDTV combines the two sets of lines into one frame that is displayed all at once. The problem is that the two sets of lines are not meant to be shown at the same time, and any fast moving object will appear with jagged edges, as shown in Figure 9-1.

Figure 9-1. An interlaced video frame shown on a progressive-scan display device

In order to properly show interlaced video on a progressive-scan display device, the two sets of lines (called *fields*) in the video frame must be combined into one single set, and some technique must be used to compensate for any movement of objects between the fields. This is a huge field of development for the television and broadcast industries, as deinterlacing becomes more and more necessary for converting NTSC video for display on HDTV sets.

Software for the Windows OS called DScaler can deinterlace video in real time for HTPC output to a progressive-scan display. You can configure DScaler to use one of several algorithms to create progressive video output, or you can let it automatically pick the best method for the current program. DScaler is freeware and is available for download from the http://deinterlace.sourceforge.net Web site.

DScaler will work for outputting video with any AGP video card, but it is written to work with the video inputs of television tuners and video capture cards that are based on the Conexant bt848/878/879 processor. Deinterlacing video while capturing it to the HTPC is a preferable way to capture it, but if the machine does not have a television tuner card or a video capture device based on the Conexant chip, then deinterlacing can be done when outputting the video. The Conexant chip is fairly common in television tuner cards, and you can find more information about supported capture devices on the DScaler Web site.

The output quality that DScaler can achieve is excellent, and it rivals expensive deinterlacing machines. Since DScaler works on video in real time, the performance of the CPU in the HTPC has some bearing on the video quality. A fast CPU can perform more complex deinterlacing algorithms and still keep up with the video, but a slower CPU will have to settle for less impressive deinterlacing, or else settle for video with stuttering, jumping, and other signs of dropped frames.

DScaler is an excellent software tool for use with an HTPC that is connected to a progressive-scan display, such as an HDTV set. With standard television programs, VHS tapes, or other NTSC video sources, the interlaced video will look bad when objects on the screen are moving. Many HDTV sets have a built-in line-doubler that deinterlaces video when an NTSC source is connected, but since the HTPC is not an NTSC source, the HDTV's line-doubler is not active. The HTPC must deinterlace the video for output to the HDTV set. DScaler can deinterlace the video, and on fast HTPC machines, it can do it as well or better than the HDTV's own line-doubler.

Remote Control Software Utilities

In Chapter 7 we looked at using an infrared (IR) or a radio frequency (RF) remote control to control the HTPC. The major benefits of these remote controls are the small size, the ease of use and, for RF units, the ability to control the machine from a different room or from behind a soundproof barrier. Most devices that are meant for remotely controlling a computer already come with software that can do some basic tasks, such as start or stop a DVD movie, or control the sound volume. Some remotes even have mouse pointer controls that let the user point and click like a conventional PC mouse. Using a handheld remote control device with an HTPC is a great way to make it more convenient to use in the home theater.

The bundled software is not the only choice for use with a remote control device, however. In some cases, the bundled application cannot be customized or used with every application on the HTPC. Usually, the bundled software is unable to control OS features such as shutting down the system, switching screen resolutions, or logging on and off with different account information. In some cases, there is no software bundled with a remote control device—this is often the case with USB IR receivers, which are meant to work with any typical consumer electronics IR remote control. Fortunately, there are alternative remote control applications available.

Girder

A few PC software applications are available that are meant for use with a remote control device. Some of them are available as shareware, such as PC Remote Control (http://www.pcremotecontrol.com), which you can evaluate for a short period before you decide to purchase it. These products are meant for use with multimedia PCs in business environments where laptops are used to give presentations or product demonstrations at tradeshows, but they are perfectly suited for use with HTPC systems. Several excellent products are available, but the one that seems to be most popular is Girder.

Girder is a freeware application that claims to be "The Ultimate Windows Automation Tool," which is a pretty excellent description of what it does. Girder can invoke any OS event or application command when it receives input from almost any kind of device: a remote computer, an attached device, a keyboard or mouse, or a remote control. Since Girder can interact with the computer at a very low level, it works with all the applications installed on an HTPC.

Girder allows mouse movements and buttons to be mapped to any remote control device. This is a great convenience for HTPC hobbyists who prefer to use a single universal remote in their home theater. One disadvantage of using such a remote control with an HTPC is that each desired action must be preconfigured to a button on the remote control. By using Girder to map the mouse movements and buttons, the remote control becomes a mouse that can navigate through application screens, scroll through Web sites, or configure setup dialog windows without any specific preprogramming. This saves the hassle of scrambling for a keyboard and mouse when surfing the Internet or fine-tuning the HTPC configuration.

The architecture of the Girder software allows it to be compatible with a wide variety of hardware. Girder can see every event that occurs in the system, and it can trigger almost any event in the OS or application software. A remote control requires a receiver to communicate to the HTPC. The receiver is usually a small IR or RF device that connects to a USB or serial port, and it needs to have a driver installed to the OS. Girder can receive the transmitted commands from the driver no matter what type of receiver hardware is used. Girder also supports plug-ins, which are extensions to Girder that allow any user to make a file that will configure Girder to work automatically with a particular remote control (the ATI Remote Wonder, for example). The plug-in simply preconfigures Girder for the set of commands that a remote control is capable of sending. These commands are then easier to map to the actions that should be performed in the HTPC when a button on the remote control is pressed.

Like most powerful software, Girder is complicated to learn and set up. The online help is pretty good at explaining the procedure for a simple command configuration, but most users need to perform the configuration a few times before they begin to understand what is happening. Lots of plug-ins are available for popular HTPC tasks, and these are worth checking out to extend the functionality of Girder and of the HTPC. Girder can also send IR, X10, and serial signals depending on the hardware used.

Since Girder is software that lets the user control the HTPC, it is best to install it after the other applications in the HTPC have been set up and configured. Girder does not have to be the last utility or application added to the system, but it adds more value to a machine that has most of the multimedia software already installed. You can find the Girder software and more information at http://www.girder.nl/ as well as a sampling of plug-ins and a discussion forum.

Bundled Remote Control Utilities

The ATI Remote Wonder that comes with the ATI All-In-Wonder Radeon 7500 includes a software utility that connects the buttons on the remote control to features in the ATI software. The ATI All-In-Wonder products are very HTPC-friendly and suitable for almost all multimedia functions of the system. The products include a software DVD player, computer audio and video file players, television tuning and recording software, and a file organizer. The Remote Wonder software has preprogrammed buttons for all of these applications, which saves a lot of configuration and fine-tuning for the HTPC hobbyist.

Most people will find that the ATI Remote Wonder and its bundled software is a sufficient package for the HTPC when used with the ATI All-In-Wonder video cards. The software allows a minimal amount of custom configuration, so it is not strictly limited to the ATI Multimedia Center software. The Remote Wonder can be used to kick off other applications, and it features a mouse pointer and mouse buttons, so it does not lack any versatility. Though the Remote Wonder software is not as powerful as Girder, the complete integration of the hardware and software with the ATI All-In-Wonder package is a very quick and simple way to get an HTPC up and running with a remote control.

Applications

The other category of software that is required for an HTPC is the multimedia player. This type of application performs the main function of the system: playing a DVD movie, playing CD audio, or flipping through digital pictures. In fact, the development of these applications is what compelled the evolution of the HTPC in the first place. Since this software is so critical, users are very critical of this software. Finding a great DVD movie player is an all-consuming pastime of hardcore HTPC hobbyists, who delight in comparing the same movie scene played by different software DVD players until they find the best player. It is not the intention of this chapter to deprive any hobbyist of this great experience, but there are some basic features of multimedia software that are worth reviewing before jumping into the subtle differences between players.

Media Players

The least functionality an HTPC can have is to play video, play audio, or display digital picture files. Even an old original Intel Pentium-based system has a place in the home theater if it can play MP3 or CD audio files. Most people who want to build an HTPC will want it to play DVD movies, downloaded video files, and music. All of these functions are core to the purpose of an HTPC and are accomplished by installing the proper media players in the system.

DVD Players

The software DVD player installed on an HTPC is usually the most important application in the system, and finding the right one is therefore an important task. Several software DVD players are available for the Windows OS, and although they are mostly the same, each one has a slightly different set of features, compatibility, or picture quality. Since there are no free software DVD players, it is not cost effective for many HTPC hobbyists to own more than one or two such applications. It is vital to identify which features take priority and which player is most compatible with the hardware in the HTPC.

The Decoder

The most important part of a software DVD player is the MPEG-2 decoder. Anyone selling software that decodes MPEG video must pay licensing fees, so there is no MPEG-2 decoding software included with the Windows OS. Each software DVD player must include its own software code to play video, and the differences between the code for each player have a sometimes noticeable effect on the picture quality of DVD movies. Also, anyone selling software that decrypts the protected information on a DVD must pay licensing fees, which is why there is no DVD playback capability in the Windows OS without the installation of a DVD player application.

Hardware Support

The other important part of a software DVD player is the support for the video hardware installed in the HTPC. Many software DVD players are compatible with popular video cards, but the compatibility depends on other factors such as the video card drivers, the OS, and the other software in the machine. If the player is not compatible, all of the MPEG-2 decoding is done through software, which can be slower and cause stuttering or dropped frames. If the player is compatible, then the hardware in the card can perform some of the decoding, which means the HTPC system is less stressed, and the performance of the DVD playback is smoother and looks better. Most software DVD players list the compatible video cards on their Web sites, but issues with video card drivers or software versions usually require a lot of reading and research at popular HTPC discussion areas such as AVS Forum (http://www.avsforum.com).

Most software DVD players use a Windows feature called DirectShow. This is an application program interface (API) that is part of the DirectX package, and it allows applications to access hardware resources in the system directly for the best performance. The software DVD player installs a DirectShow filter for DVD video and audio. The filter is essentially the software code for playing MPEG-2 video, audio, or any other type of media stored in a computer file. When a DVD movie is playing, it is actually DirectShow that is doing the work.

 **TIP** *DirectShow DVD filters allow software DVD players to play the video and audio streams from a DVD disc. This means that with the right filter, any player that uses the DirectShow architecture can decode the Dolby Digital audio track to an S/PDIF output on a sound card or the system motherboard.*

Since DirectShow filters are available to other applications in the system, installing a DVD movie player allows other applications to play MPEG-2 video and DVD movies. Recent versions of the Windows Media Player can play DVD movies after a DVD player is added to the HTPC, and some freeware DVD players actually depend on other players to install filters for them. This can be a great advantage to HTPC hobbyists who want to experiment with freely available MPEG and DVD players, since only one player needs to be purchased to install the DirectShow filters for other players to decode and display MPEG-2 video files.

NOTE *Many video codecs for the Windows OS are implemented as DirectShow filters. The MPEG-4–based DivX codec (not to be confused with the short-lived Divx proprietary video disc format) is also a filter, which means that installing it will allow other applications to play DivX-encoded files. With the right filters, Windows Media Player can be the only video playback application you ever use!*

PowerDVD

Among the commercial software DVD players available for the Windows OS, one popular player is PowerDVD from CyberLink (http://www.gocyberlink.com). PowerDVD has all the features of a consumer electronics hardware DVD player such as repeat play, zooming, color adjustments, full navigation controls, and onscreen display, and it is compatible with VCD and SVCD discs. It also has the special features that only software DVD players can offer, such as the ability to place bookmarks anywhere in a movie and then jump back to them later. Software DVD players can also capture still images from a DVD program and save them as picture files to the computer's hard disk drive, and many DVD movies include special selections to connect to Web sites that are only available on a PC. PowerDVD also does Dolby Digital and DTS surround sound decoding for output to an external digital audio receiver. Many people find that PowerDVD has an unbeatable set of features for its price.

TheaterTek DVD

The software DVD player that is generally regarded as the best player available is TheaterTek DVD (http://www.theatertek.com). The DirectShow filters installed by the TheaterTek player are from Ravisent, and they are absolutely unmatched in picture quality, even by expensive progressive-scan hardware DVD players. The TheaterTek DVD player includes all the features of a software DVD player, such as bookmarks and screen captures, but it also has a Movie Start feature that lets the user set the starting point of a movie so that it skips the opening advertisements and menus and just begins playing the program. This is a fantastic quality of the player that is well appreciated by those who watch the same movies frequently, and especially by those of us who are forced to watch the same movies *very* frequently by kids who are fascinated with their favorite Disney title!

The picture quality of the various DirectShow filters is difficult to compare without spending a lot of time watching the same scenes with different filters. Most movie watchers will not notice the differences between one filter and another, and even enthusiasts with a keen eye for detail usually have to watch carefully and repeatedly to determine the nature of a deficiency. Selecting a software DVD player with a flexible configuration for setting the aspect ratio of the movie picture often makes a big difference in perceived picture quality for HTPC systems that output video to an HDTV set. With multiple available resolutions, the software DVD player will need to be configured to display an undistorted video picture on a variety of screen sizes to find the best setting for horizontal and vertical resolution. The TheaterTek DVD player has great aspect ratio controls for just this reason.

DVDLobby Pro

A new type of software is becoming popular for watching DVD movies on HTPC systems: DVDLobby Pro (http://www.webpromotion.com/cinemar/dvdlobby.html). This new type of software lets the user copy a collection of DVD movies to the hard disk drive of a computer and then watch the movies by playing them back from the hard disk or from a DVD jukebox drive. This is essentially just a way to catalogue and store DVD movies the same way that it is possible to store audio CDs, but the DVDLobby Pro software also lets the user configure title screens, Web links, and intro clips for each movie. This is a great way to turn an HTPC into the ultimate home theater movie machine, with movies available instantly and lots of extra information from Web links and movie trailers or featurettes. Of course, storing just one DVD movie takes an average of 4GB of hard disk space, so having a collection of movies requires either a huge hard disk capacity in the HTPC or a fast network connection to a file server. It is a way of experiencing movies that is unavailable from any device except an HTPC.

Bundled Software

Software DVD players are sometimes bundled with video cards, and these players can be great features that make a video card more attractive for use in an HTPC. The ATI All-In-Wonder Radeon series of cards includes the ATI DVD player, which includes DirectShow filters from Ravisent, the same company that provides the filters for the TheaterTek DVD player. Though the Ravisent filters for the ATI player are not the exact same ones for the TheaterTek player, they do provide very good picture quality.

The ASUS GeForce4 MX card includes a software DVD player called ASUSDVD2000, which is a version of the PowerDVD player. The advantage to using a bundled software DVD player such as those that the ATI and ASUS video cards include is that the hardware acceleration is guaranteed to be compatible. The disadvantage is that if the video card is changed, the player will no longer work. These players install DirectShow filters that are made specifically for the video hardware with which they are bundled, and they will not function with other video cards, so the HTPC system can lose the critical ability to play DVD movies if hardware is changed. For this reason, a commercially available software DVD player is a recommended addition to every HTPC that plays DVD movies.

Zoom Player

One more software DVD player that is worth your consideration is the Zoom Player. This media player can use the DirectShow filters installed by other software DVD players to play DVD movies. The unique thing about the Zoom Player is that it allows you to manually select the filters that are used, giving you a great level of control over the playback of the video and audio from a DVD disc. The Zoom Player includes no filters of its own, so it will not work without another software DVD player installed, but it does support all media types via DirectShow filters, so you can use it to view almost any video file.

CD Audio and MP3 Players

Many audio formats are available to the HTPC hobbyist. Fortunately, they can all coexist on the same system, so there is no need to forego any of them. CD audio is the original digital audio format that almost every computer system can play, but in the last few years the most popular format has become the MP3 audio file.

The MP3 audio file format has become a target for critics who claim that PCs make it easy for people to make and distribute illegal copies of protected music and audio programs. Though this is a problem for artists, copyright holders, and the computer industry, it is not the MP3 format that is to blame for this illegal activity. Music files can be compressed by a number of techniques into a number of different file types, so eliminating the MP3 format will not correct the problem. Also, the laws of most countries allow people to make copies or backups of copyrighted material for personal use, so eliminating the MP3 format will reduce legitimate personal liberties. Finally, the MP3 file format can be used to digitize and compress noncopyrighted material such as personal recordings and works in the public domain. The criminal stigma attached to MP3 files is irrational and undeserved.

In the early days of the MP3 format, it was necessary to install special software onto a computer in order to play an MP3 file. Several popular players emerged, including WinAmp, WinMP3, FreeAmp, and MUSICMATCH. These players quickly added features that catalogued and converted audio CD tracks to MP3 and other formats. The result is a variety of full-featured media players that play every type of audio and video file, and can search the local hard disk drive or the Internet for free or fee-based music. Some of these applications, such as RealPlayer and MUSICMATCH, remain popular with devoted fans.

All of the recent versions of the Windows OS include the Windows Media Player, which can play MP3 and WMA compressed audio files. This means that the Windows-based HTPC no longer needs extra software to play MP3 files. The latest version of the Windows Media Player even supports playlists and has a number of bemusing and entertaining screen patterns that pulse and flicker to the music (WinAmp has this as well). The HTPC is easily transformed into a home jukebox without adding any extra software.

There are a few reasons to keep using the alternative audio players, though. Some formats, such as Real (http://www.real.com), are not supported by the Windows Media Player because of licensing issues, so the RealOne Player software is required to playback files of this type. Some users prefer the simple interface and small program size of WinAmp, which has many great features, including playlists, a sound equalizer, visual screen patterns that change with the music, and lots of free plug-ins to download. Others have grown accustomed to the music-cataloguing feature of the MUSICMATCH software and also appreciate its ability to create MP3 files from audio CD tracks. Music playback on the HTPC is a personal choice for the right combination of features, functionality, and convenience.

Digital Picture Viewers

The newest version of Windows, Windows XP, includes a feature that lets you jump from image to image in a collection of digital pictures. Previously, you had to open, view, and then close each file before you could view the next. This inconvenience was overcome by a number of image viewers that featured a "slide show" mode. The slide show could progress through every image in a folder automatically on a timer or manually with a key press or mouse click. Such applications as Irfan-Viewer (freeware) and ACDSee became popular because they make viewing a collection of images very convenient. ACDSee even has a great file navigation interface that makes finding pictures on a crowded hard disk drive easier by showing thumbnails and previews. Though these applications remain popular, the Windows OS is slowly but surely integrating all of these features with each new release. The HTPC based on the latest version of Windows XP already has features that make it perfect for family slide shows and vacation picture viewings.

Media Recorders

An HTPC can do more than just play media files. You can give almost any HTPC system the power to record media files by installing the right software. Most hobbyists will want systems that can play DVD movies and various audio files, but some more ambitious HTPC owners want systems that can record video and audio files. Recorded media can also be edited, processed, and archived, which makes the HTPC far more versatile than a simple VCR or an audiocassette recorder.

Recording Video

Capturing video to an HTPC is generally done for one of two purposes: to record programming that will be viewed later or to record video that will be edited, compressed, or otherwise manipulated. Recording video has been the province of the VCR for decades, and though recordable DVD is slowly becoming available, the price is still too high for most people to buy into it. Editing video is also expensive—proper video editing equipment is costly and not easy to use. In the past few years, however, the personal computer has changed the business of video recording and editing. The HTPC can do both of these tasks with the right software installed, and for a reasonable cost.

Digital Video Recorders

Though the term is rather generic, the digital video recorder (DVR) is a very specific type of device. It is a video recorder that stores video on a hard disk drive. The DVR can simply play back programs like a VCR, allowing you to fast forward or reverse, or jump ahead to skip segments (such as commercials). Unlike a VCR, the DVR can jump instantly to any point in the program because the information is stored on quickly accessible hard disk drives. The DVR can also record a program while you are watching it. When you pause the playback, the DVR keeps recording, and you can then continue to watch the program from where you paused it while the machine keeps recording. This allows for rewinding and replaying programs while you are recording them. The DVR has added many new convenient features for the viewer, and DVR software for recording programming from television broadcasts is now so full-featured and powerful that the HTPC can compete with the TiVo and other digital recorders.

WinDVR is an application from InterVideo (http://www.intervideo.com) that turns a PC into a DVR. This software is a great addition to an HTPC with a television tuner or video input adapter. The WinDVR software has all the features of a full DVR system, including recording, timers, pausing and replaying live programs, and high-quality video. By integrating DVR features into an HTPC, the cost of the DVR is reduced, since adding WinDVR to an HTPC is much cheaper than buying a TiVo or UltimateTV device.

The greatest disadvantage of a TiVo or UltimateTV device is that no matter how much hard disk drive space is inside the box, once it is full, you must erase something to record more programming. You can play back the stored programs to a VCR to record them permanently (or as permanently as magnetic media will allow), but this requires a VCR and the time it takes to play a program to tape. A DVR-enabled HTPC with a CD-R drive installed can burn recorded programs to a blank CD-R to free up disk capacity. The CD-R is a more permanent storage media than a videotape, and blank CD-Rs are cheaper than VHS tapes. At typical VCD quality, a CD-R can hold about an hour of programming. Plus, with DVD-R prices steadily falling, this larger capacity storage medium will become even more appealing.

Most television tuner cards come with bundled software that can add some DVR features to an HTPC. The bundled software is usually able to record programming on a timer and lets the viewer fast forward or reverse the video and jump around to various points. Some of the bundled applications actually offer "live television" features, such as the ability to pause and restart programs while they are being recorded, or the ability to skip commercials by starting to view the program after it has started, and then jumping ahead over commercial breaks until the DVR catches up to where the program is actually playing. Though these bundled DVR applications may limit the video formats that can be captured and may not work with all types of video inputs in the system, they are usually sufficient for most casual HTPC users.

Video Editing Tools

The other use for capturing video into the HTPC is for editing it with any of the various digital editing applications. Editing video before the PC multimedia revolution required several pieces of expensive studio equipment to mix video streams and add transition and audio effects. All of this equipment has been replaced by video editing software, though with some trade-off in performance. Whereas the studio equipment could add special effects in real time, the video editing software usually requires all of the effects to be programmed, and then it takes a lot of time to render the effects and produce the final video file. Given the cost difference, almost every home-video maker chooses the PC method.

Video editing tools all work essentially the same way. Video is imported from a camcorder, VCR, or other video source to provide the raw material for the final video. A timeline is used to arrange video clips and the transitions between them.

Multiple audio tracks can be added to the timeline, along with text titles, digital pictures, slow motion or fast motion effects, or anything else that the video editing software allows. The completed timeline is then processed into a final video file. To simply convert home movies on a camcorder to digital video files, you can place the raw video on the timeline without any edits (usually the start and ending are cropped to remove unrelated scenes that may be before or after the desired segment) and then rendered into a format such as Video CD (VCD) or Digital Video (DV). These file formats are suitable for burning to a CD-R or writing back to a digital camcorder tape for storage.

Some software video editors, such as Adobe Premiere, are very full-featured. This application allows multiple video streams to be mixed into one stream, which provides for some excellent cross-fading transition effects and great background/ foreground combinations. Premiere also has multiple audio tracks on the time-line, which makes it easy to synchronize the background music or an audio commentary. The one feature that Premiere is lacking is the capability to create MPEG format video files in one step, which is a widely compatible format used by DVD players for DVD, VCD, and SVCD video discs.

Simpler (and less expensive) video editing applications are available that have just enough features to make casual movie makers happy. MGI VideoWave is a popular application because it is bundled with several video-capturing devices. Though it lacks the full-featured timeline that Premiere uses, its timeline does allow for some simpler transitions and video effects. It is possible to add multiple audio layers to the edited video, but it is difficult to carefully synchronize the audio. The great thing about VideoWave is that it can output the final video file in almost any format. This is helpful for those home movie makers who want to create high-quality versions of their movies for archiving and low-quality versions for e-mailing or for uploading to their Web sites. VideoWave could even be used to render the video produced by other applications, such as Premiere, into the preferred format.

A lot of video editing tools are available, and if you want to edit video on your HTPC, you should search the Internet and other sources of information for the one that suites your needs best. When you select video editing software, look for support for importing video from digital and analog sources, and at various reso-lutions. The features of the video timeline are important—if you will use the software to simply convert home movies to digital formats, then a simple timeline is sufficient, but if you will edit the video into entertaining and artistic clips, then a timeline that allows precise control over the video and audio elements is prefer-able. Finally, consider how you will use the final video file. If you plan to archive the video to VCD, SVCD, or DVD, then the video editing software you purchase must be able to create MPEG and MPEG-2 format files. If you are going to simply copy the video files to a CD-R or back to a digital tape, then these formats are not important.

Recording Audio

By far the largest audio recording activity on the PC currently is the conversion of audio CD tracks to MP3 or some other compressed digital audio format. As we mentioned earlier, this has gained the stigma of being a dishonest or illegal activity, but it is not illegal or dishonest as long as the audio files are not distributed or shared with others. Many people have vast collections of audio CDs that are inconvenient to search through, especially if the CDs are not cataloged or even sorted alphabetically. Storing music on an HTPC allows for an almost unimaginably immense collection of music that is searchable and playable instantly.

Those who like to listen to hours and hours of music are forced to switch discs every hour or so, and even a CD carousel cannot hold as much music as an HTPC and cannot switch between discs as fast as an HTPC can jump from song to song. Compressed digital audio formats such as MP3 have become so popular that portable players are widely available, and even car stereo systems feature MP3 playback from CD-R or hard disk drives. There is just no substitute for having thousands of songs instantly available at the touch of a button.

To convert the tracks on an audio CD to MP3 files, you'll need special software. When MP3s were first introduced on the PC, it was a difficult process to find software that could read the digital information from an audio CD and then find compressing software that could compress raw digital audio files to MP3 format. Fortunately, this is a much simpler process today. Many applications simply wait for an audio CD to be loaded into the computer, and then they read the tracks and write MP3 files out to the hard disk drive in one step. Thanks to the Gracenote online database (http://www.gracenote.com), you don't even have to supply the album or song names—the software just connects to the Gracenote Web site and looks up the audio CD to get the track information.

Quality

You can manually configure the quality of the MP3 files that are produced, and you'll often do this to suit your personal tastes after some experimentation. Since audio CD is a stereo format, MP3 files made from audio CD tracks should be stereo or joint stereo. *Joint stereo* compresses some of the redundant information from the left and right tracks into one track, though for some types of music this technique is not suitable. Most people find that a bit rate of 128 Kbps is sufficient for joint stereo tracks, and higher bit rates must be used for true stereo; half the bit rate is used for each side of a true stereo track, so a 128 Kbps file in true stereo has two 64 Kbps audio tracks, which is not generally sufficient. For true stereo, 192 Kbps is a good starting rate and you can increase this as necessary. For HTPC systems with lots of hard disk space set aside for MP3s, a setting of 256 Kbps is pretty much good enough for everything.

NOTE *Converting the raw digital audio tracks on an audio CD to compressed digital audio files such as MP3 is referred to as* ripping *by most hardcore enthusiasts. This term is a little misleading, as nothing is really ripped—it should be called "converting," "compressing," or "copying," though that might sound a lot less impressive.*

A popular application for converting audio CDs to MP3 files is MUSICMATCH Jukebox (http://www.musicmatch.com). MUSICMATCH Jukebox can read audio tracks from an audio CD and convert them to MP3 files on a hard disk drive. It also connects to the Gracenote database to get the album and track information, saving you the time and effort of retyping this info. You can configure and customize the software to save the MP3 tracks by artist, album, and file, or any combination of these attributes. MUSICMATCH Jukebox can then catalogue and play back all the MP3 files in the HTPC. Since the MP3 format is widely compatible with portable players, MUSICMATCH Jukebox is a great way to build a collection of audio CDs into a collection of MP3s for an HTPC and all the other MP3 devices out there.

Windows Media Audio Files

The MP3 format is not the only compressed digital audio format available for HTPC hobbyists. Microsoft offers the Windows Media Audio (WMA) file format as a close competitor to MP3. WMA is capable of compressing raw digital audio a little more than MP3 without losing quality, so it allows slightly more music to fit into the same amount of disk space. The Windows Media Player that comes with recent versions of the Windows OS has support for creating and playing WMA files, so no additional software is needed for the HTPC. The WMA file format is not as widely used and not as widely compatible with portable audio players as MP3, which makes the WMA files somewhat less useable, though an HTPC can play the WMA format just as easily as the MP3 format. Newer versions of Windows Media Player can also encrypt MP3 files as well, so they can only be played on that individual player.

Another popular format is the RealAudio format (http://www.real.com). You need the RealOne Player to create and play back this format. Though RealAudio is not widely compatible with portable devices and not tremendously popular for compressing audio CDs, it does have the advantage of supporting video and audio media types, and it allows for video and audio streaming from the Internet. Several Web sites provide programming for the RealOne Player, and an HTPC that is connected to the Internet is a great device for playing streaming media programs.

Finally, we'd like to make special mention of one more video and audio format available for the Windows OS. The QuickTime format from Apple Computer (http://www.apple.com) was originally developed for their Macintosh platform, but it has been adapted for the PC under the Windows OS. This format is popular because it is used to create particularly high-quality movie trailers, which are always popular with movie fans. The introduction of DVD movies has brought high-quality home theater to millions of people, and many of us wait anxiously for each new DVD release to hit the shelves. While you wait for a new movie release to appear at the video store, why not download the trailer and show it off in high-quality fashion to your friends and family? No HTPC should be without the QuickTime player to watch movie trailers.

The HTPC Project Hardware

For this book, we are installing software on two HTPC machines. The first is a fast, new machine that we want to use for much more than just watching DVD movies. We will use this machine to capture video from a camcorder and edit, render, and burn the results to CD-R discs. Since this machine will be connected to a digital audio receiver, we also want to play MP3 and audio CD music in the home theater room. This HTPC is connected to an HDTV set, so it will be used to up-convert NTSC video sources to a higher resolution and, of course, we also want great DVD movie playback.

The second machine is an older system that we want primarily to use for watching DVD movies and playing MP3 audio. This machine will be connected to a network, and with no need for a lot of hard disk drive capacity to store music or video, it will have a small disk drive and so a relatively limited amount of room to install software. Though this machine is a few years old, we expect to get great performance for movies and music.

HTPC System 1

The first software we want to install on this system is PowerStrip. Since we will use this HTPC to up-convert NTSC sources and display them on an HDTV, we need to be able to configure the video card to output the desired HDTV resolutions and to convert the interlaced source video to progressive-scan video for the display. This HDTV set has a built-in line-doubler, so the NTSC video sources could be connected directly to the set, but using the HTPC to up-convert the video lets us control the overscan and picture settings with the PowerStrip utility. It also has the advantage of allowing us to access the HTPC desktop features at any time, which lets us access e-mail, Internet chat, and Web browsing without switching the input selection on the display.

Since we assembled this system with the ATI All-In-Wonder Radeon 7500, which includes the ATI Remote Wonder, we're using the bundled ATI software to control the machine. If we find that this software is too limited for use with other applications, we'll try to configure Girder, but since this machine also has a wireless RF keyboard and mouse, Girder probably won't be necessary.

For DVD playback, the ATI video card comes with the ATI DVD Player, which is a pretty great quality player. This player supports the Dolby Digital audio track output to an S/PDIF connector, so we should get great video and audio performance from the ATI player. The ATI software also includes support for the television tuner in the video card and for other media file formats, so using the ATI bundle saves us a lot of money and work finding appropriate software to do DVR functions and video capturing.

To rip and store audio CDs, we are going to use the free MUSICMATCH Jukebox software. We can play back audio with MUSICMATCH Jukebox, though we also like to use the Windows Media Player because of the fascinating visualizations, along with WinAmp and one or two other freeware players. This is the great thing about an HTPC: We can try out different software, change our configuration, and experiment with settings as much as we want until we find the application that works best.

HTPC System 2

This system will connect to a television set through an S-video cable, so utilities such as PowerStrip and DScaler are not required. The television is actually a progressive-scan HDTV-compatible set, but it has a built-in line-doubler, so the NTSC video sent to it will be properly displayed. Eventually, this system could include a VGA-to-component transcoder, but we are trying to keep the cost down for now.

This machine features a GeForce4 MX video card, which has good MPEG-2 hardware acceleration features. We asked the TheaterTek people about the compatibility of this card with their excellent TheaterTek DVD Player, and they sent us a copy of the software to evaluate. We plan to try this software DVD player on this system through the S-video output and through the VGA-to-component transcoder borrowed from the other system.

To play music, rip audio CDs, and store compressed digital audio, we're going to use the Windows Media Player and its WMA format audio files. We're also going to use MUSICMATCH Jukebox to compress some test audio CDs to MP3 files. This should make an interesting comparison between the two formats, as it will allow us to compare audio quality and file sizes for the same discs. Ideally, we'll try to pick a preferred format to reduce the number of applications installed, but since the HTPC is a versatile machine, it easily supports a variety of file formats for audio and video, and we really don't have to pick one over another.

Installing software on our HTPC systems is easily the most complicated part of building the machine. Selecting the software is difficult because of a bewildering variety of file formats, software applications, and uses for the HTPC. Fortunately, we have decided which applications to use (for now, anyway). To find out how the systems perform when they have this software installed, see Chapter 11.

Summary

In this chapter, we examined how important software can be in creating a great HTPC. Software is at the heart of managing custom resolutions to get the best picture possible, playing MP3s, and setting up the ultimate remote control. In the next chapter, we'll look even closer at some of the software available for the HTPC—specifically, the utilities that allow you to tweak your system to perfection.

CHAPTER 10

The Power of PowerStrip

CONNECTING AN HTPC to a high-resolution display device such as a high-definition television (HDTV) brings out the best possible picture quality that the system can offer. To many home theater enthusiasts, this configuration is the reason for having an HTPC. Without an HTPC, the HDTV requires expensive equipment to get the same scaling, deinterlacing, and progressive-scan picture output. Though an HTPC is a very versatile machine with great practical application for use with a standard NTSC television, connecting it to an HDTV is the pinnacle of the home theater experience.

The HTPC is not a simple machine to mate with an HDTV-compatible display. The VGA output of a computer is not compatible with most television sets, so special hardware is required to convert it to the component input that HDTV sets accept. (For more information about the hardware connections, see Chapters 4 and 8.) Once the connections are made, special software is then required to make the output from the HTPC's video card compatible with HDTV formats. Software utilities such as PowerStrip, YXY Scaler, and DScaler are available for download and are mostly intuitive and easy to configure. PowerStrip, however, includes no manual and is notoriously cluttered with arcane settings that can confuse and intimidate new users. This chapter provides a basic guide for using PowerStrip.

PowerStrip

EnTech's PowerStrip utility (http://www.entechtaiwan.com/ps.htm) is one of the most popular and important software utilities for the HTPC industry. This software makes it possible to set a video card to display screen resolutions and timings that most Windows drivers do not support. PC users are familiar with common screen resolutions such as 640×480, 800×600, and 1024×768, but the HDTV specification does not use these PC settings. PC users are also used to setting the refresh rate as high as their monitor will allow, since most PC monitors can adjust to multiple frequencies, but HDTV devices typically run at only one frequency, 60 Hz, and cannot adjust to anything else. The one resolution and frequency timing that is shared by PCs and HDTVs is 640×480 at 60 Hz, but this is a very low resolution compared to the vast capabilities of an HDTV. Without PowerStrip and utilities like it, there would be no way to get a higher picture resolution.

Video Resolution and Bandwidth

The confusion in using a utility like PowerStrip comes from the different methods of setting computer screen formats and HDTV formats. Computer screen resolutions are pretty easy to understand: The screen is measured in pixels, and the user simply selects the number of pixels wide and the number of pixels tall, plus the refresh rate, and the computer outputs the appropriate mode. If the monitor is capable of displaying the picture that the computer is generating, then the user can see the computer image. If the monitor is not capable of displaying the picture, then it usually shows a wildly flickering and incoherent image, or it goes blank.

An HDTV, on the other hand, does not really work by setting the resolution and frequency. Instead, the HDTV works on the bandwidth of the video signal. The wider the bandwidth, the more information can be carried in the video signal, and the higher the resolution of the picture. When discussing the resolution of HDTV video, it is important to remember that resolution refers to the number of horizontal scan lines, which is a measure of the vertical resolution. The horizontal resolution does not affect the bandwidth, and almost any horizontal resolution can be used for a given vertical resolution.

NOTE *A standard NTSC video signal is (theoretically) 525 lines times 30 frames per second, which equals a bandwidth of 15.750 KHz. NTSC video is interlaced, so each frame is composed of two fields of scan lines, which means that the video signal is actually 60 fields per second. Progressively scanned video is composed of 60 complete frames per second. Thus, a progressive-scan video signal with the same number of scan lines uses twice the bandwidth, or 31.5 KHz.*

The way bandwidth determines resolution actually applies to both computer and HDTV video signals, but the PC hides this from the user by providing a predetermined selection of resolutions from which to choose. The predetermined list of available resolutions for computer displays does not match the configuration of HDTV displays, however, except at 640×480 at 60 Hz. PowerStrip converts information about HDTV video bandwidth to custom resolutions and timings that computer users can understand.

One other issue to keep in mind when you configure HDTV resolutions and timings in PowerStrip is that most consumer televisions sets suffer from at least some overscan. *Overscan* refers to the amount of the video image that is outside the display area of the set. Most televisions, including HDTV sets, have anywhere from 5 to 15 percent overscan, which means that 5 to 15 percent of the image is actually beyond the frame of the picture. This is barely noticeable for most television programming—broadcasters leave the outside of the video image empty of information—but when you're showing a computer desktop image on a television set, this means that the Windows task bar, the Start button, and anything else at the edge of the screen is not visible.

PowerStrip Settings

HDTV resolutions are based are based on three bandwidth values. These bandwidths can be used to display a progressively scanned image with a specified number of scan lines and just about any horizontal resolution, or an interlaced image with twice the number of scan lines and just about any horizontal resolution (see Table 10-1). Since a progressive-scan video signal uses the same bandwidth as an interlaced signal with twice the resolution, any HDTV that supports a given progressive-scan format should work with the accompanying interlaced format.

Table 10-1. Resolution and Bandwidth

HDTV FORMAT (SCAN LINES)	VISIBLE SCAN LINES (PROGRESSIVE)	VISIBLE SCAN LINES (INTERLACED)	FREQUENCY (VERTICAL REFRESH RATE)	BANDWIDTH (HORIZONTAL REFRESH RATE)
525	480p	960i	60 Hz	31.5 KHz
563	540p	1080i	60 Hz	33.75 KHz
750	720p	1440i	60 Hz	45 KHz

The goal for configuring PowerStrip is to set the HTPC video card to output a resolution at a refresh rate that matches one of the HDTV formats. Not all HDTV sets support all of the bandwidths specified by the HDTV standard. Quite a few seem to lack compatibility with the 45 KHz rate, which means that the 720p/1440i modes are not available. It is important to check the specifications of the display device before you connect it to an HTPC and use PowerStrip to set custom resolutions and timings, because some sets could be damaged if they try to synchronize themselves to a bandwidth that is too high.

You should install and run PowerStrip on your HTPC while the system is connected to a multisynch computer monitor instead of the home theater display. This is easier and safer, since the computer monitor can display a much wider range of resolutions and refresh rates than an HDTV, and it prevents damage to an expensive display device. One common problem that occurs when you configure PowerStrip is that an adjustment causes the HDTV to lose synchronization with the video signal, and the computer desktop is no longer visible. This makes it rather difficult to correct the situation, since there is no way to tell what is happening on the screen. Using a multisynch computer monitor will save you a lot of frustration and guesswork.

Hotkey Manager Configuration

The first configuration that you should do in PowerStrip is to set the safe mode of 640×480 to a keyboard hotkey so that you can reset the HTPC to a visible display even when the screen is corrupted. PowerStrip features a Hotkey Manager that lets you map many of its functions to keyboard commands. For example, the command Ctrl-Alt-O is already mapped to display the current screen mode. To map the video mode 640×480 to a hotkey command, switch to the screen resolution and save it as a profile. It will then appear in the Hotkey Manager window and be available for mapping to a keyboard command. To do this, follow these steps:

1. After you've installed PowerStrip and it's running, click the system tray icon to open the PowerStrip menu.

2. In the menu, select Display Profiles and then Configure.

3. In the Display Profiles configuration window, slide the Resolution selector until "640 × 480 pixels" is displayed. Click the Apply button at the bottom of the screen and let PowerStrip change the current screen mode.

4. In the Color Depth section, make sure that the color depth is set to "TrueColor (32 bit)" or the highest color depth value available.

5. In the Refresh Rate area, the refresh rate should be 60 Hz. If it isn't, change it by selecting Standard Discrete Timing from the drop-down list box.

6. In the Profiles section, click the Save As button. A dialog window will pop up to let you name the profile—use the default name "640 × 480 pixels, TrueColor (32-bit)".

7. Now that the profile is saved, it is available in the Hotkey Manager. Close the Display Profiles configuration window. Click the PowerStrip icon in the system tray to open the PowerStrip menu.

8. In the menu, select Options and then Hotkey Manager. The window shown in Figure 10-1 will appear.

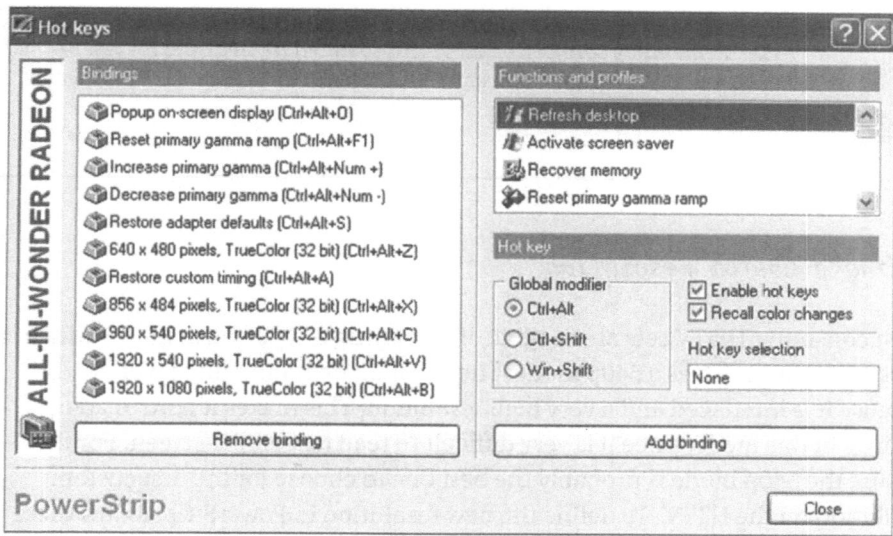

Figure 10-1. The PowerStrip Hotkey Manager window

9. In the Hot Keys window, scroll down the "Functions and profiles" list to find the "640 × 480 pixels" mode that you just added and select it.

10. Assign a keyboard command by picking a global modifier (Ctrl-Alt is the default) and typing a keystroke in the "Hot key selection" field. Many PowerStrip users map a number of screen modes to a series of keyboard commands, and it's a good idea to select a series of keys that are grouped together for this purpose. The bottom row of letters is suitable for this, as those letters aren't already used by PowerStrip for anything.

11. Close the Hot Keys window.

With this keyboard command available, it is a little safer to proceed with further custom resolutions and timings. It is also a good idea to add to the Hotkey Manager the video modes that have been configured and are known to work properly. This is a fast and convenient way to switch between modes.

To set up the first new custom resolution in PowerStrip, leave the HTPC connected to the multisynch computer monitor. You can do the configuration with the monitor attached, and then you can connect the HDTV to try it out. It is always a good idea to turn off the computer and display device when you connect and disconnect them, but most people encounter no problems when changing connections while the computer is running.

TIP *Remember, connecting an HTPC to an HDTV requires a VGA-to-component transcoder. PowerStrip is useless when used with S-video or composite video output.*

Adding a Custom Resolution

Most consumer HDTV sets are capable of displaying a 1080i video mode, which is the same bandwidth as a 540p mode. The 1080i mode is difficult to work with because it is interlaced and a very high resolution. This makes it hard to adjust settings in this mode, since it is very difficult to read text on the screen. For this reason, the 540p mode is probably the best one to choose for the first custom resolution on the HTPC. To define the new resolution in PowerStrip, follow these steps:

1. Click the PowerStrip icon in the system tray to open the PowerStrip menu.

2. In the menu, select Display Profiles and then choose Configure to open the Display Profiles configuration window.

3. In the Display Profiles configuration window, click the Advanced timing options button.

4. In the Advanced timing options window, click the Custom resolutions button.

5. The Custom resolutions window is where new resolutions are created. There is a list of predefined resolutions on the left-hand side. A radio button below the list allows you to see the User Defined custom resolutions—these are the video modes that have been set up already. The right-hand side of the window contains the various customization controls for the video modes.

    On the left-hand side of the window, scroll through the list of predefined custom resolutions to find the first 960×540 resolution listed. This should be the "960×540p (HDTV standard)" resolution, but any 960×540p resolution will do.

6. When you select the 960×540p resolution, the right side of the window will show the settings for this resolution. Note that the "Refresh rate" fields should show 34 for the horizontal field and 60 for the vertical field.

7. The "Front porch," "Sync width," and "Back porch" settings control how the picture is centered and sized on the HDTV screen. These settings are easier to adjust later, so leave them alone for now.

   When you set up further custom resolutions, you can set the porch and sync values to match values for existing video modes with the same horizontal bandwidth.

8. You should leave the "Polarity," "Composite sync," and "Sync on green" controls at their default settings. The "Interlaced" check box should be off because the vertical refresh rate is 60 Hz, which indicates that this is a progressively scanned, not interlaced, video image.

9. Click the Add new resolution button. PowerStrip will display a message that says the computer needs to be restarted to see if the display driver will accept the new resolution. Click the Restart button and let the HTPC reboot itself.

10. After the system has rebooted, click the PowerStrip icon in the system tray to open the PowerStrip menu.

11. On the PowerStrip menu, select Display Profiles and then choose Configure to open the Display Profiles configuration window.

12. Move the Resolution slider control to find the new "960 × 540 pixels" resolution that you just added.

13. Click the Apply button to switch to the new display mode.

14. If the screen comes up in the new resolution, click the Yes button to stay in the new mode.

15. Click the Advanced timing options button to open the Advanced timing options window.

16. With the display in the new mode, you can use the Advanced timing options window (see Figure 10-2) to make minor adjustments to the location of the screen in the display. It is not a good idea to change the width or height of the display in this window—you should do this by setting a "resolution inside a resolution," as explained in the next section. You can adjust the picture to the left and right or up and down in this window.

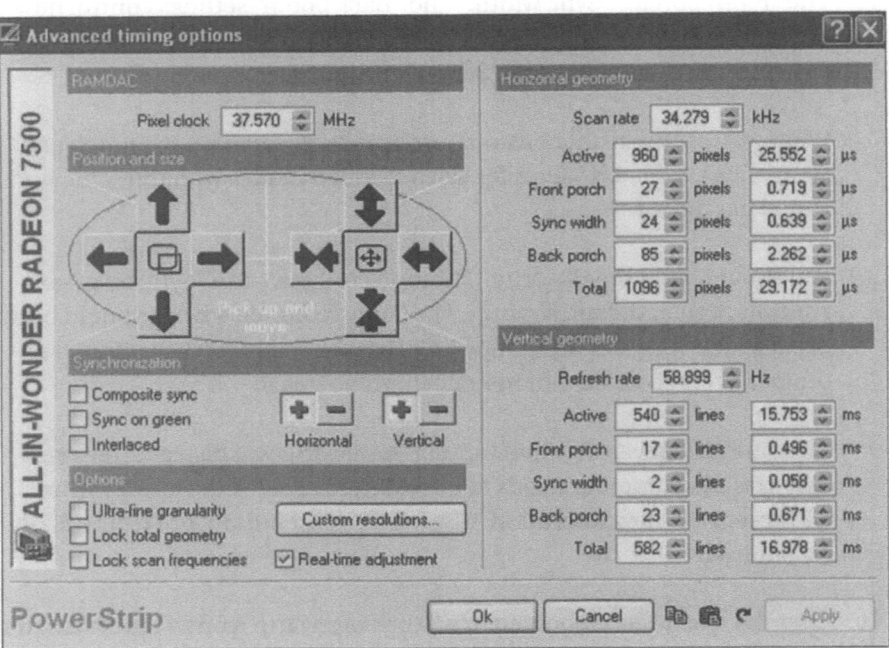

Figure 10-2. The PowerStrip Advanced timing configuration window

17. After the picture is properly centered, click OK to get back to the Display Profiles window.

18. Save the resolution by clicking the Save as button and using the default name. This resolution will now show up on the PowerStrip menu available from the system tray icon, making it easier to switch to it.

19. Click OK again to return to the Windows desktop.

The HTPC should now be set to display the new 960×540 resolution mode. You can connect the HDTV display via the transcoder to confirm that the mode works on the television set. If the picture is visible after a second or two, then the configuration is working. If the picture does not stabilize or is not visible at all, then the television is not capable of displaying the 540p or 1080i HDTV resolution. As this is a very common mode for consumer HDTV sets, most should support this resolution.

The exact vertical and horizontal refresh timings depend on the video card and the HDTV set in use. Each model is slightly more or less tolerant of custom timings, and tweaking the picture will result in different values for different hardware, even for the same video modes. Those with rear projection HDTV sets or three-tube front-projector sets will notice picture geometry and color convergence problems unless all custom resolutions are set up with the same (or very similar) vertical and horizontal refresh values. Keeping the front porch, sync, and back porch values the same is also important. If you create a new resolution with twice the horizontal resolution, then you should double the porch and sync values (e.g., it is possible to create a 1920×540p mode from the 960×540p mode—the horizontal and vertical refresh rates should be the same, the vertical porch and sync should be the same, but the horizontal porch and sync should be doubled).

Unless you have adjusted the HDTV to reduce overscan, the 960×540 mode will leave the edges of the computer desktop invisible off the screen. This makes it practically impossible to find the Start menu or the system tray icons. Use the hotkey mapping to return the display to the 640×480 mode if that makes it easier to see the edges of the desktop, or reconnect the multisync computer monitor to continue setting up more custom resolutions.

Resolution Inside a Resolution

To compensate for overscan, you can have your HDTV set professionally adjusted, or you can create a PowerStrip custom resolution that uses the porch settings to reduce the number of pixels displayed vertically and horizontally. This leaves the outside regions of the image blank, which is where the overscan makes them invisible anyway. Creating such a resolution makes it easier to use the HTPC desktop and other PC applications. Reducing the overscan also gives interesting results when you watch broadcast television or DVD movies, as the overscanned areas will be visible.

The best way to create a resolution inside a resolution with PowerStrip is by using the Custom resolutions window, where you first created the previous 960×540 custom resolution. It is possible to reduce the size of the display area in the Advanced timing options window, but because the controls on this window are all interrelated, it is difficult to get to the proper settings, even with the "Real-time adjustments" check box deselected.

In the Custom resolutions window, click the "User defined" radio button and select a resolution that will be used for the base or "outside" resolution of the new inside resolution. This will configure the right side of the window with the correct bandwidth settings for a resolution that has already been set up. Then click the "Lock total geometry" check box so that there is a check mark in it. Now you can adjust the horizontal and vertical "Active pixels" fields to create the inside resolution. It is best to start with a 540p or 720p bandwidth resolution and create a smaller resolution inside of this. Creating a smaller resolution inside of 480p would result in a video mode that is too small for most HTPC uses.

The new inside resolution can be any value, but it should fit inside the bounds of the outer resolution. If the overscan on the HDTV set is 10 percent, then setting new values 10 percent less than the original resolution should create a new mode with no overscan. Because it is difficult to guess the precise overscan amount, you will likely need to experiment to find a resolution that fits the desktop nicely into the display area, though most people find that leaving a small amount of overscan is preferable. Don't forget to save the new resolution in the Display profiles window and assign a hotkey if desired.

Keep in mind that configuring custom resolutions in PowerStrip is about the most difficult thing that any HTPC hobbyist will do. It is not easy to learn how to use the utility, and it takes a lot of time and experimentation to learn it well enough to create new resolutions. A good approach is to try to set up the "standard" 480p resolution and one higher resolution such as 960×540p first, and then worry about other resolutions later. The resolution inside a resolution of 856×484p inside of 960×540p works well for the Windows desktop and makes the HPTC easier to use, so it this is also a good custom resolution to add next as part of a minimum configuration.

There are many great Web resources for PowerStrip configurations for specific hardware. The AVS forum (http://www.avsforum.com) has a searchable discussion group for HTPCs that includes a lot of postings about PowerStrip settings for Toshiba, Sony, Hitachi, and other brands of HDTV sets. This is a good place to start when you're looking for solutions to PowerStrip problems.

Summary

PowerStrip is one of the key utilities that your HTPC will need. This chapter showed you the intricacies of PowerStrip and examined the various areas where you can put it to work for your HTPC. In the next chapter, we take a look at the results and conclusions we've come to in assembling our HTPCs.

HTPC
Systems
Wrap-Up

Part Four

CHAPTER 11

Results and Conclusions

BUILDING AN HTPC for the home theater is a much different experience than unpacking and installing a DVD player. Though the HTPC machine has more features and capabilities than an off-the-shelf player, it is also more frustrating and takes much longer to tune to perfection (if "perfection" is even possible!). This book has dealt with selecting hardware and software, and has given you some suggestions for installation and configuration, but it has not covered the lengthy process of experimentation, fine-tuning, and problem-solving that goes into an HTPC. For most hobbyists, this process is the fun part—making improvements to a machine that was already superior to a consumer DVD player is ultimately satisfying. It can also be difficult to puzzle through the unknown and learn from mistakes. This chapter, then, is a summary of the troubles and triumphs we had while building our HTPC machines for this project.

Expectations have a major bearing on the success of any HTPC project. Anyone new to the world of PCs or expecting a "plug it in and play it" experience with an HTPC, even a prebuilt system, will likely be confounded. Even a well-tuned and configured machine needs more poking and prodding than an off-the-shelf DVD player. The advantage of this is that the HTPC is almost infinitely tunable—even when it seems that the DVD picture is perfect or the MP3 sound is ideal, new hardware, new software, new drivers, or some new utility will come along to improve it. For this reason the HTPC machine is never really "finished." Those home theater enthusiasts who expect to buy it, plug it in, and forget about it will be disappointed with such a system.

We expected the HTPC systems that we built for this project to change continuously. We evaluated a lot of hardware in both systems to see what worked well, including video cards, sound cards, and even CPUs of different speeds and capabilities. Additionally, we did not try to assemble a completed HTPC all at once. It took many months of configuring hardware and software before we even had one machine to try in the home theater room. The reason we refer to building the HTPC as a "project" in this book is that it cannot be done in a weekend, or even a week. Assembly of an HTPC is a long process, especially for those of us new to the hobby, and allowing for plenty of time makes it much more pleasant.

Hardware

Putting together the hardware for our HTPC machines took a lot longer than we expected. Since we are experienced PC builders, we thought it would be quick and simple to assemble the parts we selected into two HTPCs. In general, the assembly was easy, but we found that we were constantly disassembling and reassembling our systems to try out different CPUs, video cards, sound cards, and other bits and pieces. Whenever hardware is swapped, the software in the system must be reconfigured and new drivers installed, so changing a video card, for example, takes much longer than the time to physically change the card.

HTPC System 1

This is exactly the procedure we performed on our first test system. This HTPC had been built and configured with the ATI All-In-Wonder Radeon 7500 and all of the ATI Multimedia Center software, including the ATI DVD Player. We wanted to try the GeForce4 MX video card in this system to compare the DVD playback, so we uninstalled the ATI video driver and swapped video cards. After rebooting and installing the video drivers for the GeForce4 MX card, we found (as expected) that the ATI DVD Player would no longer work. Fortunately, the GeForce4 MX card came with DVD playback software, so we installed that for our test.

Our first test system was actually two different machines during the course of this project. It began as a Pentium III/800 MHz system and then got upgraded to an Athlon XP 2100+ system. This gave us a good chance to compare performance of these two processors in systems where most of the other hardware was the same. The video card, sound card, disk RAID controller and disk drives, DVD-ROM, CD-R drive, and keyboard/mouse were moved from the Pentium III–based system to the faster Athlon XP system. Both machines had the same amount of RAM, but the Athlon XP system uses faster DDR RAM running at 333 MHz. Surprisingly, we found that both CPUs were fast enough for almost all HTPC uses, but the Athlon XP CPU really showed its performance advantage for recording and playback of uncompressed video that was digitized from the ATI All-In-Wonder Radeon 7500 television tuner. Video editing and rendering of compressed video was also much faster on the Athlon XP CPU due to its higher clock speed.

NOTE *An Intel Pentium running at a comparable speed would also perform well for video editing and rendering. Based on our testing of the hardware available to us, we found that Intel and AMD CPUs are both suitable for HTPC uses.*

It is important to emphasize that there was no difference in DVD playback quality or reliability between the Pentium III/800 MHz system and the Athlon XP 2100+ system. We tried both with the ATI All-In-Wonder Radeon 7500 and could not see any difference in performance or picture quality with a variety of DVD movies. This is not surprising, since the video card does a lot of the work of decoding and scaling the DVD picture to the screen, so the CPU does not need to be very powerful. One key reason for this is that the screen resolution we used with our high-definition television was based on the 540p HDTV format. Compared to typical PC screen resolutions, this is pretty low, so the HTPC has fewer pixels to draw and less data to process and push around. For HTPC systems that are used primarily for playing DVDs and watching television, an older and slower CPU is fine.

We had one problem with the hardware in our first HTPC machine. When this machine was based on the Pentium III/800 MHz CPU, we tried to put the GeForce4 MX video card into it, but the video card did not work. The motherboard for the Pentium III chip was an older board that could not support the proper AGP slot voltage setting for the new GeForce4 MX card, and the system would not boot up. When we switched this machine to the Athlon XP CPU, the motherboard in the new system worked fine with both the ATI All-In-Wonder Radeon 7500 and the GeForce4 MX video cards. This is a concern for those who are building HTPC systems based on older hardware, but there are plenty of excellent video cards that still work with the older motherboards available.

HTPC System 2

The second HTPC system that we built for this project is based on a Pentium III/450 MHz CPU, and we found this system to be a little slow. The DVD playback would occasionally stutter or jerk when we used a DVD player that used a software-only mode. When the DVD player supported the video hardware, playback was completely smooth. The system took several seconds to start up an application, so switching from watching television to watching a DVD movie or listening to MP3 music was not as fast as we liked. It performed most HTPC functions fine once they were started, but the quick response of our faster HTPC system spoiled us for a faster CPU.

One important performance issue that we were concerned about with this second HTPC system was the capability of the DScaler software to deinterlace the television channels from the Hauppauge WinTV-HD HDTV tuner card. Though this system is connected to our home theater display via an S-video cable, which means that it is outputting an interlaced video signal to the display, we wanted to try it with our VGA-to-component transcoder to compare progressive-scan picture quality with that of our first HTPC system. The Pentium III/450 MHz CPU did an acceptable job running DScaler to convert the television video signal to our progressively scanned display, but a faster CPU would probably be better for systems that run DScaler, as we were unable to get good results with some of the DScaler video filters.

One other quirky thing about the second HTPC system we built was finding drivers for the network card we used. This system is based on the Windows 98 SE operating system, which has excellent support for almost all computer hardware made in the last 5 years. However, for some reason, Windows 98 did not recognize the network card we installed. We were able eventually to find the proper drivers from the manufacturer's Web site, but anyone who has built a computer for a network knows that installing third-party drivers into a machine with no functioning network card is a challenge because there is no way to access the Internet or copy the software across the network to the affected PC. Fortunately, we had other PCs available to help. This became an important issue while building our HTPC systems; it is very helpful to have another computer nearby that can access the Internet to get information or software for the HTPC while it is under construction.

Software

Assembling hardware was a slow process during this project, but compared to installing software, it was quick and easy. Even experienced PC hobbyists will probably find that setting up the software for an HTPC is a slow and challenging task. The utilities and applications that are meant specifically for home theaters are very specialized and, in some cases, not well polished or well documented. This is due to the nature of the hobby: PCs in the home theater are still relatively new and much of the software is distributed as freeware or shareware, not commercial software. That is not to say that the specialized HTPC software is inferior or unstable—in fact, it is mostly excellent—but it requires much understanding and knowledge from the user to work properly.

HTPC System 1

This machine features the ATI All-In-Wonder Radeon 7500 video card, so the main multimedia software installed is the ATI Multimedia Center, including the ATI DVD Player. We were skeptical about this suite of multimedia applications because bundled software tends to be lightweight, short on features, and inferior to task-dedicated applications. After experimenting with the various applications in the ATI suite, we changed our minds. The ATI Multimedia Center software performs very well, has all the features we wanted, and integrates different media functions together easily and conveniently.

The ATI DVD Player uses Ravisent DirectShow MPEG-2 filters to play the compressed digital video stream from the disc. The Ravisent filters are widely regarded as among the best available, and the ATI player certainly benefits from this. The picture quality is fantastic, and the performance is smooth and does not stutter or jerk during slow landscape pans or fast action sequences. In addition, the ATI software enables all of the hardware features within the video card.

The display device used for this HTPC is a Toshiba TN55X81 HDTV-ready television set, which is a standard 4:3 aspect ratio set. Before the HTPC was built, we used a stand-alone DVD player to watch movies in this home theater environment. The stand-alone player caused very noticeable picture problems for anamorphic movies (16:9 aspect ratio, or "wide-screen"), where fine details looked blocky and seemed to shimmer as they moved. This is due to the lack of resolution—in order to fit the wider picture on the screen, it must be shrunk, so that it occupies fewer of the scan lines in order to leave the lines at the top and bottom blank. The result is that a picture meant to use all of the horizontal scan lines is reduced to using just the ones in the middle area of the screen.

The HTPC overcomes this problem on 4:3-shaped HDTV sets. The video mode is set to a higher resolution format—540 scan lines instead of 480—so that there are more scan lines, and the shrunken picture still occupies an area with enough horizontal scan lines to display fine details without shimmering. The ATI DVD Player lets the user control the aspect ratio, so that a video mode of 1920×540 can be used without distorting the DVD video image. This is our favorite resolution for DVDs on this 4:3 television, since it displays enough resolution horizontally and vertically to show fine detail. As we mentioned earlier, the 1080i mode does not work well with the ATI video card drivers—the video picture is stretched so that the top half of the image takes up the whole display area, and the bottom is not visible at all. We had to limit ourselves to progressively scanned modes, but this was not much of a problem because the 540p modes looked fantastic. The HTPC is far preferable to the stand-alone player for watching movies now.

The ATI DVD Player has one limitation that affected the audio playback capabilities of our HTPC. The ATI All-In-Wonder Radeon 7500 has a coaxial digital audio output (an S/PDIF port), and the ATI DVD Player can pass the digital audio stream through to the S/PDIF port on the video card, but that is the only digital audio output that the DVD Player will support. The software would not send the digital audio signal directly to the M-Audio Delta Dio 2496, which we would prefer, as this card is connected via an optical cable to our digital audio receiver. Fortunately, the M-Audio card has a coaxial digital audio input, so we patched the digital audio output on the ATI video card to the input of the Delta Dio, which then output it to the digital audio receiver. Those HTPC systems without an S/PDIF input cannot use the ATI DVD Player to output digital audio to any other device, so the ATI video card S/PDIF output will have to be connected to the digital audio receiver whenever DVD movies are played.

The ATI All-In-Wonder Radeon 7500 features a television tuner with composite and S-video inputs. The television tuner software is comparable to the software that we've seen for other television tuner cards. It has a "television on demand" feature that works like a personal video recorder, allowing you to pause live television, skip backward and forward, and record shows like a VCR. A timer feature lets you program the television tuner to record events on a daily, weekly, and yearly basis. The timer can schedule not only television recordings, but also playback of any multimedia file at any time. The digital VCR feature can record video in a variety of formats, including MPEG-1 and MPEG-2, uncompressed video, and the proprietary VCR format that ATI uses. Compressed formats require a fast CPU to record video without dropping frames, but uncompressed video uses a lot of disk space. Experimenting with the settings allowed us to find a nice balance of compression and disk space that the machine could record without dropping video frames.

Perhaps the best thing about the ATI television tuner is the fantastic deinterlacing that it does to convert the interlaced NTSC video signal to a progressively scanned video image. This deinterlacing works on the television tuner and the composite and S-video inputs. Even fast-action sports programs such as football games were flawlessly deinterlaced, scaled to any resolution, and displayed on our HDTV set.

The ATI File Player is an application that can take the place of the Windows Media Player. It can play back all types of video and audio format files, including VCD, SVCD, AVI, and the proprietary VCR files that the ATI television tuner uses to record shows. The ATI File Player can unlock the aspect ratio of the video image so that it displays correctly regardless of the screen aspect ratio, which is a feature that the Microsoft Windows Media Player lacks. This means that SVCD format video files (480×480 pixels) can be stretched to fill a 4:3 screen. Without stretching, the SVCD video makes everything look too tall and skinny. The ATI File Player can also be used to queue up a list of files for playback, like Windows Media Player. The only thing we liked better about Windows Media Player is the variety of screen visualizations for audio files.

We did encounter one problem with the ATI Multimedia Center software that we were not able to solve. The television tuner circuits on the video card send the analog audio from the television channel or composite/S-video capture connector to a ministereo plug that is supposed to be plugged into the analog line-in input of a sound card. This works fine for HTPC systems with a standard sound card that has an analog line-in connector, but the M-Audio Delta Dio 2496 does not. We had to add a Creative Labs Sound Blaster Live! card to this HTPC system in order to get the analog television tuner sound from the ATI All-In-Wonder Radeon 7500 television tuner. We then had to connect this sound card to the digital audio receiver's analog sound input ports, since the Sound Blaster Live! analog line-in does not get automatically digitized and sent to the digital audio output of the M-Audio sound card. If the ATI television tuner software could send audio to a digital S/PDIF port, or if we had selected a sound card with digital and analog sound inputs, we could have avoided the extra step of switching the audio receiver between analog and digital inputs when watching television or DVD movies.

The last issue worth mentioning with the ATI software for our first HTPC system is the ATI Remote Wonder utility. The ATI video card came with the remote control and the appropriate ATI Multimedia Center software to use it. We down-loaded the updated version of the ATI Multimedia Center software, which instructed us to uninstall previous versions of the software before upgrading. Unfortunately, the updated version does not support the ATI Remote Wonder, so the remote control no longer worked after we upgraded the software. After some research and experimentation, we found that we could install the updates without uninstalling previous versions, and the remote control still worked. This meant uninstalling all the updates, reinstalling the original version, and then reinstalling all of the updates. However, it was worth the effort, as the ATI Remote Wonder is a great remote control that makes the HTPC easy and convenient to use, and it is preconfigured to work with all of the ATI Multimedia Center software.

The first HTPC system that we built for this project uses the ATI software for most multimedia features. Overall, we really like the ATI All-In-Wonder Radeon 7500 and the software bundle with which it came because the applications are high quality, full-featured, well integrated, and easy to set up and configure. We had some issues with the software for the remote control, but once we figured it out, we really liked using it. Compared to installing separate applications for DVD playback, television tuner features, file playback, and a remote control, the ATI package is an easier and less expensive choice.

Besides the ATI software, there is not much HTPC-specific software added to our first system. The video output is controlled by PowerStrip, which was challenging to learn and configure. (For more information about PowerStrip, see Chapter 10.) The operating system is Windows XP, so it came with the latest version of the Windows Media Player and an image viewer that allows the user to move from image to image like a slide show. The video capture and editing software uses the ATI video card hardware to import and digitize video, and we installed a CD-R drive and the CD burning software that it came with to make video and data discs. It is a testament to the ATI software bundle that few other HTPC applications are needed to run the machine as the heart of our home theater.

HTPC System 2

This system uses the GeForce4 MX video card, which has MPEG-2 acceleration features that improve DVD playback, so we wanted to use DVD player software that was compatible with the video card hardware. DVD playback is not a primary requirement for this system, though, as we mainly wanted to use this machine as a video recorder and a general multimedia file player. We had some challenges finding, installing, and configuring all of the software to perform these functions.

The TheaterTek DVD Player is widely regarded as one of the best software applications for DVD playback on PCs. It uses the most recent Ravisent Direct-Show filters and the video quality is excellent. The TheaterTek DVD Player works well with the GeForce4 MX card, allowing this Pentium III/450 MHz system to play DVD movies smoothly. Without the hardware support enabled, we found that this system was not fast enough to play DVD movies smoothly without jerking and pausing during action scenes. This player can also pass the digital audio stream to the coaxial digital audio output on the Creative Labs Sound Blaster Live! sound card, which is connected to a digital audio receiver. Though DVD playback is merely a convenience of this system, it is as good as any stand-alone player connected through an S-video cable to the home theater display.

This system includes the Hauppauge WinTV-HD HDTV tuner card for receiving television broadcasts from an analog cable service and HDTV from over-the-air broadcasts. The card comes with television tuning software and the Gemstar Guide Plus+ to view program listings for the coming week, which allows us to set up recording times far in advance. The Hauppauge software works well for viewing and recording television, and for capturing still images from frames in the video stream.

We wanted to try out some personal video recorder software on this machine, and all of the various DVR programs worked well, including WinDVR 2 and Snap-Stream Personal Video Station. Because the machine is underpowered by today's standards, we were unable to get adequate high-quality (DVD level) recordings with this HTPC system; however, the machine performed well when we turned down the desired quality level and screen size. This machine is also used to play MP3 and audio CDs in the home theater room, so we wanted to use the most recent version of Microsoft Windows Media Player. Since this machine is using Windows 98, the most recent version of Windows Media Player available is version 7.1, not the new version 8.0 that comes with Windows XP. Though version 7.1 is an improvement over the one that comes with Windows 98, it is evident that this version of the Windows operating system is not going to be current or supported for much longer. This hardware is pretty slow for Windows XP, so it may be necessary to upgrade the hardware when Windows 98 is no longer capable of running the applications we want to use.

Overall, this second HTPC system is a little sluggish and slow to respond. It takes an almost unbearably long time for some applications to start up, and compared to our first HTPC, it is downright slow. Though it performs satisfactorily when doing one thing such as displaying television or playing a movie, it is not peppy at changing tasks or doing multiple things at once.

Conclusions

To wrap up our discussion of the HTPC machines we built for this project, we want to answer three questions:

- Did we achieve our goal of getting better DVD playback?

- Is the HTPC system as convenient and full-featured as we thought?

- What features were most important and least important?

Did We Achieve Our Goal of Getting Better DVD Playback?

The answer to the first question is yes for the first HTPC system. This HTPC is connected via a VGA-to-component transcoder to an HDTV set, and the DVD playback is fantastic. The higher resolution and progressive-scan format of HDTV provides much better video picture quality than the stand-alone DVD player we used before. The sound quality is at least as good as the digital surround sound was with the stand-alone player. The DVD video is played smoothly and without jerking or other problems.

The answer to the first question is no for the second HTPC system. Though the DVD playback is mostly fine and is at least equal to a stand-alone player, this machine is connected to a television set via an S-video cable, so it does not surpass the DVD movie quality of other players. With hardware acceleration, this machine is able to play DVDs smoothly, but some DVD players that we tried did not support the video hardware in this machine and did not perform well. We are satisfied with the DVD performance of this system, but it is not better than a stand-alone player, though the HTPC has many other features that make it a great choice to play DVDs.

Is the HTPC System As Convenient and Full-Featured As We Thought?

The answer to the second question for both HTPC systems is yes. These machines proved to be very versatile media machines. Both of our systems are connected to the Internet via broadband cable modems, so we have access to a wide variety of movie trailers, video clips, streaming media, and online services for entertainment. The popularity of Internet radio is almost enough reason to put a PC in the home theater and is a great feature of any Internet-connected HTPC. The only consideration to make is how much disk space to build into the machine, because our collection of media files is growing much faster than we expected as we convert our audio CDs to MP3 and digitize our home movies.

What Features Were Most Important and Least Important?

The first system we built has ended up being used mostly for watching television and digitizing home movies, even though it is optimized for playing DVD movies at high resolution. The excellent ATI Multimedia Center software came in more useful than we expected, especially the remote control, which made the machine more useable to other members of the household. We also use the digital image viewing software built into Windows XP quite a lot, and we often use the Windows Media Player to provide background music or streaming audio from Internet radio stations.

One important software utility on the first HTPC system is PowerStrip, which was crucial for controlling the output of the video card to make it compatible with the HDTV-ready television set in the home theater. Using PowerStrip to set up a resolution-in-a-resolution allows us to display television channels with no over-scan, so that the whole video image is shown on the screen.

Although DVD playback is an important part of the first HTPC system, it ended up being less important than the television tuner or media file playing software. In a typical week, this machine plays one DVD movie, but many hours of television and music. Also, we didn't need the software utilities Girder and DScaler at all, since the ATI software came preconfigured for use with the ATI Remote Wonder, and the ATI television tuner automatically deinterlaced the NTSC video from television channels and the composite and S-video inputs. We also expected that playing computer games on the big screen in the home theater would be a popular use of the HTPC, but most games did not work at the nonstandard resolutions based on the 540p video format, and the 480p format resulted in screen resolutions that were low quality. We will experiment more with high resolutions, but since these are interlaced, we don't know if many PC games will work properly or look very good.

We found similar results with the second HTPC system we built for this project. Although we concentrated on making the DVD performance very smooth and reliable, the machine is mainly used to watch television and play media files. This machine lived for a short while in the home theater and then was transplanted to the den, where it serves as a great secondary media machine in the home office. For this reason, Internet access to e-mail and Web browsing are important features on our second HTPC system.

We installed a wireless keyboard and mouse set on the second HTPC system, but this turned out to be unnecessary. Because this system is used in an office setting, it is easily accessible. We still use the wireless controllers, as they function as well as conventional devices, but they are barely far enough from the machine to require wireless connections. The digital audio output from this HTPC is no longer used, either, since it is connected to a small stereo system in the den through analog audio connections. Fortunately, the Creative Labs Sound Blaster Live! sound card in this system features digital and analog audio outputs and did not cost a lot, so we don't feel that we wasted any money on the digital audio capabilities. This machine might move back into the home theater room someday if it gets an upgraded processor, so the digital audio output might be useful again after all!

Summary

The exercise of building an HTPC is more suited to the world of the computer hobbyist than the home theater consumer, as only a real enthusiast will have the time and determination to achieve the benefits of using such a machine. This does not mean that HTPC systems are too complicated or too time-consuming for the average user—it's just that building one takes more time and effort than buying a DVD player. Unlike a DVD player, however, an HTPC has a limitless number of uses and the potential for endless entertainment from constant upgrades and improvements. Though there are some frustrations and failings along the way, the road through the HTPC construction zone leads to a world of fantastic DVD playback quality and amazing multimedia versatility.

Online Resources

AT THE TIME we wrote this book, only a handful of companies were producing home theater PCs for commercial consumption. We do, however, assume that this number will increase greatly in the coming months, so if you're interested in finding more information on HTPCs on the Internet, you can go to a search site such as Google (http://www.google.com) and search on the term "HTPC." Still, we have a few HTPC sites that we'd like to mention here.

HTPC Retailer Web Sites

The following is a list of the companies that will create and ship an HTPC. We imagine that this list will change considerably in the coming months, but during the writing of this book, this was what we found to be available.

Amptron International: http://www.amptron.com
(Amptron sells a PC configured to be an HTPC—you can find their HTPC specifications at http://www.amptron.com/html/HTPC.html)

Digital Connection: http://www.digitalconnection.com/shopper_htpc.asp
(HTPC components for sale)

Ez-HomeTheater.net: http://www.ez-hometheater.net

Heimkino: http://www.heimkino.com (not in English)

Hivizone.com: http://www.hivizone.com

HTPC-Related Web Sites

The following list of Web sites includes forums, general information sites, and other sites we thought would be helpful to you in your quest for the best HTPC possible:

AVS Forum: http://www.avsforum.com (English forum)

Collins' Cinema: HTPC!: http://www.myhometheater.homestead.com/HTPC.html

The Home Theater Computer Board:
http://homepage1.nifty.com/straylight/ bbs/ (Japanese board)

HTPC Headquarters: http://www.berrybros.net/htpc/htpc_home.htm

Multimedian.com: http://multimedian.com/school/htpc.html (HTPC FAQ)

Rootnix.de HTPC Forum: http://www.rootnix.de/board/main.php3
(German board)

Other Important Web Sites

The following list of Web sites includes sites we referenced, enjoyed, glanced at, or otherwise viewed during the writing of this book. We also include URLs for the Web sites of companies that supplied the key products we discuss in this book.

Adobe (Adobe Premiere): http://www.adobe.com

Apple Computer (QuickTime): http://www.apple.com

ATI Technologies: http://www.ati.com

Audio Authority: http://www.audioauthority.com

Creative Labs: http://www.creative.com

CyberLink (PowerDVD): http://www.gocyberlink.com

Dazzle Video Creator: http://www.dazzle.com/main.html

Digital Connection's Brief History of the HTPC page:
http://www.digitalconnection.com/FAQ/HTPC.htm

Dolby Laboratories: http://www.dolby.com

DScaler: http://deinterlace.sourceforge.net

DVDLobby Pro: http://www.webpromotion.com/cinemar/dvdlobby.html

Ed Reitan's Color Television History site:
http://novia.net/~ereitan/index.html

EnTech (PowerStrip): http://www.entechtaiwan.com/ps.htm

Girder: http://www.girder.nl

Gracenote online database: http://www.gracenote.com

Hauppauge: http://www.hauppauge.com

Hoontec: http://www.hoontech.com/english/index.html

InterVideo (WinDVR 2): http://www.intervideo.com

Keohi HDTV (YXY Aspect Ratio Controller):
http://www.keohi.com/keohihdtv/htpc/yxy/yxy.html

Matrox: http://www.matrox.com

Microsoft NetMeeting: http://www.microsoft.com/windows/netmeeting

MUSICMATCH (MUSICMATCH Jukebox): http://www.musicmatch.com

Nanocosmos (nanoDVR): http://www.nanocosmos.de

NVIDIA: http://www.nvidia.com

PC Remote Control: http://www.pcremotecontrol.com

Pinnacle Systems Studio: http://www.pinnaclesys.com

Real (RealOne Player): http://www.real.com

ReplayTV: http://www.replaytv.com/

Roxio: http://www.roxio.com

SnapStream (Personal Video Station): http://www.snapstream.com

TheaterTek: http://www.theatertek.com

TiVo: http://www.tivo.com/

Tom Genova's Television History – The First 75 Years site:
http://www.tvhistory.tv

Tom's Hardware Guide: http://www.tomshardware.com

UIRT2: http://www.caseserve.com/ht/UIRT/uirt2.htm

Ulead: http://www.ulead.com

UltimateTV: http://www.ultimatetv.com

Virtual Network Computing (VNC): http://www.uk.research.att.com/vnc/

VirtualDub: http://www.virtualdub.org/index

Index

Apress Titles

ISBN	PRICE	AUTHOR	TITLE
1-893115-73-9	$34.95	Abbott	Voice Enabling Web Applications: VoiceXML and Beyond
1-59059-061-9	$34.95	Allen	Bug Patterns in Java
1-893115-01-1	$39.95	Appleman	Dan Appleman's Win32 API Puzzle Book and Tutorial for Visual Basic Programmers
1-893115-23-2	$29.95	Appleman	How Computer Programming Works
1-893115-97-6	$39.95	Appleman	Moving to VB .NET: Strategies, Concepts, and Code
1-59059-023-6	$39.95	Baker	Adobe Acrobat 5: The Professional User's Guide
1-59059-039-2	$49.95	Barnaby	Distributed .NET Programming in C#
1-59059-068-6	$49.95	Barnaby	Distributed .NET Programming in VB .NET
1-59059-063-5	$29.95	Baum	Dave Baum's Definitive Guide to LEGO MINDSTORMS, Second Edition
1-893115-84-4	$29.95	Baum/Gasperi/Hempel/Villa	Extreme MINDSTORMS: An Advanced Guide to LEGO MINDSTORMS
1-893115-82-8	$59.95	Ben-Gan/Moreau	Advanced Transact-SQL for SQL Server 2000
1-893115-91-7	$39.95	Birmingham/Perry	Software Development on a Leash
1-893115-48-8	$29.95	Bischof	The .NET Languages: A Quick Translation Guide
1-59059-041-4	$49.95	Bock	CIL Programming: Under the Hood™ of .NET
1-59059-053-8	$44.95	Bock/Stromquist/Fischer/Smith	.NET Security
1-893115-67-4	$49.95	Borge	Managing Enterprise Systems with the Windows Script Host
1-59059-019-8	$49.95	Cagle	SVG Programming: The Graphical Web
1-893115-28-3	$44.95	Challa/Laksberg	Essential Guide to Managed Extensions for C++
1-893115-39-9	$44.95	Chand	A Programmer's Guide to ADO.NET in C#
1-59059-034-1	$59.99	Chen	BizTalk Server 2002 Design and Implementation
1-59059-015-5	$39.95	Clark	An Introduction to Object Oriented Programming with Visual Basic .NET
1-893115-44-5	$29.95	Cook	Robot Building for Beginners
1-893115-99-2	$39.95	Cornell/Morrison	Programming VB .NET: A Guide for Experienced Programmers
1-893115-72-0	$39.95	Curtin	Developing Trust: Online Privacy and Security
1-59059-014-7	$44.95	Drol	Object-Oriented Macromedia Flash MX
1-59059-008-2	$29.95	Duncan	The Career Programmer: Guerilla Tactics for an Imperfect World
1-59059-057-0	$29.99	Farkas/Govier	Use Your PC to Build an Incredible Home Theater System
1-893115-71-2	$39.95	Ferguson	Mobile .NET
1-893115-90-9	$49.95	Finsel	The Handbook for Reluctant Database Administrators
1-893115-42-9	$44.95	Foo/Lee	XML Programming Using the Microsoft XML Parser
1-59059-024-4	$49.95	Fraser	Real World ASP.NET: Building a Content Management System
1-893115-55-0	$34.95	Frenz	Visual Basic and Visual Basic .NET for Scientists and Engineers
1-59059-038-4	$49.95	Gibbons	.NET Development for Java Programmers
1-893115-85-2	$34.95	Gilmore	A Programmer's Introduction to PHP 4.0

ISBN	PRICE	AUTHOR	TITLE
1-893115-36-4	$34.95	Goodwill	Apache Jakarta-Tomcat
1-893115-17-8	$59.95	Gross	A Programmer's Introduction to Windows DNA
1-893115-62-3	$39.95	Gunnerson	A Programmer's Introduction to C#, Second Edition
1-59059-030-9	$49.95	Habibi/Patterson/ Camerlengo	The Sun Certified Java Developer Exam with J2SE 1.4
1-893115-30-5	$49.95	Harkins/Reid	SQL: Access to SQL Server
1-59059-009-0	$49.95	Harris/Macdonald	Moving to ASP.NET: Web Development with VB .NET
1-59059-091-0	$24.99	Hempel	LEGO Spybotics Secret Agent Training Manual
1-59059-006-6	$39.95	Hetland	Practical Python
1-893115-10-0	$34.95	Holub	Taming Java Threads
1-893115-04-6	$34.95	Hyman/Vaddadi	Mike and Phani's Essential C++ Techniques
1-893115-96-8	$59.95	Jorelid	J2EE FrontEnd Technologies: A Programmer's Guide to Servlets, JavaServer Pages, and Enterprise JavaBeans
1-59059-029-5	$39.99	Kampa/Bell	Unix Storage Management
1-893115-49-6	$39.95	Kilburn	Palm Programming in Basic
1-893115-50-X	$34.95	Knudsen	Wireless Java: Developing with Java 2, Micro Edition
1-893115-79-8	$49.95	Kofler	Definitive Guide to Excel VBA
1-893115-57-7	$39.95	Kofler	MySQL
1-893115-87-9	$39.95	Kurata	Doing Web Development: Client-Side Techniques
1-893115-75-5	$44.95	Kurniawan	Internet Programming with Visual Basic
1-893115-38-0	$24.95	Lafler	Power AOL: A Survival Guide
1-59059-066-X	$39.95	Lafler	Power SAS: A Survival Guide
1-59059-049-X	$54.99	Lakshman	Oracle9i PL/SQL: A Developer's Guide
1-893115-46-1	$36.95	Lathrop	Linux in Small Business: A Practical User's Guide
1-59059-045-7	$49.95	MacDonald	User Interfaces in C#: Windows Forms and Custom Controls
1-893115-19-4	$49.95	Macdonald	Serious ADO: Universal Data Access with Visual Basic
1-59059-044-9	$49.95	MacDonald	User Interfaces in VB .NET: Windows Forms and Custom Controls
1-893115-06-2	$39.95	Marquis/Smith	A Visual Basic 6.0 Programmer's Toolkit
1-893115-22-4	$27.95	McCarter	David McCarter's VB Tips and Techniques
1-59059-040-6	$49.99	Mitchell/Allison	Real-World SQL-DMO for SQL Server
1-59059-021-X	$34.95	Moore	Karl Moore's Visual Basic .NET: The Tutorials
1-893115-27-5	$44.95	Morrill	Tuning and Customizing a Linux System
1-893115-76-3	$49.95	Morrison	C++ For VB Programmers
1-59059-003-1	$44.95	Nakhimovsky/Meyers	XML Programming: Web Applications and Web Services with JSP and ASP
1-893115-80-1	$39.95	Newmarch	A Programmer's Guide to Jini Technology
1-893115-58-5	$49.95	Oellermann	Architecting Web Services
1-59059-020-1	$44.95	Patzer	JSP Examples and Best Practices
1-893115-81-X	$39.95	Pike	SQL Server: Common Problems, Tested Solutions
1-59059-017-1	$34.95	Rainwater	Herding Cats: A Primer for Programmers Who Lead Programmers
1-59059-025-2	$49.95	Rammer	Advanced .NET Remoting (C# Edition)
1-59059-062-7	$49.95	Rammer	Advanced .NET Remoting in VB .NET

ISBN	PRICE	AUTHOR	TITLE
1-59059-028-7	$39.95	Rischpater	Wireless Web Development, Second Edition
1-893115-93-3	$34.95	Rischpater	Wireless Web Development with PHP and WAP
1-893115-89-5	$59.95	Shemitz	Kylix: The Professional Developer's Guide and Reference
1-893115-40-2	$39.95	Sill	The qmail Handbook
1-893115-24-0	$49.95	Sinclair	From Access to SQL Server
1-59059-026-0	$49.95	Smith	Writing Add-ins for Visual Studio .NET
1-893115-94-1	$29.95	Spolsky	User Interface Design for Programmers
1-893115-53-4	$44.95	Sweeney	Visual Basic for Testers
1-59059-035-X	$59.95	Symmonds	GDI+ Programming in C# and VB .NET
1-59059-002-3	$44.95	Symmonds	Internationalization and Localization Using Microsoft .NET
1-59059-010-4	$54.95	Thomsen	Database Programming with C#
1-59059-032-5	$59.95	Thomsen	Database Programming with Visual Basic .NET, Second Edition
1-893115-65-8	$39.95	Tiffany	Pocket PC Database Development with eMbedded Visual Basic
1-59059-027-9	$59.95	Torkelson/Petersen/Torkelson	Programming the Web with Visual Basic .NET
1-59059-018-X	$34.95	Tregar	Writing Perl Modules for CPAN
1-893115-59-3	$59.95	Troelsen	C# and the .NET Platform
1-59059-011-2	$59.95	Troelsen	COM and .NET Interoperability
1-893115-26-7	$59.95	Troelsen	Visual Basic .NET and the .NET Platform: An Advanced Guide
1-893115-54-2	$49.95	Trueblood/Lovett	Data Mining and Statistical Analysis Using SQL
1-893115-68-2	$54.95	Vaughn	ADO.NET and ADO Examples and Best Practices for VB Programmers, Second Edition
1-59059-012-0	$49.95	Vaughn/Blackburn	ADO.NET Examples and Best Practices for C# Programmers
1-893115-83-6	$44.95	Wells	Code Centric: T-SQL Programming with Stored Procedures and Triggers
1-893115-95-X	$49.95	Welschenbach	Cryptography in C and C++
1-893115-05-4	$39.95	Williamson	Writing Cross-Browser Dynamic HTML
1-59059-060-0	$39.95	Wright	ADO.NET: From Novice to Pro, Visual Basic .NET Edition
1-893115-78-X	$49.95	Zukowski	Definitive Guide to Swing for Java 2, Second Edition
1-893115-92-5	$49.95	Zukowski	Java Collections
1-893115-98-4	$54.95	Zukowski	Learn Java with JBuilder 6

Available at bookstores nationwide or from Springer Verlag New York, Inc. at 1-800-777-4643; fax 1-212-533-3503. Contact us for more information at sales@apress.com.

books for professionals by professionals™

About Apress

Apress, located in Berkeley, CA, is a fast-growing, innovative publishing company devoted to meeting the needs of existing and potential programming professionals. Simply put, the "A" in Apress stands for *"The Author's Press"™* and its books have *"The Expert's Voice"™.* Apress' unique approach to publishing grew out of conversations between its founders Gary Cornell and Dan Appleman, authors of numerous best-selling, highly regarded books for programming professionals. In 1998 they set out to create a publishing company that emphasized quality above all else. Gary and Dan's vision has resulted in the publication of over 50 titles by leading software professionals, all of which have *The Expert's Voice*™.

Do You Have What It Takes to Write for Apress?

Apress is rapidly expanding its publishing program. If you can write and refuse to compromise on the quality of your work, if you believe in doing more than rehashing existing documentation, and if you're looking for opportunities and rewards that go far beyond those offered by traditional publishing houses, we want to hear from you!

Consider these innovations that we offer all of our authors:

- **Top royalties with *no* hidden switch statements**
  Authors typically only receive half of their normal royalty rate on foreign sales. In contrast, Apress' royalty rate remains the same for both foreign and domestic sales.

- **A mechanism for authors to obtain equity in Apress**
  Unlike the software industry, where stock options are essential to motivate and retain software professionals, the publishing industry has adhered to an outdated compensation model based on royalties alone. In the spirit of most software companies, Apress reserves a significant portion of its equity for authors.

- **Serious treatment of the technical review process**
  Each Apress book has a technical reviewing team whose remuneration depends in part on the success of the book since they too receive royalties.

Moreover, through a partnership with Springer-Verlag, New York, Inc., one of the world's major publishing houses, Apress has significant venture capital behind it. Thus, we have the resources to produce the highest quality books *and* market them aggressively.

If you fit the model of the Apress author who can write a book that gives the "professional what he or she needs to know"™," then please contact one of our Editorial Directors, Dan Appleman (dan_appleman@apress.com), Gary Cornell (gary_cornell@apress.com), Jason Gilmore (jason_gilmore@apress.com), Simon Hayes (simon_hayes@apress.com), Karen Watterson (karen_watterson@apress.com), or John Zukowski (john_zukowski@apress.com) for more information.